Praise for ... with School Success

"I love, love, love this book. Flattening hierarchies, decentralizing authority, and empowering front-line employees: what works in business also works in education! A must-read for anyone interested in GENUINE reform of learning and teaching." —**Scott McLeod**, associate professor, educational leadership, and founding director, Center for Advanced Study of Technology Leadership in Education, University of Kentucky

"The authors put forward a provocative argument for autonomy in our schools. Their ideas won't work everywhere but are exactly the kind of break-the-mold ideas that should be tried in an effort to make schools more professional workplaces for teachers and more learning-centered places for students." —**Andrew J. Rotherham**, cofounder and partner, Bellwether Education Partners and education columnist for *TIME* magazine

"Everyone who wants to 'reinvent' public education must read this book, if only to learn that it has already been reinvented! *Trusting Teachers* is a well-researched road map that will keep the next wave of pioneers from making old mistakes. Of course, they will make new mistakes, but that's part of the process." —**John Merrow**, education correspondent, PBS NewsHour, and president, Learning Matters, Inc.

"The message of this book is important, timely and timeless. I hope it is widely read by policy makers, school officials, and especially, teachers. The authors have got it exactly right. The constant and never-ending efforts to reform and improve our school system will never succeed, unless we change the way we treat teachers and the teaching job in this country. Teachers must be held accountable, but subsequently they must also be trusted to 'call the shots.'" —**Richard Ingersoll**, professor of education and sociology, University of Pennsylvania

"In our thirty-year effort to improve schools, we've blamed teachers, threatened them, and punished them. This clear and compelling book offers a new strategy: trust teachers and give them the autonomy and responsibility to make key decisions in teaching and learning and lead the effort to redesign schools and personalize education for every student. And it provides impressive evidence that this works." —**Ron Wolk**, chairman, Big Picture Learning, and founder, Education Week

"*Trusting Teachers* was hard to put down. When I was superintendent of Milwaukee Public Schools, we arranged for teachers who asked for it to have autonomy to design and manage schools. This book shows how teachers with collective autonomy redefine teacher quality, responsibility and accountability." —**William Andrekopoulos**, former superintendent and thirty-six-year educator, Milwaukee Public Schools

"Following sixteen years of teaching in traditional districts, I became an administrator thinking that I could be the impetus for change that I knew could help students. What I found was the system now made me the enemy to the teachers rather than their ally. So I helped create MNCS, where teachers govern themselves and the school. You can read all about the results in this book. Eighteen years later, it is still the most rewarding environment I have worked in." —**Dee Thomas**, lead teacher, Minnesota New Country School

"*Trusting Teachers* offers a compelling vision of schools led by the educators who know students best—teachers. It takes readers inside such schools and explores the innovative strategies they've used to create true communities of professionals." —**Thomas Toch**, senior managing partner, Carnegie Foundation for the Advancement of Teaching

"This was an exciting read. These teachers and these schools, while relatively few in number, have the potential to influence educational innovation and much needed change in our existing institutions. The authors capture the direct experiences of the teachers, themselves, giving voice to their concerns, challenges, frustrations, successes, and accomplishments. Amy Junge's commentary woven through the chapters was riveting and inspiring." —**Linda G. Roberts**, former director, Office of Educational Technology, U.S. Department of Education

"*Trusting Teachers* illustrates that when teachers play an authoritative role in determining schoolwide professional practices, they bring to that work a realistic perspective and a passion for continuously improving outcomes. The attitudes of the autonomous teachers documented here reflect motivation, engagement, teamwork, and most importantly—a sense of responsibility for their actions and those of their colleagues. Perhaps most surprising are their conservative assessments of their personal strengths and performance. Rather than inflating or overstating competencies, they demonstrate a strong willingness to self-assess and a critical understanding of potential weaknesses. This is a refreshing look at teachers who happen also to be professional leaders." —**Roger Sampson**, president, Education Commission of the States

"Teachers come to the MFT wanting and expecting the opportunities afforded to people in other professions. So the MFT works to make it increasingly possible for teachers to collaboratively create and manage high-performing communities like those described so vividly in *Trusting Teachers*. Teachers willingly accept accountability for student results and for quality teaching when they control what matters for school success." —**Lynn Nordgren**, president, Minneapolis Federation of Teachers

"*Trusting Teachers* is very timely for my colleagues and me as we are transitioning from traditional leadership to teacher leadership at our K–5 elementary school. We were able to draw from the book's description of the teachers' ideas and experiences related to budget, peer evaluation, collaborative culture, plus so much more! Because we truly are 'calling the shots,' we are willing to be accountable for school success." —**Joni Beliveau**, leadership team member, Reiche Community School in Portland, Maine

"Our teacher-members say they would happily embrace accountability measures if they were included in the development and implementation of reform initiatives. The authors of *Trusting Teachers* have hit this nail smack on the head! Every governor and state school commissioner in America should implement a test program that allows classroom teachers the chance to show what they can do if they were actually in charge of running schools." —**Gary Beckner**, executive director, American Association of Educators

"*Trusting Teachers* depicts autonomous teachers and school leaders who share a common purpose and embrace the characteristics of high-performing organizations. The authors make a compelling case that educators who truly take ownership over their students' learning are quite impactful and that we must empower the adults within school buildings in order to drive accountability and great results." —**Jean Desravines**, chief executive officer, New Leaders

"*Trusting Teachers* shows us how teachers develop the skills and mindset to run autonomous schools. The book is a wonderful counter-example to the policy tendency toward hypercontrol and managerialism. Trust and nurture work better." —**Charles Taylor Kerchner**, research professor, Claremont Graduate University

"*Trusting Teachers* is a perfectly timed tribute to the teacher who is not just holed away in her classroom trying to survive the next wave of reform but is instead actively creating and leading new approaches to school decision-making and management. The authors are clear proponents of teacher autonomy, but manage to show how these models are evolving and thriving around the country in realistic terms, and without dodging the difficult questions about what risks and challenges these models pose." —**Elena Silva**, Senior Policy Analyst, Education Sector

"*Trusting Teachers* is an in-depth look at teacher-led schools—why and how they work and the key ingredients of success. Every teacher should have the opportunity to work in a teacher-led environment and should read this book to find out why." —**Tom Vander Ark**, CEO, Open Education Solutions, and partner, Learn Capital; former public school superintendent and chair, International Association for K–12 Online Learning

"*Trusting Teachers* comes to us at a critical juncture in the dialogue about the future of education in the United States. The authors examine what happens when teachers not only receive authority over their individual classrooms, but become a part of the school's decision making structure. While many school systems push authority upwards to administration and accountability for results downwards onto individual teachers, *Trusting Teachers* shows us what can happen when authority and accountability are brought together and teachers have a seat at every table." —**Linda Darling-Hammond**, professor at Stanford University School of Education and founder of School Redesign Network, Stanford Educational Leadership Institute, and Stanford Center for Opportunity Policy in Education

"*Trusting Teachers with School Success: What Happens When Teachers Call the Shots* offers a compelling look at the breakthrough possibilities of teacher leadership. The next generation of schools can be places of real innovation and creativity if we will truly trust teachers." —**Dennis Van Roekel**, president, National Education Association

"Until we face the issue of trust—and not just for teachers—the democracy project will be stalled. This lively account of what it looks like in schools that have tried trusting teachers is a must read." —**Deborah Meier**, senior scholar at NYU's Steinhardt School, and forty-five-year educator in K-12 public schools in New York City (East Harlem) and Boston (Roxbury)

"In this important book, the authors turn education reform upside-down. They propose that teachers be empowered to manage their own teaching and their student's learning. Let's put teachers in charge of teaching! The distinct contribution of this book is that it takes the reader into many highly successful schools in which 'trusted' teachers already have professional responsibility for teaching and learning." —**James A. Kelly**, founding president, National Board of Professional Teaching Standards

"*Trusting Teachers* is a fantastic contribution. It will give people new to this idea a very strong grounding in what it's all about. We need ways to press the case for reform without alienating our great teachers, without turning them into the enemy, the problem, and the object of our disdain. This book describes one way to celebrate, engage and empower them." —**Michael Petrilli**, executive vice president, Thomas B. Fordham Institute

"Unleashing the collective wisdom of teachers is the best hope for improving our public schools. This provocative, sensible and practical book offers concrete evidence that it can be done and, in fact, is being done. And now that we have already tried virtually everything else, let's do the right thing and turn teacher-run schools from the exception into the norm." —**Adam Urbanski**, president of the Rochester (NY) Teachers Association, vice president of the American Federation of Teachers, and founding director of the Teacher Union Reform Network

Trusting Teachers with School Success

What Happens When Teachers Call the Shots

Kim Farris-Berg and Edward Dirkswager
with Amy Junge

ROWMAN & LITTLEFIELD EDUCATION
A division of
ROWMAN & LITTLEFIELD PUBLISHERS, INC.
Lanham • New York • Toronto • Plymouth, UK

Published by Rowman & Littlefield Education
A division of Rowman & Littlefield Publishers, Inc.
A wholly owned subsidiary of The Rowman & Littlefield Publishing Group, Inc.
4501 Forbes Boulevard, Suite 200, Lanham, Maryland 20706
www.rowman.com

10 Thornbury Road, Plymouth PL6 7PP, United Kingdom

British Library Cataloguing in Publication Information Available

Library of Congress Cataloging-in-Publication Data

Farris-Berg, Kim, 1975–
Trusting teachers with school success : what happens when teachers call the shots / Kim Farris-Berg
and Edward Dirkswager with Amy Junge.
p. cm.
ISBN 978-1-61048-509-8 (cloth : alk. paper)—ISBN 978-1-61048-510-4 (pbk. : alk. paper)—ISBN
978-1-61048-511-1 (electronic)
1. Teacher participation in administration. 2. Teaching, Freedom of. 3. Teachers—Professional relationships. 4. School improvement programs. I. Dirkswager, Edward J., 1938– II. Junge, Amy, 1976–
III. Title.
LB2806.45 .D57 2013
371.1'06—dc23
2012020475

™
 The paper used in this publication meets the minimum requirements of American
National Standard for Information Sciences Permanence of Paper for Printed Library
Materials, ANSI/NISO Z39.48-1992.

Printed in the United States of America

In memory of John E. Brandl
Teacher, innovator, legislator, academic and public policy leader, author, and friend.

"I understand policymaking to be the design of arrangements that motivate and provide incentives to people in ways that make their personal interests coincide with public interests."

"Finding out what works is not enough. Policymaking must reside not in priority setting, information gathering, or budget allocation, but in designing arrangements such that the people assigned to carry out public responsibilities are inclined to do whatever it takes to accomplish them."

—*From Common Good: Ideas from the Humphrey* (Brandl 2006).

Contents

Acknowledgments   vii

Preface   xi

1: What Would Happen If We Trusted Teachers with School Success?

1   Introduction: To Get High-Performing Schools, Maybe It's
Time to Trust Teachers   3

2   Teacher Autonomy: What It Is, Who Has It, and How It's Secured   19

3   When Granted Autonomy, Teachers Choose to Operate in Ways
That Emulate the Cultural Characteristics of High-Performing
Organizations   31

**2: Eight Practices Autonomous Teachers Embrace, Which Are
Indicative of the Cultural Characteristics of High-
Performing Organizations**

4   Practice #1: Share Purpose, Which Always Focuses on Students
as Individuals, and Use It as the Basis of Decisions Aimed at
School Improvement   49

5   Practice #2: Participate in Collaboration and Leadership for the
Good of the Whole School, Not Just a Classroom   61

6   Practice #3: Encourage Colleagues and Students to Be Active,
Ongoing Learners in an Effort to Nurture Everyone's
Engagement and Motivation   73

7   Practice #4: Develop or Adopt Learning Programs That
Individualize Student Learning   89

 8 Practice #5: Address Social and Discipline Problems as Part of
     Student Learning   105
 9 Practice #6: Broaden the Definition and Scope of Student
     Achievement and Assessment   119
10 Practice #7: Encourage Teacher Improvement Using 360-
     Degree, Peer-, and Self-Evaluation Methods as Well as Peer
     Coaching and Mentoring   133
11 Practice #8: Make Budget Trade-Offs to Meet the Needs of
     Students They Serve   149

**3: Implementation Strategies for Those Who Want to Support
   Teacher Autonomy**
12 It's Time to Trust Teachers   161

Appendix A: Evolution of K–12 Public Schools with Teacher
     Autonomy   179

Appendix B: Demographics at the Eleven Schools   191

Appendix C: Online Survey Instrument   197

Appendix D: Hope Survey Assessment Tool (www.hopesurvey.org)   205

Appendix E: Sample Project Evaluation Rubric   209

Appendix F: TAGOS Leadership Academy's Raised Responsibility
     Rubric   213

Bibliography   215

About the Authors   225

Acknowledgments

We are grateful to the folks with the Education|Evolving, a project of the Center for Policy Studies (CPS). CPS is a Minnesota-based group of policy fellows focusing on public system redesign, and was the primary funder of this book. CPS supported our project while at the same time granting us autonomy to design and carry out our work. The subject of teacher autonomy is one of serious interest to these fellows, yet they were open to learning the outcomes of the research no matter the findings.

We have been blessed with many colleagues, friends, and people who are teachers who provided advice, encouragement, and challenging critiques. Specifically Jacqueline Ball, Eileen Baumgartner, Dorothy Becker, Walter W. Enloe, Joe Graba, Curtis W. Johnson, Ted Kolderie, Dan Loritz, Thomas J. Marr, John M. Maas, Tim R. McDonald, Ronald J. Newell, Gina Pavlov, Jacob Sangiorgio, Jon H. Schroeder, Mark J. Van Ryzin, Robert J. Wedl, and Claire Zysman.

Karly Foster, a former fourth-grade teacher, provided very capable and thorough research assistance early on in this project. As we were rapidly identifying schools with teacher autonomy and sources for the review of literature, she kept all the details straight as well as accurate.

Our profound thanks go to Stacy Becker for generously providing thoughtful and detailed suggestions that led to substantial improvement of the book. She also gave the book its subtitle. Katherine F. Malkemus contributed copy editing that was tremendously useful.

Numerous teachers gave their time to be interviewed and/or surveyed for this book and answered our follow-up questions on a regular basis. We profoundly appreciate their welcoming us into their schools and their patience in educating us about what they do and how they work. Their candid and timely responses were enormously helpful. Their courage to seek teacher autonomy and use it to improve student learning and the job of teaching is the reason for the existence of this book. A list of interviewed teachers is printed on the next page.

Our deepest thanks go to our family and friends who, in addition to their understanding of how our commitment to this work interrupted their normal routines, provided their unfailing love and support throughout the preparation of this book.

While all of these people made contributions to the book, we wrote it and are responsible for its contents.

Academia de Lenguaje y Bellas Artes, Milwaukee, WI

Radames Galarza

Elissa Guarnero

Brenda Martinez

Sue Rodahl

Avalon School, St. Paul, MN

Carrie Bakken

Laura Connell

Monessa Newell

Jo Sullivan

Chrysalis Charter School, Palo Cedro, CA

Laura Bowie

Sara Crandell Hoxie

Alysia Krafel

Paul Krafel

Crystal Simons

EdVisions Off Campus, Minnesota

Catherine Diaz

Gigi Dobosenski

Karen Locke

High School in the Community, New Haven, CT

Heather George

Erik Good

Jack Stacey

Cameo Thorne

Independence School Local 1, Baltimore, MD

Helen Atkinson

Christopher French

Danny Rosvold

Jocelyn Virtudes

Mission Hill K-8 School, Boston, MA

Ayla Gavins

James McGovern

Amina Michel-Lord

Jeanne Rachko

Melissa Tonachel

Jenerra Williams

Minnesota New Country School, Henderson, MN

Nichole Kotasek

Lorie Standinger

Jim Wartman

Dee Thomas

Phoenix High School, Kennewick, WA

Sarah Ard

Tracy Money

Jill Mulhausen

Patrick Yecha

San Francisco Community School, San Francisco, CA

Nobie Camarena

Jessica Fishman

Eric Hendy

Nora Houseman

Tailoring Academics to Guide Our Students (TAGOS Leadership Academy), Janesville, WI

Stephanie Davis

Skylar Primm

Nic Manogue

Jonathan Woloshin

Preface

In our country's quest for high-performing schools and better jobs for teachers, some leaders are granting teachers the collective authority to make the decisions influencing whole school success. In one of the biggest examples of this to date, the Los Angeles Unified School District and United Teachers of Los Angeles reported in December 2011 that they negotiated a labor agreement that will give teachers—the professionals who are closest to the students—autonomy to manage their schools.

As shifts like this take place at an increasingly larger scale, new and important questions are emerging. What kind of autonomy will teachers need to have a real chance at success? What will teachers do with such autonomy once they have it? And how will we know if this strategy of "trusting teachers to call the shots" is producing favorable results?

Leaders outside of schools have also begun to ask how best to encourage teacher autonomy and support autonomous teachers. These leaders include school board members, school district administrators, chartered school authorizers, union leaders, policymakers, members of the business community, teacher trainers, and researchers.

This book is timely in that it begins to answer all of these questions and suggests a framework for moving forward. We have written it to be meaningful and useful for leaders both inside and outside of schools, whether they are considering teacher autonomy or are already in the thick of it.

Probably the most important among these leaders are the teachers themselves. Having observed schools in which teachers are already calling the shots, we know for sure that teachers must be at the forefront of the movement toward autonomy. So far, education leaders outside of schools have granted teachers autonomy only when teachers have asked for it. And teachers' decisions in the schools—how they collectively use the autonomy granted to them—will determine the schools' success. So, to the teachers, we offer a special message as we open this book.

A SPECIAL MESSAGE FOR TEACHERS

This book asserts that to get high performing schools, maybe it's time to trust you, the teachers. We ask this: what would teachers do if they had the autonomy not just to make classroom decisions, but to collectively—with their colleagues—make the decisions influencing whole school success?

Imagine what you and your colleagues would do if you had final decision-making authority to select, evaluate, transfer, and terminate your colleagues and leaders and set your school's staff pattern (including size of staff, full- and part-time positions, and giving teaching *and* administrative roles to teachers who seek the opportunity).

What if you could allocate your school's budget and determine the salaries and benefits of colleagues? If you were in power, you could even determine your school's overall learning program and choose your learning materials (including teaching methods, curriculum, and levels of technology). You could set the school's schedule and write school-level policies (including discipline and homework protocol).

There are teachers who already have the authority to do these things, and they are creating very different kinds of schools. This book explores what these "autonomous teachers" are doing and finds that they manage schools in ways that are characteristic of high-performing organizations.

As you read about their experiences, we hope you'll consider what *you* would do if you and your colleagues were in the position to call the shots.

Ultimately, teacher autonomy's success as a strategy for K–12 improvement is dependent on whether groups of teachers seek autonomy and use it to advance teaching and learning. Until there are a large number of success stories demonstrating, on balance, reasonable improvement over the current situation with our K–12 schools, teacher autonomy will remain a mostly theoretical idea. Yet it's not likely that a lot of people will want to do this right at the start. As with anything new, there will need to be early adapters willing to commit to the idea and give it a serious try.

So if you are a teacher and find the idea of calling the shots attractive after reading this book, consider rounding up a group of colleagues and negotiating an agreement, or contract, for autonomy. Or encourage a teacher you know to go for it.

First, study this book to learn from the teachers already in the thick of teacher autonomy. Then work to secure as much autonomy as you can and design your school; or design your own teacher practice and design and manage several schools. In order do this well, you'll need support. This book is full of ideas for how various leaders who support teachers can encourage successful implementation.

We urge you to find all the information you can about the kinds of schools you can create, but—just as the teachers interviewed for this book have done—take care not to limit yourselves only to the "best practices" from conventional schooling. Think creatively and innovate. Change your jobs. Improve learning. The opportunity for autonomy is a signal that you have the public's trust. We look forward to learning what you will do with it.

What Would Happen If We Trusted Teachers with School Success?

Introduction

To Get High-Performing Schools, Maybe It's Time to Trust Teachers

Sometimes we become so accustomed to the way things are, we cannot imagine a different way of doing things. In 1927, for example, one of the Warner brothers made a famously wrong prediction: "Who the hell wants to hear actors talk?" When it comes to systems vital for our future, like K–12 public schools, this myopia can be disastrous.

Lately, our nation's strategy for improving our schools is mostly limited to "getting tough" with teachers. Blaming teachers for poor outcomes, we spend almost all of our energy trying to control teachers' behavior and school operations. But what if all of this is exactly the opposite of what is needed? What if teachers are the answer and not the problem? What if trusting teachers, and not controlling them, is the key to school success?

Even some teachers have trouble imagining how things could be different. Just ask Janesville, Wisconsin, high school teacher Stephanie Davis. Stephanie is the kind of teacher every parent dreams of for their child. A highly qualified teacher,[1] Stephanie is passionate about English literature. Young and inspired, she got her first teaching job at the 1,780-student Craig High School. She looked forward each day to teaching her chosen subject to freshmen as well as sophomore honors students. Doing everything her district and school leaders asked of her, she applied the skills and knowledge gained from her training for the good of her students.

Stephanie's greatest thrill was seeing some of her students pick up her passion for English. Yet even those who did not share her passion strove to complete their assignments and behaved well in class. Very few students gave her any trouble. Moreover, she was surrounded by supportive colleagues who respected her. She felt proud to work at Craig, where everyone worked hard to make a great school. Teaching was her dream job, and at Craig, everything was just as she expected it would be. Things seemed to be going splendidly.

So Stephanie was crushed when, like so many other teachers, she was laid off by the Janesville School District amid state budget cuts. Since she did not have seniority compared to her colleagues who were laid off, she would not have top priority for placement in any jobs that became available. Stephanie feared she would not be able to find a job teaching in Janesville.

Eventually, district leaders assigned her to a school chartered by Janesville Public Schools called Tailoring Academics to Guide Our Students (TAGOS Leadership Academy). [2] But she was furious.

> My situation seemed to go from bad to worse. I thought I was being assigned to a place full of "bad" kids. The word around town was that TAGOS students got in physical fights all the time and caused problems all day long. Everyone said the students there don't want to learn and are just a bunch of slackers. I thought, "I am a good teacher. How can I do what I was trained to do in a place like that?" I also thought that being placed there was a sign that I was underappreciated.

She reluctantly accepted the position, and was determined not to like it.

> I put on a good face. The other teachers welcomed me and explained right away that teaching was different at TAGOS Leadership Academy. I barely heard them when they explained how the district had given them autonomy to collaboratively manage the school, and what a difference it makes for their jobs and for the students' learning.
>
> I didn't understand why they all were so excited about working here. I thought, "Of course it's a different job! You probably have to discipline students all day and hold their hands while they learn." I was really mad. I just wanted to bide my time until I could get back to Craig.

Stephanie immediately noticed that there was a lot of room for improvement in the way students were learning English literature. Most of her ideas about what had to change were pretty conventional at first.

Typically, curriculum choices are made by education managers outside of the schools, and teachers' jobs are to implement those decisions well. Ninth graders read and analyze *Animal Farm*, *Wuthering Heights*, and some others. They learn the ins-and-outs of the five paragraph essay. Students in other grades have other specific focuses. Stephanie's instinct—rooted in her training as well as her expectations about the profession of teaching—was to point out where the TAGOS Leadership Academy learning program was not towing the line, and suggest ways to get it back on track.

But Stephanie's fellow teachers had something else in mind. They made it clear that they had specifically sought out a colleague like her. They were looking for someone with experience and passion for teaching English literature to help them improve their learning program, and they had the autonomy to collectively make any changes needed. Their learning program focused on individualizing learning for TAGOS Leadership Academy students, not staying on a specific track. They wanted Stephanie's ideas for getting each student to his personal next level of achievement.

At first Stephanie was so focused on how things *usually* work that she failed to digest her colleagues' request. "Then we went on winter break, and I had time to reflect on what they were asking of me, and what my experiences at TAGOS had been compared to [what I did at] Craig," she explained.

> Suddenly I got it. I had a real opportunity at TAGOS. My voice mattered. I could lead [my colleagues]—work together with them—to create a learning program that would *really* change how our students learn English lit!
>
> I hadn't really thought about how prescribed everything I was doing at Craig was. I had to use the prescribed book list, in the prescribed order, at the prescribed pace, using a prescribed budget. There was so little opportunity to tailor what I was doing for the individual students I was working with, whether they were far beyond or far behind. I couldn't hook them on literature by first handing them a book that reflects their interests. But here at TAGOS was a chance to do all the things I thought might work better. I could influence other aspects of the school, too. My voice would have an impact far beyond English lit learning.

Stephanie was as nervous as she was excited. She realized that in exchange for such decision-making authority, she and her fellow teachers at TAGOS Leadership Academy would be accountable for the learning program they developed in addition to all of the other choices they made.

"It was a scary idea at first," she said. "I hadn't ever pictured myself in this position. But now that I've worked with [collective] autonomy I realize that I was missing out on professional opportunities to [decide with my colleagues] what would work for our students.

> It's not that I was unhappy at Craig, but this is just a much more satisfying job. I can make improvements for the individual students I am working with. I have students coming up to me saying they've never liked reading before and yet I'm guiding them as they are creating their own literature circles and assigning themselves difficult material and enjoying the analysis of it. [My colleagues and I] made this happen! I am a much better teacher for having worked in this way.

Stephanie says that she and her TAGOS Leadership Academy colleagues willingly accept accountability for their decisions in managing the schools, and with accountability, they work hard at improvement. "We are more willing to be accountable than we were elsewhere. We hold ourselves to a high standard. We're aware of where we're lacking, and because we have the authority we are motivated to fix [any problems]. Actually, I think *all* teachers have the willingness to do this, but at TAGOS *we will* do it because we have the ability to."

If most teachers were given decision-making autonomy, their attitudes about students like those who attend TAGOS Leadership Academy would probably change, suggests Stephanie. "There are some [students who are] slackers here, but there are slackers everywhere. It turns out that at TAGOS most of the students work hard and spend their time learning. They have a bad reputation for no good reason. Most of them are [at TAGOS] because they weren't motivated by what we have going on at [conventional] schools.

"Teachers in all schools have the skills and knowledge to reach all students, but what I didn't realize before I worked at TAGOS was that [conventional] job structures don't really let us apply any of it. It didn't really matter how good our intentions were. Most teachers are just doing what someone else told them to do; and [meeting these requirements] means we can't really reach everyone. This is why it really frustrates me when people blame teachers and students for our problems with schools."

BLAMING TEACHERS: HAVE WE MISDIAGNOSED THE PROBLEM WITH OUR SCHOOLS?

Could Stephanie be on to something? Are we blaming teachers for K–12's woes when the real problem is the way in which schools and teachers are managed?

Everyone knows that many K–12 public schools are not producing desired results. And our good intentions for our children and for our nation have inspired a frenetic hunt for ways to fix them. Anyone following the news can see that policymakers' and other education leaders' current focus is to tell teachers what to do and how to do it. Their approach assumes teachers—their behaviors, choices, and quality—are the problem. Even high-caliber people like Stephanie Davis.

Almost all of our eggs are in this basket. Those in power are standardizing curriculums, tightening licensure requirements, offering merit pay, and tying school and teacher evaluations to student performance. Most recently, state governors are taking aim at the rules established by teachers' unions; policies governing teachers' tenure, pay, role differentiation (what they will do and not do), and hours worked.

Teachers and teachers' unions are outspoken in their resistance. "These policies make us the scapegoats for other people's decisions," they argue. It seems quite plausible that they are right. Unlike most professionals, teachers are not able to collectively make many of the decisions that matter for their organization's success. Instead they mostly implement other people's decisions, as Stephanie said she was doing at Craig.

Teachers don't allocate the school budgets, for instance. They don't choose their colleagues. They don't have much say about the definition of student achievement or discipline policies. They don't determine the curriculum, materials, schedules, building layout, or class sizes, and they are mostly unable to change course even when they see things aren't working well.

We're at an impasse. As a matter of both policy and practice, we are increasingly asking teachers to accept more accountability for school improvement. Yet teachers don't want to be blamed, much less accept accountability, for choices they cannot control. This deadlock triggers the finger pointing that just keeps going around and around at our nation's expense.

WHERE DO WE GO FROM HERE?

Quality-improvement experts in healthcare, manufacturing, and education have repeatedly concluded that workers (in this case, teachers) are never fully responsible for poor outcomes of the system in which they work. In fact, they have found that workers are for the most part doing their best—using all of their skills and energy—to make the system work well.

What, then, is responsible for poor outcomes? The experts maintain that the design of every system determines the results it gets. So if the results are not the desired results, then the system needs to be redesigned to achieve what is desired (Deming 2000; Wehling and Schneider 2007; Berwick, Godfrey, and Roessner 1990; Hanna 1988).

Scholars have found these ideas to also be true in the case of our schools. In other words, teachers are not the problem. Willam G. Ouchi, professor of management at the University of California Los Angeles, wrote in *Making Schools Work*, "I have visited 223 schools in nine school systems and have carried out a carefully designed study of the management systems in all of them. I found that some entire districts are succeeding wonderfully while others are failing. What separates the successes from the failures is not different teachers, students, or money—it's their approach to managing the schools" (Ouchi 2003, 8–9).

Ouchi went on to conclude that successful school districts give principals "the freedom to be entrepreneurs, to identify and solve their own problems [and work with teachers to design] their own unique solutions, while at the same time collecting information on what is going on and intervening when necessary" (Ouchi 2003).

Richard M. Ingersoll, professor of education and sociology at the University of Pennsylvania, went one step further in his book *Who Controls Teachers Work?* Examining a wide array of data,[3] he concluded that if it's teacher accountability we seek, then we should design education to give increased power not just to principals and governing boards, but to teachers.

In an article describing his work to ASCD, the Association for Supervision and Curriculum Development, he wrote, "It makes no sense to hold people accountable for something they do not control or to give people control over something for which they are not held accountable. Accountability without commensurate power is unfair and can be harmful. To upgrade teacher quality, schools need to go beyond just holding teachers more accountable. They need to give teachers more control" (Ingersoll 2007, 20, 25).

Ingersoll also concluded that, in the system of education, the workers are not the problem.

> Policymakers and reformers often question the caliber and quality of teachers, telling us time and again that teachers lack sufficient engagement, commitment, and accountability. However, the data suggest just the opposite—that teachers have an unusual degree of public service orientation and commitment and a relatively high 'giving-to-getting' ratio, compared with those in other careers. The critics fail to appreciate the extent to which the teaching workforce is a source of human, social, and even financial capital in schools. (Ingersoll 2007, 23)

The American public is urging policymakers to solve K–12's problems, but just like the experts and scholars, the public doesn't blame teachers. The September 2011 issue of *Phi Delta Kappan* magazine reported that 71 percent of Americans profess to have high trust and confidence in teachers. Americans were far less confident about the state of our nation's schools, however. Only 17 percent of those polled give As and Bs to the nation's schools as a whole, down from 22 percent in 2008 (Bushaw and Lopez 2011).

A lot of our national dialogue asks the public to be "for teachers" *or* "for school improvement," but this data suggests that Americans don't see this as an either-or situation. They seem to be seeking an option that honors teachers *and* improves our schools. They seem to have distinguished between teachers and the systems teachers work in, as the source of the problem.

All of this evidence suggests that "blaming teachers" could be the wrong diagnosis of the problem plaguing our schools. If that's the case, we are wasting a lot of time and money on the wrong prescriptions. If we want an education system in which teachers will accept accountability, maybe we ought to put some eggs in a second basket. Maybe some leaders should try granting teachers the authority to make the decisions that influence the success of our schools. Maybe we ought to trust teachers.

THIS BOOK CONSIDERS A RADICALLY DIFFERENT PRESCRIPTION: TRUST TEACHERS

We've written this book primarily for teachers. It's also for anyone who is on the hunt for the right prescription for the K–12 crisis and has the power to support teachers. What follows is an exploration of an idea for consideration.

We suspect that teachers, like Stephanie Davis, are proud of their chosen profession. Yet they are aware of imperfections with our schools, and want to be better positioned to do something about it.

Many teachers have sought for years, through their school districts and unions and legislative efforts, to gain professional control over the decisions influencing school success. They have suggested that, with such authority, they would teach school students differently than the way they are required to do so now, which would lead to better results. They have also suggested that, for better or worse, they would be willing to accept accountability for the results of their decisions.

Our hypothesis, from our vantage point as students of public policy who are interested in how changes in the design of management structures affects school improvement, is that given the opportunity for autonomy, teachers would create high-performing schools. Our hypothesis is certainly based on our particular point of view, but as researchers we designed the investigation to leave open the possibility that we were wrong.

The essential question of this book is this: what would teachers do if they had the autonomy not just to make classroom decisions, but to collectively— with their colleagues—make the decisions influencing whole school success?

We also needed a framework for investigating what autonomous teachers do, in order to answer a second question: can we trust autonomous teachers to make good decisions?

Before we explain further about the nature of our investigation, and preview the results, it will help you to have a background of the current state of teacher autonomy.

THE CURRENT STATE OF TEACHER AUTONOMY

Some policymakers and education leaders in states and school districts around the country are trusting teachers to radically improve our schools. Given that it's a new idea with inherent risks and high stakes, they are trying parallel strategies: they continue to run conventional schools, but at the same time they are granting groups of teachers who request it the collective autonomy to make the decisions related to whole school success.

Are all states and school district leaders granting teachers autonomy handing over the reins completely? No. Do all groups of teachers who are granted autonomy take full advantage of it? No. Is the strategy foolproof? No. This book is not about idealizing the idea. Instead, it is about understanding the strategy, learning how it is playing out in the United States, and raising questions about its potential for radically improving our schools.

While major news outlets have touted some recently opened schools as "the first" with teacher autonomy, the reality is that this idea has been in practice for four decades. In fact, teachers in at least two public schools have had autonomy since the 1970s. Some policymakers have been dialoguing about the idea's potential impact on public schools and the teaching profession since the 1980s. States' creation of chartering laws in the 1990s increased take-up of the idea in both chartered and district schools, with both unionized and nonunionized teachers. [4]

Growth hasn't been coordinated. The groups of teachers doing this see themselves as islands, not knowing others exist. Yet today we are aware of around fifty schools with teacher autonomy in a variety of settings. That's more than enough experience for the idea to deserve serious consideration as a strategy for K–12 improvement.

Sometimes the idea of granting teachers collective autonomy is confused with other strategies—such as decentralization, site-based management, and professional learning communities—and dismissed with "been there, done that." The movement to decentralize district schools has brought attention to the role of autonomy in successful school management. Efforts like site-based management and professional learning communities have acknowledged that teachers' input is important, as is teachers' partial autonomy over their own classrooms.

But all of these strategies assume that any change in K–12 must be within the conventional concept of "school." Teachers can have more input but principals must make the final decisions, for example. Teachers must work conventional hours in conventional classrooms for conventional pay. Teachers can have some discretion within their own classroom and students, but should not decide matters dealing with the entire school. And even in their classrooms, teachers must only draw from best practices proven to work for most students in conventional settings.

Those who are trusting teachers, granting them autonomy, contemplate something entirely different. The teacher autonomy strategy is about giving groups of teachers—the professionals who work most closely with students—the opportunity to choose—even invent—the learning methods and job structures they think will best improve learning for the students at their schools.

The state, school district, chartered school board, or person who grants autonomy is responsible for holding teachers accountable for meeting mutually determined goals; however, teacher autonomy means that no one is telling the teachers *how* to meet the goals. Teacher autonomy assumes that because teachers are professionals they know how to meet them, and allows for teachers to try highly unconventional things if they judge them warranted.

Common reactions to this strategy have been, "It will never take off because teachers are not interested. Plus some single leader, like a principal, *must* be 'in charge.' Teachers don't want to take on all that administration and have too much to do already." But there is evidence to the contrary.

In 2003, Public Agenda tested a national sample of teachers' attitudes for new arrangements as reported in *Stand By Me: What Teachers Really Think About Unions, Merit Pay and Other Professional Matters* (Farkas, Johnson, and Duffett 2003). Fifty-eight percent of teachers were somewhat or very interested "in working in a [chartered] school run and managed by teachers"; this included 65 percent of teachers surveyed who had worked less than five years and 50 percent of teachers surveyed who had worked more than twenty years.

And, as this book will reveal in detail, many groups of autonomous teachers elect one or more leaders from their group to handle administration and/ or to be a lead teacher. These leaders *can and do* figure out how to handle administration. Some selected leaders simply have a talent for and desire to do administrative tasks—such as committee management or ensuring compliance with special education requirements or payroll—in addition to their work with students. In other cases selected leaders are former principals of conventional schools who teachers ask to take on many of the same duties in conventional settings.

So while many journalists covering the movement have dubbed schools with teacher autonomy as "schools without principals," that characterization misses the point. It's not about avoiding principals. The distinction is in to whom the leaders are accountable. *Teacher autonomy puts in motion an entirely different structure of accountability.* No single leader is accountable to the school district or chartered school board that monitors school success.

Instead, selected leaders are accountable to the group of teachers managing the school, which is collectively accountable to the school district or chartered school board.

This very different accountability structure is designed to ensure the leaders are working to implement the decisions of the teachers. Also, this structure makes those closest to the students accountable for school success. Teacher autonomy removes the many layers of decision making, each further and further from the classroom, thereby removing the ability to point fingers at "someone else" when things go wrong.

HOW CAN WE KNOW IF WE COULD TRUST AUTONOMOUS TEACHERS TO MAKE GOOD DECISIONS?

The central question of any K–12 improvement strategy is whether it has the potential to achieve superior results. Ideally, we'd want to know this: what strategies will help prepare students to lead lives that are successful, from an individual and societal point of view? But there are no empirical measurements for this sort of "real life" result, so we needed a proxy for measuring the results of schools created by autonomous teachers.

We considered numerous research approaches and after careful consideration we ruled out the most obvious: test scores. We decided that comparing aggregate test scores of the students in schools run by autonomous teachers with those of students in conventional schools would not be the most useful measurement—even if we could control for differences in the student populations, geographic diversity, and variances in tests used. One thing that many teachers agree on is that in many cases our prevailing system of testing does not measure students' individual progress, nor does it say much about how well teachers are performing.

Comparing test scores would also accept that as a nation we have agreed on what students should know and be able to do. Yet there is little agreement. Our nation accepts measuring students' achievement mostly in the areas of reading, writing and math, while at the same time loudly proclaiming students' need for twenty-first-century skills, such as communication and leadership, if they are to succeed in the changing economy. Many also assert the value of succeeding in other areas, such as the arts, history, and the trades.

Everyone agrees that the "three Rs" are very important, but in our quest to improve our schools the jury is out on whether that is all that's important. If autonomous teachers at a particular school collectively embrace the view that there is more to achievement than the "three Rs," then measuring the scores of their students against scores earned by conventional students accepts one definition of achievement more than others.

Ultimately, we decided that a reasonable proxy for whether a school has the potential to achieve superior results ought to be associated with the characteristics of high-performing organizations.

According to our review of literature, organizations are considered "high-performing" if they achieve results that are better than their peers' over a period of time. By inference, their cultural characteristics are associated with success. It makes logical sense that autonomous teachers' choices are "good" if they emulate the cultural characteristics of high-performing organizations. We gleaned nine such characteristics from the literature and used the detailed findings to develop survey and interview instruments that would examine autonomous teachers' approaches and behaviors in each area.

We sought to understand whether and how they

1. Accept ownership: Welcome authority and responsibility for making decisions and be accountable for the outcomes.
2. Innovate: Take risks to try creative new things, challenge old processes and continuously adapt.
3. Share purpose: Seek clarity and buy in to the mission, values, goals, and standards of practice.
4. Collaborate: Establish a culture of interdependence characterized by an open flow of ideas, listening to and understanding others, and valuing differences.
5. Lead effectively: Expect leadership from all and perceive leadership as in service to all.
6. Function as learners: Establish a culture characterized by a sense of common challenge and discovery, rather than a culture where experts impart information.
7. Avoid insularity: Learn from and be sensitive to the external environment.
8. Motivate: Be engaged, motivated, and motivating.
9. Assess performance: Set and measure progress toward goals and act upon results to improve performance.

MORE DETAILS ABOUT THE RESEARCH FOUNDATIONS AND STRUCTURE OF THIS BOOK

This book summarizes what we have come to understand about the nature of teacher autonomy and what teachers do when they have the authority to make the decisions that influence whole school success. Here is a preview of the chapters that follow:

Chapter 2: Overview, Plus a Brief Explanation of Our Methods

Before we investigated what teachers would do if they had the autonomy to collectively make the decisions influencing whole school success, we first needed to clearly define what we meant by "autonomy" and understand how it is secured. Chapter 2 explains that teachers are autonomous if they have final decision-making authority in up to ten potential areas. These areas were identified based on research examining school autonomy as well as by people who work with teachers who already have autonomy.

The ten areas include selecting colleagues; transferring and/or terminating colleagues; evaluating colleagues; setting staff pattern (including size of staff and the allocation of personnel to teaching and other positions); selecting and deselecting leaders; determining budget; determining salaries and benefits; determining learning program and learning materials (including teaching methods, curriculum, and levels of technology); setting the schedule (classes, school hours, length of school year); and setting school-level policies (including discipline and homework protocol).

Using our definition, we conducted a national search for schools with autonomous teachers from September 2009 to September 2010. The search yielded more than six-dozen leads. We then conducted telephone and e-mail interviews with teachers at forty-two schools that seemed most likely to meet the definition. Of these schools, we found that thirty-four had autonomy in at least one of the ten areas.

Ultimately we chose to conduct an in-depth survey and one-day site visits with autonomous teachers in eleven schools. In all eleven, teachers had autonomy for at least three years and in at least six of the ten areas.

The selection covers the varying arrangements by which teachers secure autonomy and represents diversity in the grade levels served; geographic location; type of school (district, chartered, alternative); teachers' affiliation with unions (some are and some are not); and environment (urban, suburban, rural, and online). Chapter 2 provides detailed information about the eleven schools and the nature of their autonomy. Table 1.1 lists the eleven schools, and detailed demographic information about each can be found in appendix B.

Each of the eleven site visits consisted of interviews with three or four teachers (mostly one-on-one), including any identified lead teachers, as well as observations of the learning environment and behaviors of teachers and students. We also informally spoke with students about their experiences with their schools. Prior to each visit we asked all teachers at the eleven sites to take an online survey in order to obtain a wider range of teachers' perceptions. Ninety-eight people took the online survey and the total response rate was 71 percent. The survey instrument is included in appendix C.

Table 1.1. Schools Visited for This Study

ALBA, Academia de Lenguaje y Bellas Artes **Milwaukee, Wisconsin** Age 3 to Grade 5	**Minnesota New Country School** **Henderson, Minnesota** Grades 6–12
Avalon School **St. Paul, Minnesota** Grades 7–12	**Mission Hill K–8 School** **Boston, Massachusetts** Grades K–8
Chrysalis Charter School **Palo Cedro, California** Grades K–8	**Phoenix High School** **Kennewick, Washington** Grades 9–12
EdVisions Off Campus **Online school based in Henderson, Minnesota** Grades 7–12	**San Francisco Community School** **San Francisco, California** Grades K–8
High School in the Community **New Haven, Connecticut** Grades 7–12	**Tailoring Academics to Guide Our Students** **(TAGOS Leadership Academy)** **Janesville, Wisconsin**
Independence School Local 1 **Baltimore, Maryland** Grades 9–12	

Following the survey and visits, we analyzed the findings to answer the book's two essential questions. Again, these are (1) what would teachers do if they had the autonomy to collectively make the decisions influencing whole school success? and (2) can we trust autonomous teachers to make good decisions? In other words, would autonomous teachers choose or invent ways of operating that emulate the cultural characteristics of high-performing organizations?

Chapter 3

Chapter 3 reports autonomous teachers' perceptions about the extent to which they emulate each of the nine characteristics of high-performing organizations, as reported in the survey and interviews. Teachers revealed that they experience both successes and struggles in cultivating and maintaining high-performance cultures.

Yet they overwhelmingly *do* cultivate and maintain them. In seven of the nine areas, more than 90 percent of autonomous teachers indicated that they emulate the characteristics. And in two areas—avoiding insularity and assessing performance—the number of teachers who said they emulate the characteristics ranged from 80 to 90 percent.

Chapter 3 concludes by reporting that our analysis of the teachers' interview responses found there are eight behaviors and approaches, or practices, teachers embrace that are indicative of the cultural characteristics of high-performing organizations.

Chapters 4–11

These eight chapters describe in great detail each of the eight practices autonomous teachers collectively embrace:

> Practice #1: Share purpose, which always focuses on students as individuals, and use it as the basis of decisions aimed at school improvement.
> Practice #2: Participate in collaboration and leadership for the good of the whole school, not just a classroom.
> Practice #3: Encourage colleagues and students to be active, ongoing learners in an effort to nurture everyone's engagement and motivation.
> Practice #4: Develop or adopt learning programs that individualize student learning.
> Practice #5: Address social and discipline problems as part of student learning.
> Practice #6: Broaden the definition and scope of student achievement and assessment.
> Practice #7: Encourage teacher improvement using 360-degree, peer-, and self-evaluation methods, as well as peer coaching and mentoring.
> Practice #8: Make budget trade-offs to meet the needs of the students they serve.

Chapters 4–11 are filled with supporting stories and experiences from the teachers themselves that illustrate the very different kinds of schools teachers create when they are granted autonomy, including how they innovate with student learning and the job of teaching. These chapters also report the questions and challenges autonomous teachers face as they practice their craft; challenges that might be addressed in future arrangements granting teachers autonomy.

Chapter 12

The book concludes that autonomous teachers do emulate the nine characteristics of high-performing organizations and that their most prominent practices flow from their cultivation of those cultural characteristics. The outcomes suggest that if we want high-performing schools then the fundamentally different incentive structure of teacher autonomy is the design change we need. It's time to trust teachers with professional authority in return for their acceptance of accountability for school success.

We then conclude that society should be open to further trial and investigation of teacher autonomy as a strategy for improving our schools. Teachers who want to succeed in their pursuit of autonomy and in their creation of high-performing schools will need support. We suggest a number of ways in which those who support teachers can encourage successful implementation.

Education managers who are outside of schools can loosen the reins and choose to hold teachers accountable via formal agreements for service instead of via mandates and other attempts at control. They can also choose to work with autonomous teachers to continuously identify and remove barriers to following high-performing cultures, including barriers to accepting accountability and innovating.

Teachers' unions can choose to support autonomous teachers by acting as advocates for increased professional roles. Leaders of teacher training institutions can choose to support teachers' migration to working with autonomy and accountability. Finally, researchers, foundations, teachers, and others can choose to establish an infrastructure of information that is necessary for understanding and supporting innovation through teacher autonomy.

These ideas are just a start. Teacher autonomy will evolve, and much more work will need to be done.

AUTONOMOUS TEACHERS CREATE SCHOOLS THAT ARE OUTSIDE THE MAINSTREAM, AND MAYBE THAT'S JUST WHAT WE NEED

This book makes the case that teacher autonomy is a promising strategy for improving our schools. We do not contend that teacher autonomy is for everyone. Nor are we suggesting that all schools ought to be transformed using this model. Coercion can actually be a very slow route to change. This strategy is intended to be optional and gradual; not a mandate or quick fix.

The number of schools with teacher autonomy is relatively small. And, yes, autonomous teachers create schools and manage them in ways that are outside the mainstream. Certainly many of their choices would never be found in most conventional schools. But why not take their work seriously? Why not be open to the possibility that we might want much more of what they produce? Autonomous teachers, and those who are granting them autonomy, are the entrepreneurs of their field. As you are about to learn, they have shown themselves to be reasoned risk takers, on a constant search for the best means to high performance.

We should also resist the temptation to classify the schools created by autonomous teachers as places only for students who can't cut it or aren't well served in conventional schools. The schools' focus on individualizing learning attracts many "typical" students, as well as large populations of students who believe they are "atypical"—they felt out of place and some-times were bullied for being different from most students.

Indeed, some autonomous teachers are creating schools specifically to serve atypical populations, including students who are far behind and far ahead of grade-level standards. Gaining the ability to create schools of this kind was one of the reasons they sought teacher autonomy. We could choose to see these efforts as a "side show" to conventional schooling. Yet we might find that the kinds of schools autonomous teachers create, and the practices they embrace, are exactly what we need for many more students.

So, as investigators who have examined this idea in detail, we challenge you to remain open to teacher autonomy and the choices autonomous teach-ers make. Innovation is about foresight. If it's improvement we seek, we simply cannot assume that doing better at the way we operate today is the only way to get there.

Remember Stephanie Davis. She went in with great reluctance, not at all impressed by her outside impressions of TAGOS Leadership Academy and its students, but today she'd have a hard time relinquishing the opportunities for students and teachers that teacher autonomy affords. For Stephanie and her colleagues, a lot of constraints and controls are a thing of the past. They are calling the shots. They are trusted with school success.

NOTES

1.   The federal No Child Left Behind Act of 2001 mandated that all teachers must be "highly qualified," meaning they have obtained full state certification or passed a teacher licensing examination and demonstrated specific content area competence.

2.   Stephanie Davis was assigned to her job after TAGOS Leadership Academy teachers requested a colleague with her skill set. Autonomous teachers in other schools have a greater level of authority to select their colleagues.

3.   Ingersoll wrote, "My research involves analyses of a wide array of data: international data from the Organization for Economic Cooperation and Development, data from my own field interviews in schools, and national data. The latter have primarily come from the Schools and Staffing Survey (SASS) conducted by the National Center for Education Statistics, the data-collection arm of the U.S. Department of Education. The Schools and Staffing Survey is the largest and most comprehensive source of information on teachers available. . . . Five cycles of SASS have been conducted: 1987–88, 1990–91, 1993–94, 1999–2000, and 2003–04. I used data primarily from the first four cycles" (Ingersoll 2007).

4.   To learn more about the evolution of the idea, see appendix A.

Chapter Two

Teacher Autonomy

What It Is, Who Has It, and How It's Secured

Education leaders in some states, as well as some district and chartered school boards, are granting teachers the autonomy to collectively make decisions influencing whole school, including every student's, success.

Their experiences, as well as the experiences of teachers and students in the schools, can inform those who are considering teacher autonomy as a potential national strategy for pursuing radical change and innovation in K–12. Chapter 1 posited teacher autonomy as an innovative design alternative for structuring and managing schools. But it is also important to clarify what we mean when we say that teachers have autonomy at a school site. Additionally, what have we learned so far about what kinds of autonomy are needed? Who has it? And how is it granted to, or secured by, teachers?

Teachers have autonomy when they are collectively granted final decision-making authority—not simply input—in areas influencing whole school success. This might occur in any of ten potential areas.

- Selecting colleagues
- Transferring and/or terminating colleagues
- Evaluating colleagues
- Setting staff pattern (including size of staff; allocation of personnel to teaching and/or other positions)
- Selecting and deselecting leaders
- Determining budget
- Determining salaries and benefits[1]
- Determining learning program and learning materials (including teaching methods, curriculum, and levels of technology)

- Setting the schedule (classes, school hours, length of school year)
- Setting school-level policies (including discipline and homework proto-col)

We identified these ten areas based on recent research conducted by RAND Education, the Fordham Foundation, and William G. Ouchi of the Anderson School of Management at the University of California, Los Angeles (Hansen and Roza 2005; Brinson and Rosch 2010; Ouchi 2003; Ouchi 2009). These works examine autonomy as a critical aspect of decentralization strategies and chartering strategies being implemented by states and school districts.

We then supplemented and refined the list using research on autonomy's effect on motivation by Daniel H. Pink (Pink 2009) as well as the observations of field practitioners and observers as reported in notes from a national meeting on school innovation hosted by the Center for Policy Studies (CPS) in June 2009.

CPS meeting attendees who most influenced our selection of these ten areas were representatives of the Center for Collaborative Education (developer of the Five Conditions of Autonomy for Schools), EdVisions Cooperative (a teacher cooperative operating with autonomy since 1994), the Minneapolis Federation of Teachers, the Teachers Union Reform Network (TURN), and autonomous teachers and leaders in Milwaukee Public Schools.

The list of ten areas is not necessarily definitive and is likely to be further refined as autonomous teachers advance their craft.

TEACHER AUTONOMY SPANS SCHOOL ENVIRONMENTS AND VARIES IN TWO MAJOR WAYS

Teacher autonomy is not exclusive to any one "type" of school. Autonomous arrangements have appeared in district, chartered, and independent schools. Some are union affiliated, others are not. There are schools with teacher autonomy in urban, rural, and suburban settings across the nation, serving students from preschool to age twenty-one.

Among the eleven schools visited for this book, seven schools are chartered. All seven are chartered by school authorizers certified by their states,[2] including three that are chartered by school districts. Four of the eleven schools are district schools: one of these is piloted[3] and one of these is a magnet.[4] Teachers in seven of the schools are union affiliated.

Three of the eleven schools serve students in grades 9–12, three serve students in grades 7–12, and one serves students in grades 6–12. Three schools serve students in grades K–8, and one serves students in grades P–5.

Five of the eleven schools are located in urban environments, two in rural environments, two in suburban environments, one in an urban-suburban environment, and one online. Appendix B contains more detailed demographic information about each school.

ONLINE NATIONAL INVENTORY OF SCHOOLS WITH TEACHER AUTONOMY

WWW.EDUCATIONEVOLVING.ORG

An outgrowth of this project's national search for schools with teacher autonomy is an online inventory.

Visitors can learn about teachers' autonomy in all of the schools identified during the search, including the eleven selected for site visits. Individual school profiles convey teachers' areas of autonomy and their arrangements for securing autonomy. There is also a national map of schools as well as a greater selection of photographs from the eleven site visits than what is included in this book.

At this time the Center for Policy Studies Education|Evolving initiative appears to be the exclusive tracker of this information.

Teacher autonomy varies in two major ways in the eleven schools. First, teachers have autonomy in varying combinations of the ten potential areas. According to teachers' reports, teachers in four schools have full autonomy in all ten areas. Teachers in the remaining seven schools have a mix of full and partial autonomy in an average of 7.71 out of the ten possible areas.

Figure 2.1 provides an overview of the varying combinations of autonomy that teachers have in each of the schools. "Partial" means that teachers have some, not full, authority in a particular area. Academia de Lenguajes y Bellas Artes (ALBA) teachers have the ability to select leaders, for example, but cannot dismiss or terminate them once they are selected. Teachers in some schools can determine a portion—not all—of their school budget. These distinctions are clarified throughout this book.

Teachers also have varying arrangements by which they are granted, or secure, their autonomy. As is depicted in figure 2.1, the teachers' arrangement can affect each area of autonomy, determining whether it is de jure (established formally in policy or agreement) or de facto (autonomy is practiced, but informal and not guaranteed). The state, school district, chartered school board, or person who grants autonomy is responsible for holding teachers accountable for meeting mutually determined goals.

Schools	Selecting Colleagues	Transferring/ Dismissing Colleagues	Evaluating Colleagues	Setting Staff Pattern	Selecting Leaders
ALBA	DE FACTO (Partial)		DE JURE (Partial)	DE JURE	DE FACTO (Partial)
Avalon	DE JURE	DE JURE	DE JURE	DE JURE	DE JURE
Chrysalis	DE JURE	DE JURE	DE JURE	DE JURE	DE FACTO
EdVisions Off Campus	DE JURE	DE JURE	DE JURE	DE JURE	DE JURE
HSC	DE FACTO (Partial)		DE FACTO (Partial)	DE FACTO (Partial)	DE FACTO
Independence	DE JURE (Partial)	DE FACTO	DE FACTO (Partial)	DE JURE	DE FACTO
MNCS	DE JURE	DE JURE	DE JURE	DE JURE	DE JURE
Mission Hill	DE JURE	DE JURE	DE JURE (Partial)	DE JURE	DE FACTO
Phoenix HS	DE FACTO (Partial)		DE FACTO		DE FACTO
SFCS	DE JURE (Partial)			DE JURE	DE JURE
TAGOS	DE FACTO (Partial)			DE JURE	

Note: De jure refers to autonomy that is established formally in policy or agreement. De facto refers to autonomy that is practiced, but informal and not guaranteed.

Figure 2.1. Areas of Teacher Autonomy at the 11 Schools

Schools	Determining Budget	Determining Salaries	Determining Learning Program	Setting Schedule	Setting School Level Policy
ALBA	DE JURE (Partial)		DE JURE	DE JURE	DE JURE (Partial)
Avalon	DE JURE	DE JURE	DE JURE	DE JURE	DE JURE
Chrysalis	DE FACTO	DE JURE	DE JURE	DE JURE	DE JURE
EdVisions Off Campus	DE JURE	DE JURE	DE JURE	DE JURE	DE JURE
HSC	DE FACTO (Partial)		DE FACTO	DE FACTO (Partial)	DE FACTO (Partial)
Independence	DE JURE (Partial)		DE JURE	DE JURE (Partial)	DE JURE
MNCS	DE JURE	DE JURE	DE JURE	DE JURE	DE JURE
Mission Hill	DE JURE (Partial)		DE JURE	DE JURE	DE JURE
Phoenix HS	DE FACTO (Partial)		DE FACTO	DE FACTO (Partial)	DE FACTO (Partial)
SFCS	DE JURE (Partial)		DE JURE	DE JURE (Partial)	DE JURE
TAGOS	DE JURE (Partial)		DE FACTO (Partial)	DE JURE (Partial)	DE JURE (Partial)

Note: De jure refers to autonomy that is established formally in policy or agreement. De facto refers to autonomy that is practiced, but informal and not guaranteed.

Figure 2.1. *Continued*

Regardless of the autonomy arrangement, teachers are also held accountable by students and their families who are able to exercise choice regarding which school they choose to attend. Since money follows students, losing them to other schools means a depletion of the school budget. This is a powerful incentive to succeed.

Among the eleven schools, there were six arrangements:

1. *Contract between chartered school board and teacher professional partnership* [EdVisions Off Campus (EOC), Minnesota New Country School (MNCS)].

    EdVisions Cooperative, established in 1994 under Minnesota Statute 308A, enters into contracts with chartered school boards across the state of Minnesota, accepting accountability for school success in exchange for its teacher-members' authority to make decisions about the school.

    EdVisions Cooperative is known as a "teacher professional partnership," or TPP. TPPs are formal entities, organized under law (partnerships, cooperatives, limited-liability corporations, etc.), that are formed and owned by teachers to provide educational services.

2. *Chartered school contract and/or chartered school bylaws* [Avalon School (Avalon), Chrysalis Charter School (Chrysalis), Independence School Local 1 (Independence), Tailoring Academics to Guide Our Student (TAGOS Leadership Academy)].

    Chartered school authorizers, including a county board of education (Chrysalis) and two school districts (serving Independence and TAGOS) approved chartered schools knowing the teachers would have autonomy. Teachers' areas of autonomy are laid out explicitly in the chartering contracts between authorizers and the school. At Avalon, teacher autonomy is made formal via the school's governing bylaws that are approved by the school's board.

3. *Instrumentality charter contract + MOU between school, district and union local* [Academia de Lenguajes y Bellas Artes (ALBA)].

    Since 2001, the Milwaukee Public School board has authorized instrumentality chartered schools that it knows will be run by teacher cooperatives. In Wisconsin instrumentality chartered schools, staff are employed by the school district and eligible for state retirement benefits, whereas staff in non–instrumentality chartered schools are employed by the chartered school board and not eligible for state retirement benefits.

    Much of the autonomy for the teacher cooperatives is arranged via the instrumentality chartering contract between the school board and the school. The teachers keep their economic life with district employment via a memorandum of understanding (MOU) with the district and union local that provides waivers from aspects of the collective bargaining agreement. In Milwaukee the term "cooperative" refers to a state of mind about collective ownership in managing the schools.

4. *Pilot school agreement* [Mission Hill K–8 School (Mission Hill)].

In 1994, Boston Public Schools (BPS) designed "pilot schools" in an effort to retain teachers and students after the Massachusetts Legislature passed a state chartering law in 1993. Under the pilot agreement, the BPS superintendent delegates authority to pilot schools' governing boards to try new and different means of improving teaching and learning in order to better serve at-risk urban students. Sometimes governing boards delegate the authority to teachers at the school, as is the case at Mission Hill.

5. *Site-governance agreement between district school board and district school* [San Francisco Community School (SFCS)].

SFCS, which operated with informally arranged teacher autonomy since 1972, formally secured autonomy via a Small Schools by Design agreement with the San Francisco Board of Education in 2007. San Francisco schools with a Small Schools By Design agreement have autonomy that is spelled out explicitly in the agreement. Sometimes governing boards delegate this authority to teachers at the school, as is the case at SFCS.

6. *Informal arrangements resting on the goodwill of a superintendent, principal, or governing board* [High School in the Community (HSC), Phoenix High School (Phoenix)].

Teachers in these schools do not have any formal agreement securing their authority to make decisions.

LIMITING ONE AREA OF AUTONOMY CAN LIMIT WHAT TEACHERS ARE ABLE TO DO WITH OTHER AREAS OF AUTONOMY

By our definition, teachers with just one of the ten potential areas of autonomy are considered to have autonomy. The ten areas of autonomy, however, are often interdependent such that when teachers have just one, then their ability to innovate can be limited. Teachers interviewed for this study made this observation based on their own experiences, echoing the findings of RAND Education, William G. Ouchi, and a long list of others who have studied autonomy.

In RAND's *Decentralized Decisionmaking for Schools*, Janet S. Hansen and Marguerite Roza wrote, "Decentralization has little chance of being effective unless it . . . embraces the full range of decisions about authority over instructional matters" (Hansen and Roza 2005, 3).

The authors cited Bruce A. Bimber's research in the early 1990s which found that decentralization efforts up until that time had limited effects. The efforts "treated decisions (about budgets, personnel, curriculum and instruction, and general operations and administration) as separable, and lifted constraints in some areas while leaving many others intact. Because many decisions are in fact highly interdependent, authority ostensibly granted in one area was limited by constraints still in place in other areas" (Hansen and Roza 2005, 3; Bimber 1994).

In *The Secret of TSL*, Ouchi found that school success is related to five pillars of school empowerment plus "not one but four freedoms that are equally essential" (Ouchi 2009, 38). He concluded, "The elements of the five pillars and four freedoms [autonomy in the areas of budget, staffing, curriculum, and schedule] must be substantially, if not perfectly, aligned with one another because the effectiveness of one element depends in part on its alignment with others" (Ouchi 2009, 272). Without alignment, he said, the effects of any one pillar or freedom are muted.

Autonomous teachers interviewed for this study reported that having the authority to determine budget, for example, can allow for increased decision-making authority regarding learning program and materials, schedule, and staffing pattern. Controlling the budget *and* staffing pattern meant they could tailor employment arrangements according to what would work best for students, even if their arrangement was unconventional. They could replace a full-time employee with two part-time employees, for example, without jumping through a lot of hoops.

Similarly, autonomous teachers said that controlling the budget *and* learning program meant they could spend on materials of most benefit to their students. Teachers in one school had limited budget autonomy and were bound to its school district's budget formula for text books. The line-item formula served most schools in the district well, as most were working with the district's required curriculum and texts. But at this school the teachers had autonomy to determine their curriculum and did not want to use books, preferring to use software and free online resources.

These teachers had hoped to reallocate that money to another planned expenditure. They found, however, that if they didn't use the money allocated for text books they would lose it. So they purchased books and questioned the extent to which they would be able to innovate with their learning program under the circumstances.

AS A TEACHER, I NEVER HAD AUTONOMY

My name is Amy Junge, and I was part of the team that researched this book. It was my role to bring the voice of a K–12 conventional school teacher and administrator into the investigation. I started my career in teaching at the elementary level and moved to a middle school three years later. Middle school was a good fit for me and after two more years I earned my administrative credential and was promoted to assistant principal. My reflections from my visits to schools with autonomous teachers are interspersed throughout this book.

I am proud to be a teacher. Teaching children gives me a sense of satisfaction that is powerful and fulfilling. My experiences in public education as a student, a teacher, and an administrator have for the most part been very positive. The schools, districts, and unions I have worked with are dedicated to helping students succeed and maintaining supportive work environments. I was fortunate. This is not the experience of many students and educators in public K–12 education.

Yet I often feel disrespected as part of the teaching community. While parents have always been respectful of me and value my role as their child's teacher, I don't feel this same respect when I tell someone outside of my school community that I am a teacher. Most education articles I read praise the individual teacher yet bash the profession of teaching.

As a teacher I never really gave much thought to teacher autonomy. It wasn't a term I heard used much in my credential classes or at any of the three schools I worked at. If I had been asked, I would have said teacher autonomy referred to classroom autonomy. It never occurred to me to think of it in terms of my colleagues and I having the autonomy to run a school.

After participating in this project I realize that I never had autonomy as a teacher. The district always chose the curriculum, my principal always supplied the budget, and the school rules were established well before my arrival. Within my classroom, I had the freedom to plan lessons and choose discipline strategies that fit my students' needs and my style, but this didn't apply beyond my classroom.

Because I wanted to make more of an impact on the whole school environment, I went into administration. If I had been aware of collective teacher autonomy, I would have been drawn to the opportunity and the potential to lead without having to completely leave the classroom. This would have satisfied my desire to make a larger contribution to more students' education.

Given my experience in teaching and administration, I can honestly say I was very surprised and impressed by what teachers are able to create with collective teacher autonomy. Their work is inspiring. Students at the schools we visited were not only succeeding, but often thriving—even students who had been failing at their previous schools. Not only is teacher autonomy a truly innovative option, it has real potential to improve schools and empower teachers as professionals and students as learners.

These teachers were not alone in experiencing limitations to one area of autonomy due to its overlapping nature with another. Other examples will be described in the remaining chapters of this book.

SOME TEACHER AUTONOMY ARRANGEMENTS ARE
MORE SUSTAINABLE THAN OTHERS

While the discussion about the interdependent nature of autonomy suggests it is ideal to get a formal agreement with all ten areas of autonomy, implementation can be tricky.

Pragmatically speaking, there is not necessarily one "right way" to grant or secure teacher autonomy. At times teachers sense they need to take what they can get both in terms of their arrangement and areas of autonomy, so they decide together how far they will push. The "right way" for each group of teachers seems to depend on a host of influencing factors, including state and local political climates, openness of states, counties, school districts, chartered school boards, and union locals to trying things differently, as well as the personal preferences of teachers in the group.

Sometimes the "right" autonomy arrangement for a particular school evolves over time as influencing factors change. Teachers at SFCS started without a formal agreement for their collective autonomy, for example, but over a number of years demonstrated their success. According to SFCS teachers, their innovative report card design indicating students' mastery of specific state standards had even been replicated throughout the school district.

SFCS teachers had done so well that, when their school board became interested in a wider implementation of decentralization strategies, they were invited to help author the formal agreement that secured their autonomy in a number of specific areas.

But the SFCS case, like many others, raises important questions about how to sustain states', counties', school districts', chartered school boards', and unions' commitment to teacher autonomy and, by extension, the innovations teachers develop with their autonomy. Before they arranged their formal agreement, SFCS teachers' autonomy might have been jeopardized had a change in school board leadership been averse, rather than friendly, to autonomy.

Case in point, teachers in other school sites reported that new district superintendents were not obligated to honor the informal autonomy arrangements they had with previous superintendents. When some new superintendents, with different management philosophies, made changes that the teachers perceived as threatening to their autonomy, the teachers became wrapped up in numerous activities hoping to avoid more intrusion. Teachers had taken for granted their informally provided arrangement.

A good number of teachers expressed regret that they hadn't pursued formal autonomy arrangements as well as one or more specific areas of autonomy when they first established their arrangements. But they stated they did not do so for one or more reasons, including the following: (1) They did not think it possible to secure a formal autonomy agreement or did not believe they would ever be granted some specific areas of autonomy, even if they had asked; (2) it did not occur to them to pursue a formal autonomy agreement; (3) they did not know which areas of autonomy to pursue; (4) they did not realize that limitations to one area of autonomy could limit the potential associated with another; and (5) they were afraid that asking for some areas of autonomy would jeopardize their ability to secure the areas which they perceived to be surer bets.

Each of these reasons highlights the fact that there is not a lot of information available to guide teachers who wish to pursue autonomy. The limited information is mostly theoretical and not rooted in the real experiences of autonomous teachers. As more teachers accept authority and accountability for school success, answering questions about how to best sustain autonomy arrangements and what levels of accountability should be associated with varying degrees of authority will be of great importance.

AUTONOMY PROVIDES TEACHERS *THE OPPORTUNITY* TO EMULATE THE CULTURAL CHARACTERISTICS OF HIGH-PERFORMING ORGANIZATIONS; IT IS NOT BY ITSELF A SOURCE OF A HIGH-PERFORMING CULTURE

With all the focus on autonomy in this chapter, it might easily be confused as a source of high-performing cultures. But it is not. Instead, autonomy structures provide *the opportunity* for teachers to use their discretion to choose or invent ways of operating that emulate the cultural characteristics of high-performing organizations. The subject of this book is what teachers do with that opportunity.

We will highlight what teachers describe are their successes and struggles, all of which might be rooted in the nature of their arrangements. As this subject is explored in the following chapters, knowing the teachers' varying arrangements and areas of autonomy—as well as the autonomy structures each could potentially have—will be helpful.

NOTES

1. While salaries and benefits are part of the school budget, they are listed as a separate area of autonomy for two reasons. First, autonomy arrangements can vary for each area as they do for the teachers at Chrysalis Charter School. Second, some teacher groups have partial autonomy to determine their budget, but definitely do not have autonomy to determine salaries and benefits. This can have an impact on teachers' ability to change school practices, as is discussed in chapter 11.

2. A chartered school authorizer is the entity that chartered school boards enter into contract with for permission to operate and oversight. Chartered school authorizers, also called sponsors (in some states), determine who should be entrusted with public funds and teaching students (Piper 2009).

3. A pilot school is a public school that is associated with a school district and employs teachers who are members of the local teachers union. The arrangement is unique in that autonomy from the district is spelled out in an agreement between the school governing board (which is responsible for overseeing progress) and the superintendent of the district (who has ultimate authority). Typically the superintendent holds pilot schools accountable via a school quality review process based on a set of benchmarks for a high-performing school.

4. A magnet school is a public school with specialized courses or curricula. "Magnet" refers to how the schools draw students from across the normal boundaries defined by authorities (usually school boards) as school zones that feed into certain schools.

Chapter Three

When Granted Autonomy, Teachers Choose to Operate in Ways That Emulate the Cultural Characteristics of High-Performing Organizations

Teacher autonomy isn't a silver bullet means of attaining school success. Autonomy simply provides teachers at each school *the opportunity* to collectively use their discretion to choose or invent ways of operating that are associated with high performance. As we consider whether granting teachers autonomy ought to be part of a national strategy for addressing problems with K–12, a major question is this: what will teachers do with this opportunity?

Answering this question first requires a definition for "high performance." In chapter 1 we stated that organizations are considered "high performing" if they achieve results that are better than their peers' over a period of time. By inference, their cultural characteristics are associated with success.

To learn more about these organizations, we conducted a review of literature—twenty-three studies and professional articles examining private and public sectors, but mostly the private sector (see bibliography). The findings suggest that high-performing organizations have nine cultural characteristics. Managers and workers:

1. Accept ownership: Welcome authority and responsibility for making decisions and be accountable for the outcomes.
2. Innovate: Take risks to try creative new things, challenge old processes, and continuously adapt.

3. Share purpose: Seek clarity and buy in to the mission, values, goals, and standards of practice.
4. Collaborate: Establish a culture of interdependence characterized by an open flow of ideas, listening to and understanding others, and valuing differences.
5. Lead effectively: Expect leadership from all and perceive leadership as in service to all.
6. Function as learners: Establish a culture characterized by a sense of common challenge and discovery, rather than a culture where experts impart information.
7. Avoid insularity: Learn from and be sensitive to the external environment.
8. Motivate: Be engaged, motivated, and motivating.
9. Assess performance: Set and measure progress toward goals and act upon results to improve performance.

As explained in chapter 1, we decided that a reasonable proxy for determining whether autonomous teachers make choices associated with high performance is to examine to what extent teachers emulate these cultural characteristics.

There was not any literature available regarding autonomous teachers' choices, but we were able to find and review literature—another twenty-four studies and professional articles (see bibliography)—examining the choices of teachers who have a higher-than-average voice in determining school-level improvement strategies. These teachers work in what education leaders call professional communities, learning communities, and learning organizations.

The results of this second portion of the literature review showed that when teachers have choices about how they work they do, to some extent, emulate the nine cultural characteristics of high-performing organizations. The implication for this study was that examining the choices of *autonomous* teachers, who have the authority to collectively make the decisions influencing whole school success, would be a worthwhile endeavor.

Let's examine the extent to which autonomous teachers emulate each of the nine characteristics:

1. Accept Ownership: Welcome Authority and Responsibility for Making Decisions and Be Accountable for the Outcomes.

Autonomy gives teachers the authority and responsibility for making decisions, which teachers said incents them to accept accountability and responsibility for their schools' outcomes. In their survey responses 92 percent rated their colleagues' willingness to individually accept responsibility for decisions as excellent (29.7 percent), very good (36.3 percent), or good (26.4 percent). An equal percentage rated their willingness to collectively accept responsibility as excellent (37.0 percent), very good (40.2 percent), or good (15.2 percent).

Ninety-two percent also rated their colleagues' willingness to individually accept accountability for student performance outcomes as excellent (24.4 percent), very good (38.9 percent), or good (27.8 percent); and 91 percent gave the same rating for their colleagues' willingness to *collectively* accept accountability for student performance outcomes (excellent [30.8 percent], very good [40.7 percent], or good [20.9 percent]). One hundred percent of teachers with complete budget autonomy rated their colleagues' willingness to collectively accept accountability for the school's financial outcomes as excellent (40.0 percent), very good (48.6 percent), or good (11.4 percent).

Teachers don't have a problem with being held accountable for results when they are allowed to determine, as professionals, the means of achieving them. Teachers explained that in the areas they have autonomy they are able to take pride in what works well and refine what doesn't. This is very different from their prior arrangement, they said. They perceive that in conventional arrangements, as a matter of both policy and practice, teachers are blamed for problems they don't have the authority to address.

Alysia Krafel at Chrysalis School (Chrysalis) observed of her school, "There is no one going over teachers' heads and ignoring our advice," she said. "We have ownership of our decisions, and the consequences—good or bad—are right in our face. With the freedom to address the bad, we're willing to take the responsibility." Jill Mulhausen at Phoenix High School

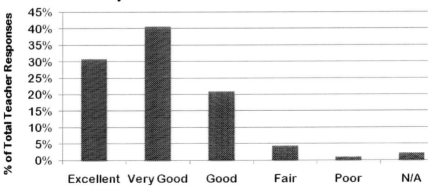

Teachers' willingness to collectively accept accountability for student performance outcomes

(Phoenix) stated, "[In the areas we have autonomy] we do not have the ability to blame the system, the students, or the parents. We made the decisions. There isn't a bureaucracy handling them. So we'll accept accountability."

And there are people making sure that they do. Autonomous teachers are accountable to the state, school district, authorizer, chartered school board, or person who grants them autonomy. Those granting autonomy are responsible not for telling teachers *how* to practice their craft and achieve goals, but for holding teachers accountable for meeting mutually determined goals.

Teachers are also held accountable by students and their families who are able to exercise choice regarding which school they choose to attend.

Teachers reported that these accountability frameworks provide powerful incentives to make the choices necessary for success.

Carrie Bakken at Avalon School (Avalon) explained, "Without students we wouldn't have a budget. That need to retain students dramatically affects our sense of accountability, and our willingness to do what it takes to keep students at Avalon."

Nichole Kotasek at Minnesota New Country School (MNCS) said,

> There is no one to blame. We're not members of the union here, so there is no one to make a case for me if things aren't going well. *I* have to change what's not working, both for the students and for myself. *I* have to step it up or risk facing the consequences. I also have to place a lot of faith in my colleagues, that they'll do the same. Since we are all accountable together, we find ways to ensure everyone is working toward our school's success.

2. Innovate: Take Risks to Try Creative New Things, Challenge Old Processes, and Continuously Adapt.

Teachers report that their sense of accountability for school success encourages them to innovate. Most are constantly on the lookout for what's not working well and most willingly put in extra effort to find new ways of doing things. They are not satisfied with the status quo when the responsibility for students' outcomes falls on them.

Nora Houseman at San Francisco Community School (SFCS) reported, "[As autonomous teachers] we know we can't be mediocre. We need to be exceptional. If we're not then there is no meaning; no connection between our autonomy and students' [outcomes]. [Plus, our outcomes] have a direct impact on me. My job and being able to work the way we work here depends on us doing well."

Sarah Ard at Phoenix said, "We have a willingness to say, 'We did a terrible job.' We have a willingness to look at ourselves period! The students in this school depend on us to make a difference. If we can't show that we are, they'll leave. So we need to come up with real solutions. Real solutions for *our* students aren't always the ones being recommended for the district as a whole."

Erik Good at High School in the Community (HSC) said, "We understand the responsibility we have, and we'll go out of our way to do what it takes to be successful."

Almost 97 percent of teachers surveyed said they and their colleagues are excellent (40.0 percent), very good (43.3 percent), or good (13.3 percent) at creating innovative means to improve performance.

Teachers gave similar rankings, in the mid-90th percentile, for the following: our culture's encouragement of teachers to search out opportunities to change and improve (excellent [37.1 percent], very good [40.4 percent], or good [18.0 percent]); our culture's encouragement of trying new things (excellent [62.2 percent], very good [22.2 percent], or good [12.2 percent]); commitment to continuous improvement and adaptation in the way we work (excellent [48.3 percent], very good [37.1 percent], or good [10.1 percent]); acceptance of teachers' innovation in their individual work with students (excellent [57.8 percent], very good [35.6 percent], or good [4.4 percent]); and implementation of creative, new ideas (excellent [54.4 percent], very good [28.9 percent], or good [12.2 percent]).

Eighty-five percent of teachers indicated that they had done an excellent (34.8 percent), very good (39.3 percent), or good (11.2 percent) job of removing bureaucratic processes standing in the way of implementing good ideas for improvement. The majority of the teachers who said that bureaucratic processes were standing in the way of improvement were working in schools where interviewees had reported recent challenges to or reduction of their autonomy. Leaders from their school districts or unions had reasserted their authority.

Teachers described a number of ways in which bureaucratic processes and structures limited their innovation. Teachers in schools affiliated with school districts, for example, said that their ability to create relevant professional development is hindered by their autonomy arrangements' failure to remove the requirement that they attend and pay for district-wide professional development that assumes teachers are in conventional roles.

Some teachers want to require peer evaluation for all teachers in their schools—including new teachers and veteran teachers—but are not able to because districts, teacher unions, and/or administrator unions require that an administrator conduct evaluations. Also, some teachers reported that measuring individual students' learning growth is superseded by time-consuming requirements to assess students' aggregate performance on adequate yearly progress (AYP) as defined by the federal No Child Left Behind Act of 2001.[1]

3. Share Purpose: Seek Clarity and Buy in to the Mission, Values, Goals, and Standards of Practice.

Teachers have a shared purpose when they collectively buy in to a mission, values, goals, and standards of practice which are commonly understood. All autonomous teachers report that they collectively abide by written statements outlining their shared purposes.

Almost 98 percent said they have specific goals for the school. Nearly 92 percent said their schools' cultural reinforcement of teachers' stated values is excellent (37.2 percent), very good (39.5 percent), or good (15.1 percent). And 95 percent rated teachers' personal commitment or buy in to standards of practice—guidelines for determining what they should do and not do in practicing their craft at the school—as excellent (43.8 percent), very good (41.7 percent), or good (9.4 percent).

Autonomous teachers who were interviewed said they commit to continuous and reflective dialogue about how to improve the school so they will better meet their shared purpose. Teachers know continuous dialogue can lead to innovation that better achieves their purpose, and this knowledge fuels their interest in participating.

Just over 95 percent said they are excellent (50.0 percent), very good (37.2 percent), or good (8.1 percent) at engaging in reflective dialogue. Ninety-eight percent said their inclusiveness of teachers, whether new or veteran, in setting school goals is excellent (60.4 percent), very good (30.2 percent), or good (7.3 percent). These choices are reflected in teachers' ratings of their colleagues' personal commitment and buy in to the purpose. Nearly 98 percent said their personal commitment and buy in is excellent (63.9 percent), very good (26.8 percent). or good (7.2 percent). Almost 96 percent rated teachers' excitement about their goals as excellent (33.3 percent), very good (42.7 percent), or good (19.8 percent).

To the extent possible, teachers hire new colleagues based on their perceptions about candidates' ability to commit to the shared purpose and associated culture. Teachers who had limitations in their hiring autonomy expressed that their ability to hire people who would be a good match for their shared purpose is at times compromised. This can affect autonomous teachers' ability to emulate many other cultural characteristics of high-performing organizations.

Teachers conveyed that sometimes it seems their longer-term goals can get lost as they take care of day-to-day needs. Also, teachers reported that individuals have different ideas about how the collective can best meet their shared purpose in carrying out their work, which can lead to intense disagreements between colleagues.

One source of disagreement, for example, is to what extent status quo expectations about students' academic achievement should affect their learning program choices. Some teachers think their schools ought to be radically different from the status quo while others are more conservative. Yet teachers said they willingly carry out what the group decides, even if they don't always agree with the decisions, because they know their ideas have been considered. Autonomous teachers also continuously dialogue about their work, so they know there will be an opportunity to change course if the selected ideas don't work well.

4. Collaborate: Establish a Culture of Interdependence Characterized by an Open Flow of Ideas, Listening to and Understanding Others, and Valuing Differences.

Autonomous teachers reported that they believe collaborating for the good of the whole—not just for the good of their own classrooms—is essential to school success. Since whole-school success is their responsibility, they commit to nurturing a collaborative culture that involves consultative behavior, listening, openness to differing opinions, mutual respect, and working together.

Almost 98 percent of surveyed teachers rated their culture as excellent (58.7 percent), very good (29.3 percent), or good (9.8 percent) at fostering teamwork, consultation, and engagement. Nearly 98 percent and 94.6 percent, respectively, rated their cultures as excellent, very good or good at having an open flow of ideas (excellent [53.3 percent], very good [31.5 percent], or good [13.0 percent]) and interdependence (excellent [38.0 percent], very good [44.6 percent], or good [12.0 percent]).

Most autonomous teachers warned that collaboration is not always easy, however. Maintaining a collaborative culture requires a lot of patience and tolerance, and a willingness to work on collaborative skills. Almost 96 percent rated their collective willingness to invest the time and effort it takes to develop a collaborative community as excellent (47.8 percent), very good (35.9 percent), or good (12.0 percent). And the same percentage rated their value for differences, as evidenced by a culture of listening to and understanding others regardless of status or function, as excellent (45.7 percent), very good (39.1 percent), or good (10.9 percent).

When union-affiliated teachers' authority to work extended hours is limited, they report that it can be difficult to maintain a collaborative culture. They need extra time to make decisions, and are often willing to put in the time, but the union work rules prevent them from doing so. This problem can be exacerbated when hiring autonomy is limited. When teachers must hire those who were "first fired" they aren't always able to hire people who are willing to participate as everyone else does. This can erode collaborative culture.

5. Lead Effectively: Expect Leadership from All and Perceive Leadership as in Service to All.

Since autonomous teachers have collective accountability for whole school success, leaders get their authority and power from the collective. Teachers often select their own leaders—principals, lead teachers, committee leaders, and others—who are accountable to the group for their actions. In this arrangement the leaders aren't "in charge" of teachers but are instead obligated to act collaboratively, frequently consulting with and carrying out the wishes of the group. The conventional hierarchical leadership triangle, in which teachers are accountable to their leaders who are accountable to off-site leaders, is inverted.

About 78 percent of teachers surveyed said they strongly agreed (41.5 percent) or agreed (36.6 percent) that their leaders are selected by all and accountable to all, while another 14.6 percent neither agreed nor disagreed. Almost 89 percent said that their leaders' commitment to being in service to all is excellent (41.4 percent), very good (33.3 percent), or good (13.8 percent), and 87.3 percent said their understanding of leadership roles is excellent (35.6 percent), very good (33.3 percent), or good (18.4 percent).

Almost 91 percent reported that their trust and confidence in their leaders is excellent (40.2 percent), very good (36.8 percent), or good (13.8 percent). Just 79 percent, however, reported that their distribution of [selected] leaders is diverse and complimentary (excellent [24.4 percent], very good [36.0 percent], or good [18.6 percent]).

Sometimes autonomous teachers don't delegate all of their authority to single leaders, and instead make some or all decisions democratically as a whole group or by committee. Teachers said they are willing to participate in these leadership functions because they believe that collaboration is essential to whole-school success.

But whether decisions are made by single leaders or the whole group, almost 92 percent of surveyed teachers said they were excellent (32.2 percent), very good (42.5 percent), or good (17.2 percent) at expecting that all are leaders. Fewer teachers, 83.8 percent, said that as a group they were excellent (33.3 percent), very good (33.3 percent), or good (17.2 percent) at including all teachers as important decision-makers.

6. Function as Learners: Establish a Culture Characterized by a Sense of Common Challenge and Discovery, Rather Than a Culture Where Experts Impart Information.

Teachers said they create learning cultures in which they see themselves as unfinished learners rather than experts who know all there is to know about teaching students. Almost 89 percent of those surveyed rated their attitude that they are not experts as excellent (41.4 percent), very good (32.2 percent), or good (14.9 percent). About 95 percent said their cultures support them in asking for and receiving help (excellent [29.1 percent], very good [50.0 percent], or good [16.3 percent]). And nearly 97 percent rated teachers' ability to admit difficulty without social costs as excellent (36.8 percent), very good (41.4 percent), or good (18.4 percent).

Autonomous teachers conveyed that their learning cultures support them in addressing what doesn't work by facilitating discovery of better ways to encourage student engagement and motivation. Almost 98 percent rated their commitment to continuous learning and improvement as excellent (57.5 percent), very good (26.4 percent), or good (13.8 percent). And 95.4 percent of teachers surveyed rated their cultures' support for teacher learning as excellent (39.1 percent), very good (40.2 percent), or good (16.1 percent).

While autonomous teachers see themselves as always learning, they questioned whether they have access to enough formal professional development that is relevant to the learning programs and environments they create. Teachers in schools affiliated with districts sensed they spent so much time

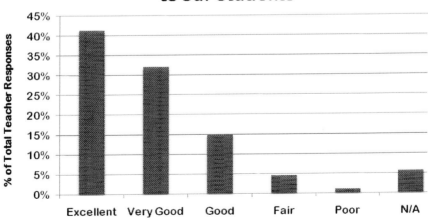

Our attitude that we are not experts whose role is to impart information to our students

and money on required professional development that wasn't relevant to their model that there was not much leftover to spend on more useful formal professional development.

Teachers who have complete budget autonomy said that they are able to access relevant professional development, but many indicated there was room for more. Professional development, many said, was not as high on their priority list as other matters and is one of the first things to suffer when time is limited.

Still, it was clear that these teachers value professional development and seek opportunities to improve their skills. Nearly 83 percent said, for example, that their intentional cultivation of teachers' leadership skills—a dimension of professional development teachers desire when working in schools with teacher autonomy—is excellent (24.4 percent), very good (38.4 percent), or good (19.8 percent).

7. Avoid Insularity: Learn from and Be Sensitive to the External Environment.

While autonomous teachers gave themselves high ratings for their cultural commitment to learning from and being sensitive to the external environment, this is an area in which they do not rate themselves as highly as they do in other areas. About 90 percent of those surveyed rated their attitude that they need to learn from others [in the external environment] as excellent (33.0 percent), very good (36.4 percent), or good (18.2 percent), and 94.3 percent rated their ability to adapt when conditions around them change as excellent (47.7 percent), very good (34.1 percent), or good (12.5 percent).

But fewer, 83.1 percent, rated their *value* for new ideas from those outside the school as excellent (21.3 percent), very good (42.7 percent), or good (19.1 percent). And even fewer, 80.9 percent, gave themselves those ratings for their invitation of new ideas from those outside the school (excellent [23.6 percent], very good [38.2 percent], or good [19.1 percent]).

About 87 percent rated their commitment to understanding what their stakeholders desire as excellent (23.0 percent), very good (36.8 percent), or good (27.6 percent). But interviewees expressed differing opinions about who their stakeholders are. About 87 percent rated their attitude that students' future employers and future educational institutions are stakeholders of their schools as excellent (31.5 percent), very good (37.1 percent), or good (18.0 percent), yet teachers who were interviewed did not report that they were particularly influenced by those groups.

Almost all said they also did not pay much attention to the ideas of business leaders, leaders of future educational institutions, state education leaders, teachers' union leaders, and school district leaders except to be attentive to changing political tides in order to avoid losing their autonomy.

Autonomous teachers' attitude was that sometimes these leaders, in the name of listening to the external environment, make too many changes, too fast. The leaders move on to the "next big thing" without allowing the previous "big thing" to take root.

Also, autonomous teachers said that sometimes these leaders' decisions are the barriers to the innovation that teachers are working to advance. Teachers reported they were open to learning from the external environment to improve their craft, but were at a loss for ideas about where useful advice might come from.

Teachers regarded students and parents as their biggest stakeholders. They said they pay a lot of attention to youth culture and their students' life circumstances as they create and refine their school models. Some also pay attention to technology trends. Teachers at one school explained that they were talking about adapting their already innovative technology practices to stay "new and different." Others spoke about constantly paying attention to whether their learning, disciplinary, and after-school programs were supporting students' individual and cultural needs.

Considering many districts and unions are now trying some of the practices that autonomous teachers took on years ago—including peer evaluation, restorative justice disciplinary strategies, and "laptops for all"—some teachers reported that they want to find ways to stay ahead of the trends in order to continue to appeal to teachers and students.

8. Motivate: Be Engaged, Motivated, and Motivating.

With accountability for school success, autonomous teachers said they collectively decide to place a strong emphasis on encouraging students' engagement and motivation. These teachers realize that students choose to learn—adults can't make them—so they need to find means of adapting to students' individual learning needs. Individualizing learning, teachers said, requires their own engagement to innovate with learning environments, learning programs, disciplinary strategies, and even their own roles.

Mostly, teachers' choices put students in a position to take responsibility for their own learning. They seek the best means of encouraging students to be active learners, not passive learners whose job it is to receive and memorize information from teachers. They also design schools and schooling methods with an eye toward accommodating students' varying levels of readiness, aptitudes, interests, and rates of learning.

Almost 98 percent of teachers said they were excellent (48.9 percent), very good (33.0 percent), or good (15.9 percent) at varying teaching methods according to the needs of individual students. And 95.5 percent reported they were excellent (43.2 percent), very good (34.1 percent), or good (18.2 percent) at varying teaching methods according to the *interests* of individual

Personalization of student learning

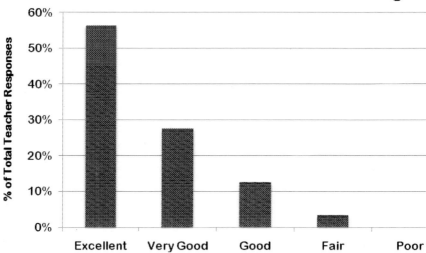

students. Fewer teachers, 86.3 percent, rated students' freedom to pursue topics of interest to them for academic credit as excellent (56.8 percent), very good (25.0 percent), or good (4.5 percent).

Cultures which value individualized learning seem to be especially engaging for students who perceived they were not served well in conventional schools, including students receiving special education, students who are bored or bewildered, and students who are seeking safety. Encouraging students' *motivation*, however, takes much more time. Teachers said that many students really struggle with their motivation as they discover what it takes to be active learners in individualized learning environments. They prioritize forming strong relationships with students in order to understand what makes each one tick.

All teachers surveyed rated their value for knowing students as whole persons is excellent (72.4 percent), very good (21.8 percent), or good (5.7 percent). And almost 97 percent rated their understanding of the differences among students as excellent (51.1 percent), very good (34.1 percent), or good (11.4 percent). Knowing students and their differences allows them to personalize learning, something 96.6 percent of them said they were excellent (56.3 percent), very good (27.6 percent), or good (12.6 percent) at achieving.

9. Assess Performance: Set and Measure Progress toward Mission, Values, and Goals and Act upon Results to Improve Performance.

Autonomous teachers assess their students' performance as well as their own to determine their progress toward their mission, values, and goals. They also assess both student and parent satisfaction. About 87 percent of teachers surveyed rated their commitment to measuring progress toward their success in achieving their purpose as excellent (27.6 percent), very good (37.9 percent), or good (21.8 percent).

Over 94 percent rated their commitment to acting on results to improve performance as excellent (37.9 percent), very good (39.1 percent), or good (17.2 percent). And almost 92 percent said they were excellent (34.9 percent), very good (38.4 percent), or good (18.6 percent) at committing to understanding their reasons for success. Finally, about 81.5 percent and 83.8 percent, respectively, said they were excellent (26.4 percent; 26.4 percent), very good (40.2 percent; 33.3 percent), or good (14.9 percent; 24.1 percent) at assessing student and parent satisfaction.

Autonomous teachers view the outcomes of student assessments as feedback on individual students' progress as well as feedback on the overall design of their learning programs and environments. Many reported that they use the feedback to make any necessary adjustments. About 86 percent rated their use of information gathered from student assessments to improve their performance as excellent (25.6 percent), very good (40.7 percent), or good (19.8 percent).

Teachers take their students' scores on state standardized tests and, where applicable, district standardized tests seriously, but focus more intently on individuals' learning growth than on raising aggregate student achievement to make AYP.

Eighty-six percent of teachers said their commitment to setting specific, measurable goals for individual students is excellent (36.0 percent), very good (31.4 percent), or good (18.6 percent). Teachers are not interested in defining their schools or their students with labels such as "good enough" or "needs improvement." Labels, they say, take the focus off individual growth and can squander the motivation of students at all levels of academic achievement.

Focused on their mission, values, and goals, autonomous teachers also elect to assess students' achievement in areas beyond academics. Almost 98 percent of teachers surveyed said they were excellent (34.9 percent), very good (47.7 percent), or good (15.1 percent) at assessing student performance using their own standards. Many conveyed in interviews, for example, that they require students to learn to manage their own learning, develop disciplined approaches to learning, build confidence in their ability to solve their own problems, recover from failure, communicate effectively, and be contributing members of their communities.

Not all teachers have autonomy to determine the methods for evaluating their own performance, but most who do have it reported that they choose to do self-, peer-, and 360-degree evaluations. Teachers in almost all of the schools said that their evaluation rubrics help identify individual teachers' areas for improvement.

With accountability for school success, teachers decide that all will be coached and mentored in these areas (only informally in schools without evaluation autonomy) in order to improve the school. In fact, about 93 percent of teachers surveyed said their leaders' commitment to coaching and facilitating is excellent (37.9 percent), very good (39.1 percent), or good (16.1 percent). Receiving coaching and mentoring isn't seen as a punitive action, they said—*everyone* has areas needing improvement.

Assessment of teacher performance, however, is an area in which surveyed teachers did not rate themselves as highly as they did in other areas. About 75 percent of the teachers who had autonomy in the area of evaluation said they are excellent, very good, or good at assessing teachers' performance as it relates to their students' performance.

The same percentage said they are excellent, very good, or good at assessing teachers' strengths and weaknesses, in part, as they relate to the school's overall performance. About 79 percent of all teachers surveyed rated themselves as excellent (27.6 percent), very good (34.5 percent), or good (17.2 percent) at assessing teachers' collective performance as it relates to school success.

AUTONOMOUS TEACHERS EMBRACE EIGHT BEHAVIORS AND APPROACHES THAT ARE INDICATIVE OF THE CULTURAL CHARACTERISTICS OF HIGH-PERFORMING ORGANIZATIONS

This chapter began with a question: will teachers collectively use their autonomy to choose or invent ways of operating that are associated with high performance? Autonomous teachers' responses to the survey and interview questions suggest that the answer to this question is clearly "yes." Our analysis of their interview responses also revealed that with collective autonomy teachers embrace eight behaviors and approaches, or practices, all of which are indicative of the cultural characteristics of high-performing organizations. Part 2 of this book dedicates one chapter to each of the eight practices:

Practice #1: Share purpose, which always focuses on students as individuals, and use it as the basis of decisions aimed at school improvement.

Practice #2: Participate in collaboration and leadership for the good of the whole school, not just a classroom.

Practice #3: Encourage colleagues and students to be active, ongoing learners in an effort to nurture everyone's engagement and motivation.

Practice #4: Develop or adopt learning programs that individualize student learning.

Practice #5: Address social and discipline problems as part of student learning.

Practice #6: Broaden the definition and scope of student achievement and assessment.

Practice #7: Encourage teacher improvement using 360-degree, peer-, and self-evaluation methods as well as peer coaching and mentoring.

Practice #8: Make budget trade-offs to meet the needs of students they serve.

NOTE

1. The federal No Child Left Behind Act allows state education agencies to develop target starting goals for AYP. After those are developed, states must increase aggregate student achievement in gradual increments in order for 100 percent of students to become proficient on state assessments by the 2013–2014 school year.

2

Eight Practices Autonomous Teachers Embrace, Which Are Indicative of the Cultural Characteristics of High-Performing Organizations

Chapter Four

Practice #1

Share Purpose, Which Always Focuses on Students as Individuals, and Use It as the Basis of Decisions Aimed at School Improvement

Autonomous teachers said that the purposes they collectively create—their mission, values, and goals—are similar to the purposes created for most schools across the country: educate students so they are prepared for life and work.

When they worked as teachers in conventional settings, they were somewhat familiar with their school's purpose, but they did not feel accountable for using it as the basis for their own daily decision making and behavioral choices. Nor was the purpose statement the basis of an ongoing, collective dialogue about how best to meet students' needs. Most decisions, such as which curriculum to use and how to allocate the budget, were made by state and school district leaders with a focus toward *most* students.

Ayla Gavins at Mission Hill K–8 School (Mission Hill) pointed out a major consequence of this way of operating: "People can really move away from making students the center of decision-making." Eric Hendy at San Francisco Community School (SFCS) illustrated further, "When decisions are made top down, things are scripted for you. When teachers know that certain mandates are irrelevant to the students at the school we are working at, we think, 'We don't need to do that.' But in many cases teachers don't have much choice."

Nichole Kotasek at Minnesota New Country School (MNCS) said teachers *do* have a choice. That is, to follow or ignore the mandate. "When things operate like this, teachers are inclined not to follow through. Then we say, 'We knew this idea from [off site] was dumb. It was never going to work.' There's just no buy in when we're not involved."

When teachers are accountable for school success, however, they make the shared purpose a living commitment that guides their decision making. Alysia Krafel at Chrysalis Charter School (Chrysalis) said, "A school purpose can so easily become just words that someone else wrote. In cultures where people don't have authority to make decisions, why would anyone bother remembering what the basic mission and goals are?" When Chrysalis teachers gained collective authority to make decisions related to school success, she said, "Our commitment to the purpose started permeating everything."

FOR AUTONOMOUS TEACHERS, SHARED PURPOSE PROVIDES THE FOUNDATION FOR A CONTINUOUS, REFLECTIVE DIALOGUE ABOUT SCHOOL IMPROVEMENT

Autonomous teachers consistently said that they intentionally create school cultures focused on how best to carry out their shared purpose. There is a willingness to define what's hindering progress and to consider and commit to new ways of doing things, all within the context of their shared mission, values, and goals. Almost 97 percent perceived that their school culture's reflection of the purpose was excellent (49.5 percent), very good (33.7 percent), or good (13.7 percent), and almost 96 percent said teachers have an excellent (38.5 percent), very good (38.5 percent), or good (18.8 percent) ability to see connections between the purpose and its implications for teaching.

Kotasek at MNCS said, "Day to day we are more honest about what works and what doesn't. Our commitment to students' learning feels far more authentic."

Others echoed Kotasek, citing their observations about teachers' tendency to get off purpose when they don't have much influence about how to implement the school purpose structurally and culturally.

Skylar Primm at Tailoring Academics to Guide Our Students (TAGOS Leadership Academy) said, "When I attend reflection-based trainings with teachers who are in traditional schools they aren't talking about learning. They go on and on about their encounters with students who are using cell

Our school culture's reflection of our purpose

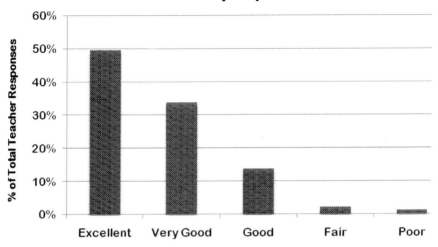

phones and wearing hoodies to hide headphones. These things don't have to matter, but this is their focus! It makes me grateful we have a huge amount of freedom to implement our [purpose]."

Sarah Ard at Phoenix High School (Phoenix) reported that, compared to her teaching experiences in other schools, "We spend a higher percentage of time focused on how to educate the kids. We avoid trainings that aren't aimed at this purpose. We don't spend our time worrying about who is chewing gum. Our time is spent to develop a culture that believes in the kids and their ability to do high-level work."

To maintain their focus, teachers in several schools put their statements of shared purpose front and center when they make decisions. Jo Sullivan at Avalon School (Avalon) said, "We keep a paper with our mission and goals in front of us at meetings to keep ourselves aware. Each agenda item is put under a section of the mission. If an item doesn't fit well, it gets dropped from the agenda."

Other schools have aspects of their shared purpose painted boldly on their walls. At MNCS the painted words remind teachers of their four main re-sponsibilities: Choice. Passion for learning. Relationship. Responsibility. Teachers reported that they frequently invoke school purpose statements dur-ing conversations. They ask themselves questions such as, "How is our pur-pose living in the school? How would it live if we were to make these specific changes?" Jessica Fishman at SFCS said, "We have a culture of asking ourselves, 'Is this in the best interest of our students?'"

These discussions can be challenging, even difficult. Autonomous teachers describe themselves as very passionate about choosing paths that are best for students, and sometimes their ideas about what's best vary. Teachers also disagree about the best means of school improvement. They reported they are not shy about expressing their anger and disappointment when they don't get their way. But teachers also reported that most of them willingly do what the group decides collectively, even when their own ideas aren't the ones taken up by the group.

Why? In the position of accountability, they see how their cooperation can make or break school success, teachers said. Also, they know the reasons why decisions are made because they were part of the process. Their culture of continuous dialogue also allows for them to raise their points again if initial decisions don't lead to desired results. "Since we're accountable for school success, we know that everyone here wants to make sure we are putting out a school that is the best we can make it. If things don't work, we know people will be open to ideas for how to make things better," said Laura Connell at Avalon.

WHEN AUTONOMOUS TEACHERS HIRE NEW COLLEAGUES, THEY STRONGLY CONSIDER CANDIDATES' POTENTIAL TO COMMIT TO THE SHARED PURPOSE

Teachers reported that they look for new hires who will both fill gaps in what the school is able to offer to students (academically speaking) *and* be a "good fit" as far as buying into and carrying out the shared purpose and the associated standards of practice regarding the learning program, environment, and culture. To make a good diagnosis of one's potential "fit," teachers choose to involve the community, including students and parents, in the hiring process. At High School in the Community (HSC), Avalon, and MNCS, teachers even give student participants an equal vote.

The whole community considers this: Does the candidate understand the purpose of the school, and the standard of practice we use to achieve it? Will he or she embrace it and add to the culture? Does this person have the ability to learn from mistakes and the humility to work toward improvement? How does the candidate reflect the purpose in his or her treatment of students? How do students react to him or her?

"We've interviewed people who were really excited about what they were teaching, but had a low effect on students' excitement. We didn't hire them," said Jill Mulhausen at Phoenix. "We hire people because they are a good fit for the [purpose and] culture. At our school, students do self-directed projects and Sarah, for example, showed herself to be a project-based learner in her own life. She converted her Land Rover to diesel herself. She runs a working ranch. She organized a children's marathon. She's not afraid to take on something she's never done before. That's the kind of person we need to inspire the students we work with."

Carrie Bakken at Avalon (where students are also self-directed learners) made a similar point. "We look for people capable of directing their own learning in their own lives," she said. Gavins at Mission Hill said, "People who buy in to Mission Hill's purpose are willing to be like first year teachers again and again; always facing new challenges. We hire from the pool who shows they are willing." Chris French at Independence School Local 1 (Independence) said, "Everyone we've hired is a lifelong learner. It sounds [like a] cliché, but it's the truth."

The survey validated that the vast majority of teachers do a good job of hiring colleagues who embrace their shared purpose. Nearly 94 percent said teachers were excellent (43.6 percent), very good (33.0 percent), or good (17.0 percent) at hiring based on compatibility with their shared purpose. Almost 98 percent rated teachers' personal commitment and buy in to a shared purpose as excellent (63.9 percent), very good (26.8 percent), or good (7.2 percent). And about 95 percent indicated the same about teachers' commitment and buy in to established standards-of-practice (excellent [43.8 percent], very good [41.7 percent], or good [9.4 percent]).

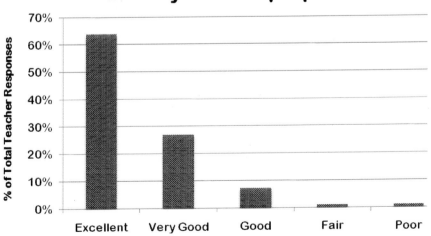

Teachers' personal commitment and buy-in to our purpose

AUTONOMOUS TEACHERS GENERALLY CREATE AND ACT ON SHARED PURPOSES THAT SUPPORT INDIVIDUAL STUDENTS' SUCCESS

Most autonomous teachers interviewed for this book said that their shared purpose includes a strong commitment to individual students' success. As Paul Krafel at Chrysalis put it, the goal is to nourish individuals for who they are such that individuals don't go home feeling devalued for not being the same as everyone else. In general, teachers reject the idea that all students must be on the same path to success.

Karen Locke at EdVisions Off Campus (EOC) said, "Our job is to help kids find *their* place in the world versus the same place in the world. College and certain kinds of jobs aren't the right goals for everyone." Patrick Yecha at Phoenix said, "The students here are neat individuals. We don't have 'bad apples,' just people who don't fit into any mold. Because we acknowledge and accept individuality, there are not any outcasts here. No one hates school."

Teachers explained that honoring a commitment to nourishing individuals is possible because they have the autonomy to make and later adjust structural and cultural decisions based on their on-site observations about what works and what doesn't. They are able to try different ways of carrying out their purpose to best serve the individuals who attend their particular school.

SFCS teachers, for example, have been engaged for some time in a deep dialogue about the meaning of equity. They said they are pressured to give into the conventional definition that equity means offering all students the same amount of time with teachers. But SFCS teachers believe equity involves spending more time with some students and less with others, so this is how they practice their craft.

Heather George at HSC said,

> We are in the trenches every day. We know more about our students than administrators working at the city. We know when a student didn't get enough to eat, and when another has been raped. We know who is getting beat-up on a nightly basis. The teachers here can help students make the best decisions for their own life context. If we stink we move on and try something else. We know we're responsible for making the changes. We don't blame the students.

THESE SCHOOLS AREN'T SIMPLY HIRING TEACHERS
FOR GRADE-LEVELS AND SUBJECT AREAS

When I applied to be a teacher I submitted applications to districts, included recommendations, and waited to be called for interviews. I chose districts based on their reputations and locations. If I wanted to be at a specific school, then I built a relationship with the principal so that when an opening came up at his site that I was qualified for, he would pick me to be interviewed. I mostly chose schools based on the principal and the student population. The other staff members were an afterthought. What would happen in my classroom was more important.

In my experience, conventional schools hire to fill the empty position (either grade level or subject area) with the most qualified person for the job within their budget. "Qualified" has a lot to do with credentials. Principals screen applicants from a district pool based on recommendations, college degrees, and/or certifications. Interview panels I've participated in mostly asked candidates about their experience with classroom management, lesson planning, discipline strategies, and parent communication.

At schools with teacher autonomy a central part of the interview process is figuring out if the candidate will contribute to the unique environment and buy into their shared purpose. Of course applicants need to be qualified to teach, but beyond that these schools are looking for staff members who will contribute to their schools and cultures *beyond* the classroom. They are looking for a community member who will add value to their school, commit to their mission and goals, and work well in a highly collaborative environment for the success of all students.

Autonomous teachers expect their colleagues to be more than their job titles. These teachers are far more than a "math teacher" or a "second-grade teacher." They are an integral part of the learning process for all students—even if they never officially have some students on their roll sheet.

Not all of the teachers I know would want to work in the kinds of schools autonomous teachers are creating. But just as autonomous teachers create schools to serve the needs of students not being well served in conventional settings, they also create jobs that appeal to educators who are seeking something different.

The autonomous teachers I met desire enlarged professional roles not only for themselves but for their colleagues. They also want the ability to innovate so that they can better meet the needs of their students. And they are willing to take full accountability for the schools they create. For these professionals, teacher autonomy is an answer that should be more widely available.

AUTONOMOUS TEACHERS CREATE AND ACT ON SHARED PURPOSES THAT ACKNOWLEDGE AND ACCEPT STUDENTS' CULTURAL IDENTITIES AND EXPERIENCES

Teachers described a variety of cultural identities among the students they serve. They reported that the identities seem to evolve from students' expectations for themselves based on their socioeconomic circumstances as well as from students' experiences with digital technology, finding their own social identity, identifying and practicing their own talents and interests, and making decisions as young adults. Autonomous teachers consciously choose for their shared purposes to include acknowledging and accepting students' cultural identities. To fail to do so might hinder students' success, they said.

Sometimes students' identities are rooted in youth culture, embodying characteristics that are separate from what is recognized in dominant culture. The philosophy of many middle and high school teachers interviewed is that fighting youth culture is an unnecessary distraction from staying on purpose.

French at Independence echoed teachers' statements from earlier in this chapter that their shared purpose guided their choice to spend energy on building trust and learning rather than on enforcing norms from the more dominant adult culture. "Our students want to drink coffee or wear hats or hoods or lay on the floor while they're learning," he said. "We've decided we're not going to distract from their learning to fight it."

French and other teachers said that when students sense their identities are accepted by adults they don't feel they need to spend so much time fighting for acceptance. So they learn to trust the adults, and are more open to making learning their focus.

Autonomous teachers demonstrate their commitment to acknowledging youth culture in their learning program choices and implementation. David Rice at MNCS said that teachers who have created self-directed learning environments at the middle and high school levels make an effort to stay alert to trends in youth culture and how they are affecting students' individual curriculum choices.

"We have to stay credible in their eyes," Rice said. "If we can help them channel what they are learning about themselves and their environment into their academic learning we can get them to move [from engagement to motivation]." Teachers at Avalon noticed that students were showing an affinity for their MP3 players, for example, so they invited students to submit proposals for how to positively incorporate them into the learning environment.

Teachers offering other kinds of learning programs acknowledge youth culture with customized courses. HSC teachers offer Hip Hop Poetry as well as a course on the Vietnam War that lets students explore the time period's similarities and differences with their own cultural experiences. When Phoenix teachers noticed an uptick in students getting tattoos, they created a health seminar for students to explore associated risks and how to manage them.

Sometimes teachers' purposeful acknowledgment and acceptance of students' cultures attracts students who share a particular cultural identity to their schools. Chrysalis teachers reported their schools' appeal to formerly homeschooled students who seem to enjoy their teachers' tolerance for their highly inquisitive nature and desire for independent exploration.

Avalon teachers said that a good percentage of gay and lesbian students attend their school because word is out that students who attend don't need to hide their identity. Avalon teachers supported marching as a school in the local gay pride parade and cooperated with students from the school's Gay-Straight Alliance when they wanted to plan and implement a school dance.

Avalon students shared that they had spent some time in their advisory groups discussing a string of suicides committed by homosexual teens in nearby Anoka, Minnesota, and what to do if they were being bullied. Students recognized that their ability to discuss this was due to a choice made by their teachers. Their perception was that teachers were acting on their stated shared purpose.

Other schools appeal to large numbers of students living in poverty. Teachers at HSC, TAGOS Leadership Academy, Phoenix, and other schools thought this might be because they acknowledge students' culture that is rooted in their socioeconomic experiences and expectations. They purposefully don't communicate to students an assumption that everyone is going to college. Some students don't perceive this to be an affordable option from either a social or economic perspective. Teachers have learned that communicating that college is the only legitimate next step can cause students to stop engaging in high school.

Cameo Thorne at HSC said,

> Our [dominant] culture assumes we're preparing everyone to go to college, and that this group of students in particular [who attend HSC] should want to leave their lives for college. Everything is built on that assumption. But the truth is they're afraid to leave. They wonder, "Who will be alive when I come back?" Yesterday one student went to her seventh funeral this year. We have others living in apartments without water or heat. [Dominant culture] doesn't acknowledge this. We do. So they stay here.

Jon Woloshin at TAGOS Leadership Academy said, "[In some communities] education is not seen as a way up and out. The General Motors plant closed here [in Janesville, Wisconsin] and even educated people are out of work. The incentive to achieve is low. Here we help students discover a reason to achieve and teach them to avoid stopping their learning at age eighteen."

QUESTIONS AND CHALLENGES

Teachers reported two primary questions and challenges in the area of shared purpose.

1. To what extent is formal hiring autonomy related to teachers' capacity to root their decision making in a shared purpose?

Autonomous teachers in most schools affiliated with districts have partial autonomy to select their colleagues. They are able to make recommendations about which candidates would be a good match, and most of the time these recommendations are honored. But with a struggling national economy some teachers worry that their partial autonomy will no longer be enough.

The prevalence of "last hired, first fired" policies in collective bargaining agreements has posed a challenge as the people who must be hired back first are insistent on securing employment wherever they can. Candidates who aren't interested in teacher autonomy, much less the shared-purpose cultures autonomous teachers create, have been placed in some of the eleven schools.

In the past teachers who weren't a good fit caught on right away and either adjusted to the culture or left on their own. In this economy, however, autonomous teachers worry that people who are a poor fit will stay because they need employment, even if they don't adjust. In some places teachers reported this is already happening, at the expense of having a collective commitment to shared purpose and perhaps ultimately their success as autonomous decision makers.

Teachers' willingness to accept accountability diminishes, they said, when they can't trust that their colleagues will be on board with the purpose. Without formal agreements allowing teachers to choose candidates who are both willing to take on the responsibilities of teacher autonomy and to buy in to the cultures teachers establish, there is little anyone can do.

Teachers at Mission Hill did not report that they experience these problems; they have full formal hiring autonomy formally arranged via their pilot agreement with Boston Public Schools. Similarly, teachers in the chartered Avalon, Chrysalis, EOC, and MNCS have full hiring autonomy and did not report any concerns of this nature.

2. Are teachers able to pay adequate attention to setting and reaching long-term, overarching goals?

Autonomous teachers evaluated themselves harshly at keeping their eye on how they're doing in setting and reaching long-term goals. They worry that their commitment to overarching mission, vision, and goals might get lost as their attention is drawn toward day-to-day urgencies. "We need to focus more on strategic planning and less on nuts and bolts," said Dee Thomas at MNCS.

We had a visitor recently who asked, "This is called Minnesota New Country School. What are you doing that's new?"

I had to stop and think. I'm not really sure any more. At one point our offering every senior a computer was a big deal, but I worry we're getting complacent. We might be resting on our laurels while we could be taking on matters that will make this school even better. Students coming in this year won't leave until seven years from now. Will the school be the same when they leave?

Teachers at Chrysalis are working through similar fears. This year they set four long-term goals designed to help them keep their shared purpose in focus, and they've made certain individuals responsible for leading the group in addressing the goals and bringing them into the day-to-day dialogue. One of these goals is to strengthen field study. Chrysalis emphasizes nature-based learning, but with recent staff turnover some worry that the value for learning out in the field has decreased as new teachers push for goals and strategies that they grew accustomed to when they worked in more conventional settings.

"It takes time for teachers to transition out of the culture that focuses on test-prep," one teacher said. "Now we have a few new teachers coming out of that culture, so we have to start over at getting commitment and buy in to our purpose here."

Veterans in several schools indicated that in situations like this they feel the need to balance the school purpose they've upheld for years with an attitude of openness to hearing what might work better.

Almost 98 percent of all teachers said their colleagues are collectively excellent (60.4 percent), very good (30.4 percent), or good (7.3 percent) at including both new and veteran voices in setting school goals. Even so, veterans said they frequently encourage new teachers to learn "what works" in the environment they're in now. The healthy tension between "what's always worked" and "what could be better" helps teachers to remain alert to their shared purpose and focused on related long-term improvement.

Chapter Five

Practice #2

Participate in Collaboration and Leadership for the Good of the Whole School, Not Just a Classroom

With a strong sense of accountability for the success of the entire school, autonomous teachers collaborate for the good of the whole. When these teachers taught in conventional settings, they said, they felt accountable for their classrooms but not for their schools. Their principals were accountable for whole-school success, so teachers saw it as the principal's job to support other teachers' success and students' overall success.

Stephanie Davis at Tailoring Academics to Guide Our Students (TAGOS Leadership Academy) explained autonomous teachers' behavior.

> Here we actually collaborate. [In the conventional school] where I worked before this there was little-to-no collaboration. There you're only responsible for your own class. A little for what's happening in your department. Not for the school. Here it's all teamwork. We're accountable for the whole thing, so we work together. . . . It makes us feel like, "This is my school." It's *mine*. I'm committed to it. It's not just a place where I work.

Sue Rodahl at Academia de Lenguaje y Bella Artes (ALBA) said, "Collaboration at ALBA happens because of the structure that makes adults accountable to one another. There is more than one person accountable. I am a stakeholder. *I'm* accountable. If I made the decisions, then I'm willing to collaborate to make them work." Nichole Kotasek at Minnesota New Country Schools (MNCS) said, "Elsewhere, you don't have as much at stake. Here you feel obligated to participate. . . . [As individuals] we're more likely to seek help and others are more likely to offer it. We know the school's success depends on it."

Autonomous and accountable teachers know that whole school success requires them to collaborate for students' success outside of their own classrooms. Teachers work together to know their students as individual learners who have varying needs. "We're all responsible for every student," said Jack Stacey at High School in the Community (HSC).

Stacey and his colleagues remind themselves of this at every staff meeting. They spend thirty minutes discussing two individual students, one who is doing well and one who is struggling. Everyone collaborates to understand what works and what doesn't work for those individuals, and implements those strategies whenever they see the students. "We all learn how to be better teachers," said Heather George.

Laura Bowie described a similar collaborative culture at Chrysalis Charter School (Chrysalis).

> In other schools we collaborated to discuss what curriculum we'd offer to all students in the grade level and subject we were teaching. We didn't think a lot about what teachers in other departments were doing and how students were doing in other classrooms.
>
> [To be successful here] we *have to* communicate about students' whole experience. We need to know: Are students' grades suffering in other areas? Are they managing well in other classroom settings? How do we differentiate learning so each student is challenged, but not overwhelmed? We're always trying to make sure that every student has the right mix.

AUTONOMOUS TEACHERS CREATE COLLABORATIVE CULTURES CHARACTERIZED BY CONSULTATION, LISTENING, BEING OPEN TO DIFFERENT OPINIONS, WORKING TOGETHER, AND MUTUAL RESPECT

Most autonomous teachers expressed that sharing accountability for whole school success makes it necessary to create collaborative cultures in which they feel free and comfortable to participate, suggest new ideas, ask for help, and disagree with their peers. Nora Houseman at San Francisco Community School (SFCS) said, "Staff collaboration is unique. We plan together. We help each other. We question each other. We support each other."

Ayla Gavins at Mission Hill K–8 School (Mission Hill) said, "Everyone is paying attention to how we can improve. Whenever necessary someone can call for a discussion [about what's not working well] and if change is needed we can make it right here, right away."

About 98 percent of teachers surveyed rated their cultures as excellent (53.3 percent), very good (31.5 percent), or good (13.0 percent) at having an open flow of ideas. Almost 96 percent of teachers said their cultures were excellent (45.7 percent), very good (39.1 percent), or good (10.9 percent) at valuing differences, as evidenced by a culture of listening to and understanding others regardless of status or function.

Skylar Primm at TAGOS Leadership Academy said, "Everyone is comfortable participating fully. Anyone can reach out and say, 'What do you think about trying this new idea?'" Stacey at HSC said, "Everyone is willing to listen to each other and ask for help. I wouldn't characterize it as 'messy.' We value the dialogue, and we have lively conversations that lead to a better school." Rodahl at ALBA reported, "Everyone attends meetings and has a voice. Everyone can add agenda items. We're not afraid to disagree. The decisions aren't always what I want them to be, but I know my ideas were considered."

Most autonomous teachers warned that collaboration is not always easy, however. Maintaining a collaborative culture requires a lot of patience and tolerance, they said. And it is time consuming, as people aren't always on the same page. At times the loudest or most senior person steers the conversation. Veteran teachers wish their newer colleagues would participate more, and newer teachers wish veterans wouldn't be so insistent with their statements about what's been tried before and what works best. Sometimes people storm off when they don't get their way, and conversations need to be tabled while people negotiate how they want to proceed.

Yet most teachers also emphasized that the results of collaboration are worth their investment of time and energy. They reported that they feel valued and supported. When they know that they have reached agreement about how they will run the school they find it easier to share accountability. They can trust that their colleagues will work toward whole school success.

About 96 percent rated teachers' willingness to invest the time and effort it takes to develop a collaborative community as excellent (47.8 percent), very good (35.9 percent) or good (12.0 percent). Ninety-six percent (excellent [62.5 percent], very good [23.9 percent] or good [9.1 percent]) also said that they had pride in being part of their team. The collaborative culture, teachers say, leads to job satisfaction.

Dee Thomas at MNCS said, "We talk about the struggles, but in the end it is a much better job." Sarah Hoxie at Chrysalis said, "People are really happy here. The job satisfaction here is super high because people feel a part of it." George at HSC said, "I was unhappier and more stressed in the conventional school I used to work at. Here I enjoy my job more, so I don't mind the work." Another HSC teacher wrote, "The motivation of the teachers at this school is outstanding. We work with a collaborative approach more impressive than I have ever seen before in an educational institution."

AUTONOMOUS TEACHERS SET ASIDE TIME FOR COLLABORATIVE DECISION MAKING, AND LOOK FOR WAYS TO MAKE THESE PROCESSES MORE EFFICIENT

While autonomous teachers collaborate formally and informally all of the time, they explained that they need to set aside special time for focused collaborative dialogue and decision making. With waivers from union rules about work hours, and/or using their other autonomy arrangements, many teachers arranged to participate in decision-making processes before and after school several times a week, and often during the summer.

Some teachers described changing school schedules to make time for their discussions. At HSC and Independence School Local 1 (Independence), for example, teachers added an extra half hour to school on Monday through Thursday. This change allows them to dismiss students at noon on Friday and use the afternoon for dialogue.

As they gain experience, some autonomous teachers find ways to make more efficient use of time. Avalon School (Avalon) teachers used to meet every day after school for indefinite lengths of time, for example. These days they have two, one and a half hour staff meetings for collaborative dialogue and decision making per week. They've even participated in trainings for running effective meetings.

Another efficiency tool adopted by teachers in several schools is the "fist of five" rating. To gauge how close they are to having a final decision, the discussion leader calls for all teachers to indicate their level of agreement using their hands. If a teacher is completely in favor of a proposed decision he or she displays all five fingers. But he or she can also close his or her fist to block action completely, or use one to three fingers to say he or she is not fully convinced but is willing to support the idea if it is what the majority wants.

Jill Mulhausen at Phoenix High School (Phoenix) said, "If someone will sabotage a decision, or too many people are at a one or two, then we keep the conversation alive. If people don't budge, it's probably not a great idea."

TAGOS Leadership Academy teachers have improved efficiency by agreeing to carry out lengthy dialogues using Google Docs. Google Docs is an online collaboration tool where multiple people can contribute to the same document. It is a way for teachers to dialogue without needing to be in the same room together, and at times convenient for each individual.

AUTONOMOUS TEACHERS' WHOLE-SCHOOL ACCOUNTABILITY AND COLLABORATIVE CULTURES INFLUENCE THE NATURE OF LEADERSHIP: LEADERS ARE SEEN AS ACCOUNTABLE, AND IN SERVICE, TO ALL

When there is collective accountability for whole-school success, leaders get their authority and power from the collective. Leaders take on specific duties delegated by the group of teachers that manages the school.

Many assume that, to be effective, teachers must have a single leader who has ultimate authority. Individual teachers must be accountable to a single leader for their actions. But in almost all of the eleven schools the group of autonomous teachers has ultimate authority. They select their leaders—principals, lead teachers, committee leaders, and others—who are accountable to the group for their actions. In this arrangement the leaders aren't "in charge" of teachers but are instead obligated to act collaboratively, frequently consulting with and carrying out the wishes of the group.

Autonomous Teachers Invert the Conventional Hierarchical Leadership Triangle

In ten of the eleven schools, leaders are selected by and accountable (formally and informally) to the group of teachers. Teachers are in turn accountable to their school boards, who are accountable to their school district leaders or school authorizers, who are ultimately accountable to the state for school success. As figure 5.1 illustrates, the conventional hierarchical leadership triangle—with teachers accountable to school leaders who are in turn accountable to their school boards, who are accountable to their school district leaders or school authorizers—is inverted.

Autonomous teachers reported that they are frequently confronted by people who doubt that the inverted triangle model can work in schools. People worry it is inefficient and that teachers don't have the training necessary to guide and carry out school leadership, including administrative work. Some further assume that teachers don't want to be cultural and professional leaders, don't want decision-making authority, and don't have the time to do administrative work, especially if they have to do it collaboratively.

But autonomous teachers said that the doubters misunderstand how they work. To stay efficient most groups of teachers delegate some cultural and professional leadership, decision-making authority, and administrative responsibilities to specific, qualified, trained people or groups. Having a collaborative culture doesn't mean everyone has to be involved in making every decision. As Houseman at SFCS summed it up, "People assume we focus on

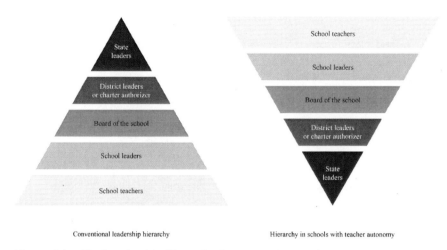

Conventional leadership hierarchy   Hierarchy in schools with teacher autonomy

Figure 5.1.   The Leadership Hierarchy Pyramid Is Inverted

management all the time. But we delegate a lot to [qualified] people we choose." Teachers said that this works well so long as there is a clear shared purpose guiding all the players.

Leaders of all kinds know their success depends on collaborating with their colleagues and making decisions within the boundaries their colleagues set. Of administrative leadership at Avalon, Monessa Newell said, "Two women have taken on administrative roles [for our school]. We call them lead teachers. They teach part-time and administrate part-time, and we've carved out their duties based on their strengths. One of them went to law school before becoming a teacher, so she has some specific skills that we put to use. But the lead teacher role is not like a traditional principal's role. These two are not our bosses. They are responsible to all of us."

Stacey at HSC said, "Our head teacher is one of us. He is accountable to us. He knows that if he messes up then he is out the next election." Another HSC teacher reported, "Because we elect our leaders, we have a strong vote of confidence in their work, and because [we require] those leaders to include us in all decision making and troubleshooting, we have a significant under-standing of what makes this ship run. I am proud to be a part of this team."

Teachers' autonomy to select and remove leaders, and thus the extent to which the leadership triangle is inverted, varies among the eleven schools:

1. Full, de jure authority (established formally in policy or agreement):

- Avalon
- EdVisions Off Campus (EOC)
- MNCS

• SFCS

In these four schools teachers have full, formal authority to collectively select and remove one or more leaders who are responsible for making and implementing specific decisions. Leaders are accountable to the teachers. At Avalon, EOC, and MNCS, teachers don't have to select leaders, but choose to do so. At SFCS teachers must select a leader who is certified to perform certain duties, specifically evaluation (see chapter 10).

2. Full, de facto authority (autonomy is practiced, but informal and not guaranteed):

• Chrysalis
• Independence
• HSC
• Mission Hill
• Phoenix

At Chrysalis, teachers are able to select their leaders (but do not have to select a leader), and the school board approves teachers' decisions. Their arrangement is very similar to that of Avalon, EOC, and MNCS.

In the other four schools—Independence, HSC, Mission Hill, and Phoenix—school district administrators require that there are one or more leaders at the school who are ultimately accountable to a district administrator, such as a superintendent of schools. The four school districts require also that leaders must have an administrative credential (i.e., the license to be a principal).[1] Within these boundaries, teachers have full de facto (informal) authority to collectively choose who these leaders will be. That is, they can select *and* remove leaders.

In practice, the leaders at these four schools act accountable to the teachers. Gavins at Mission Hill said, "I am accountable to the teachers and to the district. Among the teachers at the school, I am expected to think like a teacher. There is no line for 'this is what I do and this is what I don't do.' I don't see myself as a boss, but as a facilitator, coach, and liaison between the teachers and the school district."

At times, however, Gavins and others feel caught between what district leaders ask them to do versus what teachers at the school collectively determine to be best. This challenge will be further discussed later in the chapter.

3. Partial, de facto authority:

• ALBA

Teachers at ALBA have the same authority as those at Independence, HSC, Mission Hill, and Phoenix, with one exception. At ALBA, the leader cannot be removed by teachers once selected.

4. No authority:

• TAGOS Leadership Academy

At TAGOS Leadership Academy teachers do not have authority to select the school leader. Instead, a principal is appointed by the school district. Teachers report that so far appointed leaders have been "fans" of the model and rarely override teachers' recommendations. They get involved in day-to-day decision making only on a minimal basis.

Even minimal intervention, however, can have a large effect on the school. At TAGOS Leadership Academy, for example, school district leaders hold the principal accountable for ensuring that teachers are making students do very specific practice exercises for state tests despite teachers' collective sense that this isn't best for their students.

Autonomous Teachers Sometimes Share Leadership: Many or All Teachers Take On Leadership Functions and Participate in Democratic Decision-Making Processes

Sometimes teachers don't delegate all of their authority and responsibility to single leaders and instead make some or all decisions democratically as a whole group or by committee. Teachers said they are willing to participate in these leadership functions because they believe that collaboration is essential to whole-school success. Committee leaders and members view themselves as accountable to all teachers at the school. In most cases, all teachers at the school select the committee leaders and pay them a stipend for their work.

MNCS has one of the most elaborate committee structures, including committees for personnel, finance, building and transportation, special education, outreach and public relations, technology, and testing. Teachers at MNCS and the other ten schools also often collaborate with one another in inquiry groups to plan, develop, and evaluate learning activities. Finally, teachers in nearly all schools create task forces to address special topics. At HSC, for example, a group of teachers is designing an entirely new learning program.

Each teacher is usually a member of more than one committee at a time, and has a lot of say about which committees she or he will serve on. Some groups of teachers have implemented policies requiring committee memberships to have a balance of teachers who have been autonomous for a while and teachers who are new to having autonomy. Some also have policies requiring that teachers gain experience serving on various committees over time. When teachers learn what goes into managing all aspects of the school they are better collaborators, teachers said. They have a deeper respect for decisions committees make.

Long-term autonomous teachers we interviewed said that it is especially important to the health of collaborative cultures that teachers gain experience on personnel committees because members must handle issues that can be contentious, such as evaluation and documentation, conflicts between teachers, and personal matters. When teachers know how personnel decisions are made they are less likely to engage in gossip and distrust outcomes.

QUESTIONS AND CHALLENGES

Teachers reported four primary questions and challenges having to do with collaboration.

1. Do teachers have the skills necessary to collaborate?

Autonomous teachers acknowledged their general lack of experience with collaboration when they first started at their schools. But teachers said that building their skills is a worthwhile commitment, given that they are accountable for school success. Erik Good at HSC said, "Everyone doesn't always know how to participate, but they feel responsible so they keep trying."

Some veteran teachers shared their personal journeys in learning collaboration skills over time. Nic Manogue at TAGOS Leadership Academy said, "I'm less bossy now than when I got here. I was a control freak. I'm good at being 'in charge.' What I'm doing at this school is my calling, though, so I'm learning to be a better collaborator. I'm listening more." Jim Wartman at MNCS described that he has learned not to fret so much over every small decision. He has gotten better, he said, at saving his criticism for the proposals that he believes will really threaten school success.

Veterans report they encourage and coach new teachers who need to build confidence and camaraderie before they can collaborate well. Jo Sullivan at Avalon said, "We encourage everyone to speak up. The more we are on the same page the more it helps the students." Her colleague Carrie Bakken said, "We give new teachers a grace period to warm up, but pretty early we make clear that the expectation is that they start participating."

Crystal Simons, a Chrysalis School teacher who is new to autonomy, said positive reinforcement from her peers really encouraged her. "At first it felt weird to have a voice at all. It was out of my comfort zone. But the more people asked for my opinion and reinforced that my ideas were useful, the more I wanted to participate."

2. In schools affiliated with school districts, lead teachers or other single leaders are formally accountable to school districts. By virtue of being selected by their fellow teachers, however, they are also accountable to, and serve at the wishes of, their colleagues. When school districts and teachers have differing ideas, leaders sometimes are at risk of being in a precarious position.

When teachers have autonomy to control what matters for school success, their judgment of "what's best for students" sometimes differs from what is required by federal governments, state governments, unions, and school districts. At times teachers are collectively willing to stick to the methods that they know work well for their students, despite potential objection from the authorities holding them accountable for school success.

When the teachers share formal accountability for their decisions, the risk is shared. In district-affiliated schools where only a principal or lead teacher is "officially," or formally, accountable to the school district, however, risks taken by the group can put the leaders in a precarious position. This is the case at ALBA, HSC, Independence, Mission Hill, Phoenix, SFCS, and TA-GOS Leadership Academy.

This raises some questions: If a collective decision were to fail, would only the principal or lead teacher take the fall? And, if so, to what extent is a principal or lead teacher going to jeopardize his or her job for teachers' collective decisions? Would he or she assert his or her official authority? Or would he or she stick by his or her colleagues?

The principals and lead teachers interviewed conveyed that they know the risks and accept them, at least for the time being. Most would rather have a formal autonomy arrangement that spreads accountability across all teachers. Nevertheless, the leaders stated that collaborative decision making is so essential to school success that asserting their authority for the purpose of keeping teachers in-line with outside requirements would only weaken the school.

One lead teacher said she is willing to lose her license to support teachers' collective decisions. She has witnessed teachers' work and knows that decisions are made soundly and with great care, even if they are in contrast to whatever is being required. "Teachers don't want their school and autonomy to disappear, and if there is a bad decision it *will* disappear whether I take the fall or not," she said. This lead teacher has decided that it is her duty to make the teachers aware of any requirements, but that it is teachers' collective decision to determine what to do about them.

Questions for further consideration are these: Is it appropriate to put lead teachers in this position? Will doing so hinder start-ups or diminish teachers' chances of creating a healthy collaborative culture? In district settings, could accountability for school-level decisions be formally spread across the group of teachers? Shouldn't education managers who are outside of schools ask themselves whether the best outcomes for students are produced as a result of collective decisions or conventional hierarchical decision making?

3. In schools where teachers are members of a union and do not have a waiver or other arrangement explicitly specifying that teachers have autonomy to work beyond negotiated hours, will teachers be as willing to spend the time it takes to collaborate?

Teachers in six of the eleven schools visited (ALBA, HSC, Independence, Phoenix, SFCS, and TAGOS Leadership Academy) do not have a waiver or other arrangement explicitly specifying that teachers have autonomy from union work rules that limit the number of hours that teachers can spend in staff meetings. These teachers indicated that it can be difficult to maintain a healthy collaborative culture under these circumstances.

Teachers from three of these six schools said they used their hiring autonomy to select candidates who at first said they were "on board" with the groups' collaborative practices but later said they would not work extra hours without extra pay. Teachers who do not have the authority to transfer or dismiss colleagues who are not a good match for their cultures must honor their colleagues' right to limit work hours.

Teachers in the three schools explained that for years they were generally able to hire people who were eager to do whatever was necessary to collaborate. But in today's tough economy hiring choices are constrained. Under union-negotiated rules, school district teachers who are laid off anywhere in the district must be hired back first, wherever there are positions available. Thus, candidate pools are limited and those who must be hired first are not necessarily best suited for working as part of a group of teachers who have collective autonomy and a collaborative culture.

Whereas in the past teachers who were poor matches left schools quickly, in today's job market they stick around. Waivers from negotiated work hours as well as arrangements granting teachers authority to transfer or dismiss colleagues who don't mesh with their culture might be more important tools in a weak labor market than they have been in the past.

4. How much do founders' values and aspirations guide their schools' collaborative cultures? Are teachers able to succeed when founders depart?

Several founders, who are also long-term lead teachers, expressed concern about what might happen when they leave the schools. They questioned whether their colleagues share their values and aspirations enough to be able to carry on the cultural leadership necessary to manage the schools. Some also doubted their colleagues' ability to assert unpopular points of view and to deal well with what they characterized as very strong and consistent state and school district pressures to be more conventional.

A few founders close to retirement are beginning to engage in succession planning, informing their colleagues of their pending departure and opening discussions about how specific responsibilities would be handled when they leave. Paul Krafel at Chrysalis said, "If the school and [our shared purpose] do not survive when [my cofounder, Alysia Krafel, and I] leave then we haven't done our jobs well."

At MNCS and SFCS teachers have found that rotating leaders and committee membership helps reduce the difficulty of transitions. In schools where administrators' licenses are required for principals or lead teachers, succession planning is especially important. Teachers in a few of these schools are proactively pursuing a strategy of having multiple teachers pursue an administrator license so future leaders can be chosen from within.

Teachers at Avalon, EOC, Phoenix, and TAGOS Leadership Academy reported that they transitioned well when strong founders departed. Founders carried a lot of responsibilities, but when they left these jobs were spread across more people.

A TAGOS Leadership Academy teacher said that since the founder's departure, teachers have had to take on a lot more work, but as a result they are much better at sharing leadership and accountability. "Our founder sheltered us from a lot of the annoying aspects of school management as well as the battles of being a [school with teacher autonomy] in a [conventional district]. When he left we realized how much we had been sheltered from and everyone was willing to do more. We're far more teacher-led now than we ever were."

NOTE

1. At Phoenix and HSC the leader does not need an administrative credential.

Chapter Six

Practice #3

*Encourage Colleagues and Students to Be Active,
Ongoing Learners in an Effort to Nurture Everyone's
Engagement and Motivation*

With accountability for school success, autonomous teachers collectively decide to place a strong emphasis on encouraging students' engagement and motivation. These teachers realize that students choose to learn—adults can't make them—so they need to find means of adapting to students' individual learning needs. Adapting to individual needs requires them to be open to the idea that conventional tools and training may not be sufficient. They come to see themselves as unfinished learners rather than experts who know all there is to know about teaching students.

Karen Locke at EdVisions Off Campus (EOC) said, "We're always learning how to teach in new ways. We are so challenged to try new things that will keep students interested, especially in our online setting. We have to be innovating all the time." Stephanie Davis at Tailoring Academics to Guide Our Students (TAGOS Leadership Academy) reported, "I shifted from [a focus on] teaching to [a focus on] learning when I came here. I'm constantly learning new things and [broadening] what I consider to be my responsibility to help students learn. I'm not planning lectures and grading papers."

Almost 98 percent of the teachers surveyed rated their collective commitment to continuous learning and improvement as excellent (57.5 percent), very good (26.4 percent), or good (13.8 percent). And about 89 percent said their attitude that they are not experts whose role is to impart information to students was excellent (41.4 percent), very good (32.2 percent), or good (14.9 percent).

Teachers said that autonomy greatly increases their willingness to take on a learner role. Some had been involved with improvement efforts where teachers had input, but no real authority. Without authority, they said, it wasn't worth the time investment required to learn new things and innovate. It was almost impossible to sustain their changes, they said.

James McGovern at Mission Hill K–8 School (Mission Hill) said, "We're all learners here. That's because of [the autonomy]. At my previous school there was no culture of learning among the staff. It wasn't the people. It was the structures preventing any real change. We had a progressive principal, but we couldn't move ahead. People didn't want to create something that would just be pulled back."

AUTONOMOUS TEACHERS INNOVATE WITH THE DESIGN OF LEARNING ENVIRONMENTS TO PUT STUDENTS IN THE POSITION TO BE ACTIVE, NOT PASSIVE, LEARNERS

Almost 97 percent of autonomous teachers rated their collective belief that the basic function of a teacher is to motivate students to be learners as excellent (61.4 percent), very good (29.5 percent), or good (5.7 percent). With engagement and motivation central, teachers said they realize quickly that they need to put students in a position to take responsibility for their own learning. So they design innovative learning environments in an effort to find the best means of encouraging students to be active learners, not passive learners whose job it is to receive and memorize information from teachers.

They also design the environments with an eye toward accommodating students' varying levels of readiness, aptitudes, interests, and rates of learning. Learning how to encourage individual students to be active learners, autonomous teachers expand what constitutes the physical learning environment, expand their own roles, and expand students' means of learning.

Expanding What Constitutes the Physical Learning Environment

When most people think of a school they think of a building. They think of bells telling students when to move. They remember their own classrooms with desks in tidy rows and a teacher at the front instructing a group of students who were all learning the same curriculum at the same time. They think of teachers using a white board to instruct students and teachers having a "lounge" that is their space alone. Autonomous teachers suggest that all of these set-ups assume students are passive learners. When the goal is to help students become active learners, these designs no longer make sense.

Some autonomous teachers had arranged classrooms in conventional ways, but in most schools teachers and students worked together to design spaces that were more conducive to self-directed and experiential learning programs. In these spaces there isn't a "front of the room." Instead, the schools are large warehouse-style open spaces (one a former church, one a former coffee factory, one a former storage facility) that look like a typical work office. Walls are often brightly colored and covered with student work including graffiti or other art specific to the cultures of the students attending the school.

Carrie Bakken at Avalon School said,

> The space is designed to reinforce our values. We intentionally avoided leasing an old school with traditional classrooms because an open warehouse design is vital to our educational environment. Students are learning to work collaboratively with adults and other students while managing their own individual projects. Teachers work alongside students as advisers who support learning but do not direct it. We needed a space that allows for both communal interaction and individual work.

Middle and high school students often have their own work stations situated amid students of mixed ages, complete with an office-style desk, computer, Internet access, and personal décor.

At the Mission Hill K–8 School (Mission Hill) there aren't any desks. Students regularly chose among multiple activities throughout their classrooms and school to learn their subject material. To learn physical science, for example, they could go to the art room, work with manipulative materials, build boats in one corner, or cook in another. It was perfectly acceptable for students to complete their writing and reading activities at a table or while lying on the ground.

Melissa Tonachel, a teacher at Mission Hill, said, "We give students freedom-of-movement choices. They decide where to work and what to work on. They are able to figure out where they work best." Bakken at Avalon said, "Designing our space, we had to step back and realize that not all of them are going to be earning their living while listening to lectures and working at desks."

Most schools didn't have any bells telling students when to move, opting instead for students and teachers to monitor the time themselves. Most students also had the ability to move freely throughout the day. Most teen students didn't need permission to use the restroom or get a snack, for example. They simply went by themselves.

In most schools there were few, if any, spaces that were off limits to students (except areas that housed student records). Teachers and students share bathroom, kitchen, and dining areas. In ten of the eleven schools, students called teachers by their first names. Jonathan Woloshin at TAGOS

Leadership Academy said, "We always try to signal that teachers *and* students have voice and choice in school. All of us have real ownership as one community of learners."

As will be covered in more detail in chapter 7, autonomous teachers expand the learning environments beyond physical school buildings as well. Teachers view broad physical boundaries for learning as an integral part of the learning programs they design, and say these should not be confused with occasional field tripping. At EOC, for example, students learn online, from home, without a central "building" at all. Chrysalis Charter School (Chrysalis) students learn by doing field studies using the natural environment.

Expanding Teachers' Roles

Patrick Yecha at Phoenix High School (Phoenix) said, "Everything is different about how students learn here. The bottom line being: I don't teach them everything." Many autonomous teachers do not see themselves as "instructors," but as "guides" and "coaches" in helping students to get better at taking an active role in their learning. At the high school level, for example, teachers said their role is to foster an environment in which students are challenging themselves, developing a better understanding of how their own abilities and interests lend themselves to careers, and meeting graduation requirements.

When they are guides and coaches, autonomous teachers learn four new ways of operating. First, knowing they cannot possibly be content experts in all the areas students will learn, many see themselves as lifelong learners who must act more as generalists than specialists. Dee Thomas at Minnesota New Country School (MNCS) said, "Our students see adults modeling lifelong learning. Every adult here is teaching outside their subject area expertise."

Chris French at Independence School Local 1 (Independence) said, "We're all lifelong learners. We all teach outside our subject area. Anyone who teaches here has to be willing to teach outside their comfort zone." Teachers said that subject area expertise does come in handy, but in unconventional ways. Experts train their colleagues about how to advise students well in their subject area. Also, students who are exploring their subject area frequently seek them out for coaching even if their main advisor is another teacher.

Second, many autonomous teachers said they designed their schools so each teacher is intentionally advising students from more than one—sometimes multiple—grade levels. Instructing students at every age level is difficult, and that is the point. To encourage active student learners they want to avoid instructing. Serving students from multiple grade levels *requires* them to coach more and instruct less.

TEACHER AUTONOMY GETS DIFFERENT
RESULTS THAN "SMALL SCHOOLS"

As we visited the first three of the eleven schools I was impressed with many things: the bright, articulate students; teachers' dedication; teachers' actual *acceptance* of youth culture; the community feel each school had; the open spaces; students' ability to call teachers by their first names; and more. But there was a nagging doubt in the back of my mind: wouldn't teachers and administrators in any small school be capable of creating an environment like this?

Let me explain my doubt. My teaching experiences have all been at fairly large schools—well over five hundred students at most of the sites; some closer to eight hundred. Imagining shared leadership with a staff of fifty teachers to create schools similar to the ones we visited is mindboggling, yet it seemed almost easy with a small staff. The schools we visited are all small, ranging from three to thirty-two teachers. I was quietly wondering if it was the small teaching staff that was creating these environments.

Then we interviewed Patrick Yecha at Phoenix. He said how different this school was from his previous school even though they were both small in size. He had come from a small rural school and yet he felt isolated there and disconnected from the students and fellow teachers. I started to realize then that the size of the school had little to do with what I was observing, and that it was the teachers' ability to make real choices and changes that caused them to be accountable for the schools' success and create these unique environments. During our visits to the remaining schools, more teachers convinced me of the same.

Regardless of the size of the school, when teachers operate by conventional modes there is isolation. Teachers teach "their" students, in "their" classroom, where they close "their" door for the majority of the day. In my experience, teachers want chances to interact, dialogue, and learn from each other, but the opportunities to do this are limited at best, and in reality are not a priority. This isolation makes it hard to make learning program choices that are best for the whole school.

At the schools we visited, autonomous teachers deliberately and consciously designed their schools, their physical environments, to collaborate, learn, and grow from each other and their students. Their autonomy allows them to make these choices. Their *choices* set their schools apart in the level of community and team work, not the size of their staff and student bodies.

Third, autonomous teachers prioritize building relationships. One hundred percent of teachers rated their value for knowing students as whole persons as excellent (72.4 percent), very good (21.8 percent), or good (5.7 percent). Most teachers carry a very small total student load and work with students for two or more years in a row. This allows teachers to spend one-on-one time with individual students and form deeper knowledge about their sources of motivation.

Fourth, to some extent autonomous teachers seek or create professional development that supports how *they* work in their new roles and with the students they serve. Those who have budget autonomy can and do design and participate in developmental activities beyond what is required by their states and school districts. When teachers at EOC noticed an influx of Hmong and Cambodian students, for example, they realized that they didn't understand the major cultural differences that caused friction between them. They sought diversity training for that specific issue and are now better able to support both groups of students well.

Expanding Students' Means of Learning

Autonomous teachers draw on learning resources far beyond what they and textbooks can convey. Students can use computers, software programs, the World Wide Web, and various search engines to access knowledge from all around the world in just seconds. Autonomous teachers believe that this opens enormous possibilities for learning, and they put students in the position to regularly draw on these resources for learning themselves, without waiting for guidance from a teacher.

In five of the eleven schools, for example, students learn via their own computers, situated at their own office-style desks. They use websites and software as tools that help them learn everything from algebra to simple organizational skills to more specialized interests such as architectural design and fashion design. Many autonomous teachers emphasize that realizing digital technology's potential has something to do with seeing themselves as coaches and advisors instead of instructors. Otherwise students would be learning to use technology as directed and not as a tool for directing their own learning, a skill they will need postgraduation.

But not all autonomous teachers see digital technology as the best means of engaging and motivating the students they serve. While digital technology tools are present in their schools, teachers at Chrysalis, High School in the Community (HSC), and Independence expand students' means of learning by exposing them to nature and other community resources, from weekly visits to community libraries to bird observations to biking trips along the C & O Canal.

Sarah Hoxie at Chrysalis said, "I teach kindergarteners, and they've got years of experience with technology already. My job is to get them in the dirt. When they listen to the birds and trees, they learn to recognize for themselves the infinite lessons they can learn from the environment. Those lessons are far beyond what I could convey to them in this classroom." Her colleague, Laura Bowie, who teaches students in grades 6–8, told a few stories of students rushing into the rooms with nature artifacts in order to do their own research with microscopes or other science-learning tools, which they are free to use on their own.

HSC teachers choose to use discretionary funds to pay for a social worker who helps students to learn how to access social services (sometimes just to get basic clothing) and confront emotional issues that are preventing them from taking responsibility for their academic learning. Teachers said this investment gives students the help they need; the ability to address their own problems so they can commit to academics.

At all schools visited, teachers and students made use of parents and community members as learning resources. Some teachers require students to involve community members and professionals in their self-directed learning. Many schools host community nights or parent lunches where students present what they are learning.

These events, typically held at least once per quarter, are beyond typical "open house" or "science fair" events in which parents are passive observers. Teachers ask parents and community members to visit with many students about their learning, offering positive feedback as well as real challenges to encourage improvement.

SOME STUDENTS FIND THE OPPORTUNITY TO BE ACTIVE LEARNERS IN ADAPTIVE LEARNING ENVIRONMENTS IMMEDIATELY ENGAGING. THEIR MOTIVATION, HOWEVER, TAKES MORE TIME.

Autonomous teachers reported that some students are attracted to their schools and become immediately engaged because of the opportunity to be active learners in environments where their individual and cultural needs are accepted and acknowledged. Encouraging students' motivation, however, takes much more time.

Teachers said that many students really struggle as they discover what it takes to be active learners in an individualized learning environment. Many middle and high school students arrive with habits they developed as passive learners, and these don't work well in their new environments. Students come to find out, for example, that many of their autonomous teachers don't tell them what to do and how to do it.

Some students also need to feel safe before they are self-motivated to learn, teachers explained. Many students who are attracted to their learning environments believe they are atypical—they felt out of place and sometimes were bullied for being different from most students. It takes time for them to test and trust their new environments' culture of acceptance.

Davis at TAGOS Leadership Academy said, "Students are here for a reason. We attract certain types of kids. What many have in common is the element of 'seeking safety.' Of course, some students *threaten* the sense of safety, but those students learn quickly—mostly from other students—that the culture here is about acceptance of everyone and appreciation for what each individual brings to the table."

Motivation also takes time because there's no set formula. Different students are motivated in different ways, and it can take a while for teachers and students to find the right sources of motivation. But autonomous teachers stick to the challenge and take it seriously. About 95 percent rated their [eventual] success at motivating students as excellent (23.0 percent), very good (47.1 percent), or good (25.3 percent).

Sarah Ard at Phoenix said, "They are working *toward* motivation here, [they aren't necessarily motivated right away]. This could be seen as evidence that our program doesn't work. But consider the context. Take the same student and drop him into a conventional school and he would be comatose. I've seen it myself." Woloshin at TAGOS Leadership Academy said, "The goal isn't to force them into anything, it's to help them understand that they have the adult capacity to decide and do things on their own. This doesn't happen overnight. It's a gradual progression."

Autonomous teachers in five of the eleven schools make a point to measure students' psychological adjustment in their school environments over time, including whether or not individual students are increasingly motivated to obtain goals, using a tool called The Hope Survey (described in more detail in chapter 10).

Evidence of their success with encouraging student engagement, teachers said, is that in addition to drawing in many conventional students, they increasingly draw student populations who indicate they were seeking learning programs with more potential for individualization. Families of students who receive special education and of students who were bored or bewildered in conventional learning environments seem to spread the word that their students are engaged. This causes more and more people to explore and attend the schools.

Students Receiving Special Education

Autonomous teachers reported that students receiving special education are engaged at their schools because they don't worry so much about negative attention for standing out. Students receiving special education have individual education programs (IEPs), which are legal documents designed to meet the unique educational needs of students with disabilities, as defined by federal regulations. Many teachers draw a distinction between how IEPs work in their schools compared to conventional schools.

Autonomous teachers don't try to fit a single student's individual needs into a setting in which most students are learning the same things at the same time. Instead, most autonomous teachers are individualizing learning for everyone. Thomas at MNCS said, "If a student needs to be pulled out for services, or has a tick and needs to stand up, spin around, and sit back down, no one here will even notice it. The student wouldn't be disrupting anything. Everyone is moving around all the time to complete their own learning goals."

Figure 6.1 shows that seven of the eleven schools serve higher than average percentages of students receiving special education. Erik Good at HSC wrote, "With 19.1 percent of our students receiving special ed, we are the highest of the six magnet high schools in New Haven. The next highest is at 13.8 percent and all the rest are below 9 percent. We are also higher than the two nonmagnet comprehensive high schools. They're at 12.4 and 12.9 percent."

French at Independence said that a high percentage of all the people who seek to attend Independence in the Baltimore City Public Schools lottery have special education needs. Each year he must work with the district to get the percentage of the total admitted down from 50 percent to around 20 percent, just to keep things manageable. "We don't have the capacity to have half the population on IEPs and serve everyone well. But the numbers do show demand for more schools like ours," French said.

Students Who Were Bored or Bewildered in Conventional Settings

Data does not exist to demonstrate that the schools designed by autonomous teachers are in demand for atypical students who were bored or bewildered in conventional settings, but teachers and their students describe their schools' populations this way. In schools with teacher autonomy, teachers acknowledge, accept, and accommodate whatever it is that makes them perceive themselves as atypical. As Ard at Phoenix puts it, these cultures "meet students' need for belonging."

Teachers and students reported that atypical students come from many cultural groups.

Students Committed to Pursuing Nonacademic Goals in Addition to Conventional Academics

Some students want to pursue individual nonacademic goals, such as music, art, and athletics. In conventional settings these students said they had to miss class and lectures and "make up" their missed time, but in self-directed learning environments such as Avalon and MNCS they managed their own learning and could manage both their academic and nonacademic pursuits

Schools	Site % of Special Education	District % of Special Education[1]	State % of Special Education
ALBA	10.5%	18.6%	13.7%
Avalon	26%	16%	13%
Chrysalis	6%	13%	11%
EdVisions Off Campus	20%	N/A[2]	13%
HSC	19.1%	12.3%	11.6%
Independence	27.6%	16.7%	10.9%
Mission Hill	24.1%	19.4%	17.0%
MNCS	33%	15%	13%
Phoenix HS	11.5%	12.1%	12.6%
SFCS	10.8%	11.5%	11%
TAGOS Leadership Academy	18.4%	14.4%	13.7%

Source: Demographic data was collected from each school's state department of education website. All data is from the 2010-2011 school year.

[1] For schools that are not part of a district, data for the nearest school district was used.
[2] EdVisions Off Campus is an online school that draws students from all over Minnesota, so it is not appropriate to compare their enrollment data to a nearby school district.

Figure 6.1.   Percentages of Students Receiving Special Education in the 11 Schools

without a big hassle. Often their nonacademic goals were career oriented, and some students planned to leave high school already gainfully employed or with the skills to get a job immediately.

An Avalon student was able to become a forest ranger while attending school, for example. Another was able to practice toward her goal of professional ice skating during school hours when coveted "ice time" was available.

A student at MNCS reported that she had always desired to be a cosmetologist, but knew she was lacking the outgoing personality necessary to do well. The MNCS learning model allowed her to design a project to earn academic credit for communications skills she would learn as a sales consultant for Mary Kay Cosmetics. MNCS also allowed her to tailor her academic learning toward cosmetology school rather than a four-year college without criticism, she said. She completed a research paper on how trends in women's hairstyles corresponded with women's rights, for example.

Yecha at Phoenix described a student who was able to academically complete her credits one year early, but who realized she needed to do more social development before she moved into a college environment full time. As the student's teacher, Yecha agreed with her assessment. He was able to work with the student to codesign learning activities that would allow her to develop socially while beginning to complete college credits.

Students Who Get Behind or Need Special Accommodations Due to Medical Treatments

When students must receive long-term medical treatments for serious ailments, they miss a lot of school and are faced with the stress of staying at the same learning level as their classmates. "Keeping on pace" can be especially difficult in conventional schools.

A student explained that when she missed a lecture she missed what was needed to do the homework and pass the tests. She also missed tests, and had to schedule make ups. She was continually "catching up." The associated stress wasn't conducive to her healing. What's more, she and others in her position reported that they felt pushed out of their conventional schools.

Individualized, self-directed learning programs can be far more accommodating. Sarah, a student at TAGOS, said, "I had some medical issues last year and had to miss a lot of school. It was really hard to make up that much work at my old school and I was falling way behind. Here I can catch up on my own schedule." A Phoenix student reported, "Last year I had a bad head and neck injury and was out of school for a long time. When I tried to make up the work it was hard to communicate with all of my teachers. Here I can make up the credit and get ahead."

Previously Homeschooled Students

Many families seek individualized and nonacademic learning experiences for their children and teens, and initially choose homeschooling because they were not able to find public schools offering these experiences. Aware of their potential appeal to these families, especially as the economy makes homeschooling less of a possibility for many, some autonomous teachers specifically design schools and programs with these populations in mind.

Teachers reported that many of Chrysalis's full-time students, for example, say that the differentiated learning and field study options drew them to the school. If they weren't at Chrysalis, they would likely still be homeschooled.

In addition to full-time school, Chrysalis teachers offer a homeschooling program through which families sticking with homeschooling can borrow learning resources from the school. These students can join full-time peers for nature field study or other learning options while completing other credits at home with their parents. Chrysalis receives a portion of each student's state per-pupil funding to host the program.

As an online school, EOC also appeals to many previously homeschooled families. Students are able to learn flexibly from home, as they have for years. The appeal of EOC is that the families receive publicly funded support from teachers who understand individualized learning and can advise students as they take an active role in meeting graduation requirements and staying "on track" for postsecondary education and other post–high school pursuits.

At families' urging, EOC also offers opportunities for in-person, interactive group-learning experiences. Last year there was a school sponsored outing to the Grand Canyon, for example. More locally, teachers and students attended the Renaissance Fair.

Students of Minority Cultures

Teachers explained that students in minority cultures arrive at their schools having left settings where they sensed they were not well accepted and couldn't celebrate who *they* were because the schools were more focused on mainstream culture. Students sought an opportunity to be able to discuss and explore their own cultures.

Some high schools serve what they described as large percentages of "out" members of the lesbian, gay, bisexual, and transgender (LGBT) communities—both students and parents. Teachers and students at the St. Paul–based Avalon School mentioned they had participated as a school in the local pride parade and that the student Gay-Straight Alliance handles many of the social activities for the school. In all of these schools, exploring LGBT culture is not off limits for individual and group learning activities.

Comparatively, the nearby Anoka-Hennepin School District drew national attention when five students committed suicide in the 2010–2011 school year for reasons related to bullying and harassment. Teachers in the district have publicly stated that were not able to reach out to students because the district had, via its "Sexual Orientation Curriculum Policy," in effect placed a gag order on teachers. The policy prevented teachers from discussing LGBT issues or even mentioning the word "gay" in classrooms (Crary October 9, 2010; Sun 2011). "It's just a whole different experience for me at Avalon," said an LGBT student.

Similarly, Academia de Lenguaje y Bellas Artes (ALBA) teachers said their colleagues in conventional schools would tell them they shouldn't speak Spanish with their English Language Learner students in the hallways because the students were to be focused on learning English. Colleagues also insinuated that they had "too many parties" with students and parents.

ALBA teacher Elissa Guarnero said, "They didn't understand that in order to engage and motivate students and families in learning we need to build community and relationships with them first. These people need to trust us. And mainly they learn to trust us because we *value* their first language and we *acknowledge* their culture of origin with celebrations. Since when is it bad to know two languages and understand two cultures, anyway?"

Students from Economically Downtrodden Families

Teachers in several of the schools visited described that many students and families they serve are suffering greatly in today's struggling economy. Students are affected by depression as well as hopelessness about the prospects associated with education. HSC teachers explained that some of their students are living without utilities. In survival mode, students must take care of their siblings while parents look for jobs or work. Students find that their autonomous teachers are willing to work *with* these problems rather than expecting students to act is if the problems don't exist.

Repeatedly teachers pointed out that they are aware of mixed messages. "College for all" is the national emphasis, yet four-year colleges are unaffordable for some families, which can result in the feeling that a high school diploma is meaningless. Teachers try to show students other postsecondary options that can put them in a position to support their families and serve as pathways to college in the long run.

At TAGOS Leadership Academy in Janesville, Wisconsin, for example, General Motors shut down a plant and many educated people are out of work without many job prospects. Woloshin at TAGOS Leadership Academy said, "They would just drop out if it wasn't for how we are able show them opportunities here."

Teen Parents

Most high schools visited had at least one teen parent, and EOC teachers said that a good percentage of their total population is made up of teen parents. Like all of the other atypical groups of students, they don't want to "miss" and "make up" school. Teen parents seek an opportunity to make school work around maternity and child care needs.

Gigi Dobosenski at EOC wrote in the school's 2009–2010 annual report, "It is . . . noteworthy that over half of the 5 seniors who graduated in 2009 were teen parents. . . . Although we do not [specifically seek to] cater to these students, this success can be attributed to the individualized academic plans we set forth for students."

QUESTIONS AND CHALLENGES

Teachers reported two questions and challenges associated with the changes they make to encourage students' engagement and motivation.

1. Autonomous teachers who are affiliated with school districts are often required to participate in professional development that assumes teachers and students are in conventional roles. To spend time and money wisely, how can professional development adapt to accommodate different roles for teachers and students?

Autonomous teachers in most schools affiliated with school districts say they are often required to participate in professional development that assumes teachers and students are in conventional roles. This affects teachers, especially those who are serving as leaders, at ALBA, HSC, Independence, Phoenix, SFCS, and TAGOS Leadership Academy. Notably, Mission Hill's pilot school agreement with Boston Public Schools allows for some flexibility in this area.

Teachers want to avoid giving states and school districts any reason to close their schools and limit their autonomy, so they attend. Yet they also convey that the trainings can be a waste of their time and their schools' money because the tips and tools just don't apply to their unconventional way of operating.

Autonomous teachers are open to developing or finding their own, more relevant, professional development, but doing that in addition to mandated training can be overwhelming. Teachers also said that their attendance at most mandated trainings is at the schools' expense, which limits their ability to spend professional development dollars on additional training.

For the time being, autonomous teachers who attend professional development trainings said that when necessary they adapt what they learn for how it is relevant at their schools. Adaptation can be especially important when the professional development explains state- or district-wide mandates, such as special education requirements (how to implement IEPs, for example).

Teachers said they understand that states and school districts need to do training to avoid liability. But often teachers must be creative to figure out how to apply mandates to their models, and the work can be time consuming. While most of these teachers have limited budget autonomy, some suggested that increased autonomy in the area of budget would allow them to hire consultants and attorneys to do the adaptation and customize the trainings.

Emerging questions include the following: Would increased budget autonomy as well as autonomy to decide on and arrange for their own professional development needs lead to teacher training that is more productive? And, what could be done to increase district officials' level of comfort to grant autonomy in these areas?

2. How does the requirement that teachers must be "highly qualified" to teach a specific subject, as defined by the federal No Child Left Behind Act of 2001 (NCLB), affect teachers whose role it is to guide instead of instruct students?

Teachers can become "highly qualified" to teach a subject area in a variety of ways, including completing twenty-four semester hours of subject-specific undergraduate coursework or completing a graduate degree in the subject. But autonomous teachers who are acting more as "guides" than "instructors" don't necessarily teach students in a single subject. Instead they advise students on their learning choices in all subjects. These teachers are innovating with their roles to encourage student engagement and motivation, but in doing so are not compliant with NCLB.

In some states teachers can apply for waivers from the requirement, but this can be a time-consuming hoop. Thomas at MNCS explained that since she and her colleagues opt to be guides, the school has to send out formal letters to all families annually to notify them that MNCS teachers are not highly qualified according to the federal requirements.

Families are on board, and support the learning program MNCS offers, so they aren't much affected by the letter. Still, teachers said that the letter conveys that the school is doing something wrong. "How does this requirement convey that policymakers are interested in creating an innovative environment for K–12?" asked Thomas.

Chapter Seven

Practice #4

Develop or Adopt Learning Programs That Individualize Student Learning

Autonomous teachers' decision to put students in a position to be active learners responsible for their own learning—not passive learners to whom teachers "deliver" education—was the subject of chapter 6. It is in that same vein that teachers decide which learning programs to develop or adopt.

Teachers reported that their dialogues about learning program selection and improvement typically seek to answer questions similar to those outlined by Maurice Gibbons in his popular 1974 *Phi Delta Kappan* article, "Walkabout." Those questions are, "What sensibilities, knowledge, attitudes, and competencies are necessary for a full and productive adult life? What kinds of experience will have the power to focus our children's energy on achieving these goals? And what kind of performance will demonstrate to the student, the school, and the community that the goals have been achieved?"

Answering such questions, autonomous teachers choose learning programs that individualize student learning. Almost 97 percent of all teachers surveyed reported that their schools are excellent (56.3 percent), very good (27.6 percent), or good (12.6 percent) at personalizing student learning. And nearly 98 percent said they are excellent (48.9 percent), very good (33.0 percent), or good (15.9 percent) at varying teaching methods according to individual students' needs.

Teachers' most frequently selected methods to facilitate individualization are self-directed, experiential, and differentiated. Figure 7.1 indicates that teachers in seven schools incorporate all three of these learning methods in their programs. Teachers in the remaining four schools use two or more of the methods, mixed with some conventional instruction. Teachers in two of

School	Experiential	Differentiated	Self-Directed
ALBA	B, C		
Avalon	C, P, R, T	✔	✔
Chrysalis	D, N, R	✔	
EdVisions Off Campus*	C, N, P, R, T	✔	✔
HSC	C, R, S	✔	
Independence	C, R, S	✔	
MNCS	C, N, P, R, T	✔	✔
Mission Hill	C, D	✔	✔
Phoenix HS	C, P, R, T	✔	✔
SFCS	C, D, N, P	✔	✔
TAGOS Leadership Academy	C, P, R, T	✔	✔

* EdVisions Off Campus (EOC) is an online school that offers synchronous and asynchronous learning to support an individualized and self-directed learning program.

Figure 7.1.   Learning Program Designs of 11 Schools

Experiential Key

B: Bilingual *and* bicultural
C: Cultural exploration including religious, race/ethnicity, youth, and sexual orientation
D: Developmental/Play
N: Interaction with nature
P: Projects
R: Extensive use of existing community resources
S: Service
T: Extensive use of digital technology

the eleven schools, Academia de Lenguaje y Bellas Artes (ALBA) and EdVisions Off Campus (EOC), have designed learning programs that are distinct from most existing schools in the nation.

This chapter will describe all of these learning programs and provide examples to illustrate teachers' innovative approaches. The examples are not exhaustive, however, and represent just a small portion of teachers' learning program choices.

AUTONOMOUS TEACHERS IN SEVEN OF THE ELEVEN SCHOOLS CREATE SELF-DIRECTED LEARNING PROGRAMS

Self-directed learners are responsible for their own learning. Students select and, at the middle and high school levels manage and assess their own learning activities, which can be pursued at any time, in any place, through any means, at any age[1] (Gibbons 2008). In seven of the eleven schools, students are making their own learning choices and teachers have for the most part shifted their roles to act as students' advisors rather than their instructors.

In five of these seven schools—the ones serving students in the 6–12 grade range—students plan and manage the vast majority of their learning activities themselves. Students design their own projects and audit—for credit—seminars offered at their schools, in the community and at local colleges. They must propose and get teacher-advisors' approval for their learning plans, making clear how the plans will help them progress to meet all the state graduation requirements plus any additional learning goals they set for themselves.

A student at Tailoring Academics to Guide Our Students (TAGOS Leadership Academy) said that as a self-directed learner in control of his curriculum he learns content when it is relevant to his choices and pace instead learning it on someone else's schedule "just in case" he needs it for future courses, college, or life.

Students in these five schools have their own work spaces complete with a computer and Internet access. When compared with conventional school set-ups, the schools look more like offices. Students manage multiple learning activities at once, often using software called Project Foundry to monitor their progress and communicate with teacher-advisors.

Teacher-advisors are available to interact with students verbally throughout the day as well. Advisors challenge students with suggestions for improving proposals and managing activities, but many stated they are careful not to take over or do too much leading. Sarah Ard at Phoenix High School (Phoenix) said, for example, "Students are responsible for their own curriculum, assessment, understanding, and they are often their own postsecondary counselor. They use these skills to make decisions about the future. Part of our job is to guide them in figuring this out for themselves."

Teacher-advisors award credits when students demonstrate their knowledge, or competency, in a particular content area. To pass, students must achieve 80 percent mastery of content or higher (far more than what is required to earn credit in most conventional settings, teachers pointed out). The amount of credit students earn depends on the number of hours they spent on the work.

Students assess their own work first, and then their assessment is considered by their project advisory team, which is comprised of their own teacher-advisor, one or more other teacher-advisors, and sometimes peers and community members. If the advisory team affirms a student's assessment, and the student has reached at least 80 percent mastery, then the student and his or her teacher-advisor negotiate to determine what grade will be reported on the student's transcript. If the student has not reached 80 percent mastery or earned his or her desired grade, then the student and advisory team determine what the student must do to reach his or her goal.

Teachers offering self-directed learning to students in grades K–8—at Mission Hill K–8 School (Mission Hill) and San Francisco Community School (SFCS)—operate differently. At these two schools students make their own learning choices within preselected learning themes and activities determined collectively by all teachers at the school. The themes and activities ensure that students meet standards, but still allow for individual voice and choice.

At Mission Hill, for example, students tackle three themes per year. Each theme gives students the opportunity to learn multiple content areas and Habits of Mind.[2] The goal is that after four years and twelve themes students will have learned all the state and district standards they are to learn during the corresponding four grade levels.

Students stay with the same teachers for two consecutive years, so that all students in kindergarten and first grade are together with the same teacher, and all students in second and third grade are together with the same teacher, and so on. Teachers set individual learning goals for each student and monitor progress with portfolio assessments and public demonstrations of learning.

In 2010–2011, the Mission Hill learning themes were "Physical Science," "Struggle for Justice—the African American Experience," and "Long Ago, Far Away—Ancient Egypt." On a "physical science day" all students in the school do physical science. But there are a number of ways to learn it, and individuals choose their preferred way.

From their home classroom, some go down the hall to the art room where they learn the mechanics of spin art from the art teacher. Some make pancakes. Some build and test boats. Some build and test bridges. Some study flight—from bat flight to air balloon flight to plane flight. Some work with manipulative learning tools, working to answer teachers' open questions such as, "What happens when you build on a mirror?" At the end of the day, students write reflections about their learning.

SFCS teachers structure learning in a very similar way. Students in grades K–5 stay with their teachers for two consecutive years and learn multiple subjects, standards, and life skills via four themes per year. SFCS students learn content associated with eight total themes every two years. Students in sixth, seventh, and eighth grades learn science via rotating themes, but teachers otherwise require them to shift their focus to core subjects and learn more conventionally as they prepare for high school.

Self-directed learning is often experiential and opens up possibilities for differentiation. But understanding what aspects of the learning are "experiential" and "differentiated" requires a definition of both terms. The discussions and examples revealing how such learning takes place within the context of self-directed learning programs are therefore reserved for subsequent sections of this chapter.

AUTONOMOUS TEACHERS IN ALL ELEVEN SCHOOLS ADVANCE EXPERIENTIAL LEARNING PROGRAMS

Experiential learners make discoveries and experiment with knowledge first-hand instead of hearing or reading about others' experiences (Itin 1999, 91–98). In all eleven schools teachers said they intentionally expand the means of learning beyond lectures and textbooks to give students more opportunities to have firsthand experiences.

Figure 7.1 highlights each school's means of experiential learning. The means teachers most frequently select include projects, extensive use of digital technology, service, developmental/play activities, extensive use of existing community resources, interaction with nature, and cultural exploration. In a good portion of the eleven schools nearly all of students' learning is experiential. In others it is an important yet smaller part of the learning program. Some examples follow.

Experiential Learning via Self-Directed Projects

Nichole Kotasek said that through experiences the self-directed learners at Minnesota New Country School (MNCS) develop a depth of knowledge and a connection to the material. "The experiences aren't simulated; they are completely real," she explained. Some of the students' project-based experiences at MNCS, for example, have been to design the school building, design the school green house, and plant and maintain the orchard on school grounds. Students grow food and sell it for profit at local farmers' markets, earning credit in science, marketing, and mathematics.

A TAGOS Leadership Academy student shared how he had earned physical education credit for biking to school every day. He proposed the project to include tracking his fitness improvement over time (measuring body fat, blood pressure, and more) and reflective writing. Through his reflections he learned he had unintentionally gained an improved understanding of and interest in community design. "I realized that the community was intentionally laid out in a certain way," he said. His eyes were bright when he explained that planning and design is an area of study he might now explore further.

At a public exposition of their learning, a Phoenix student explained how he had earned history credit through his study of film, which required watching films, reading and analyzing critiques, presenting his findings, and doing reflective writing. The young woman at the desk next to him had learned about Japanese cuisine to get world cultures credit. She researched and taught Japanese customs and culture in addition to cooking and tasting.

Other students learned math and science through their hands-on explorations of automobile speed and archery, which a student had recently added to his hunting repertoire. Another student learned about psychology as she delved into her interest in dream interpretation and practiced her skills on herself and her peers.

Experiential Learning with Existing Community Resources at High School in the Community (HSC)

HSC teachers reported that since the school's inception teachers have made it a priority to show students how they can be learning all the time, making use of community resources already existing all around them. Jack Stacey, for example, has been teaching New Haven history while he and the students visit famous Neapolitan pizza joints and tour local oystering businesses. Stacey made arrangements with the local history center for students to contribute research from their explorations. According to Stacey, the center is highly enthusiastic about students' reports and findings.

HSC students have a "poverty of experience," several HSC teachers explained, including limited ideas about the potential rewards of school and learning. One of their goals is to give students many experiences that build their knowledge and confidence in their own capacity to succeed. "From the moment you arrive here as a teacher you are told, 'We want you out in the community.' It's rewarding when the students take in the experiences and begin to think about what else they could learn and contribute to out there," Stacey said.

Experiential Learning via Wilderness Outings at Independence School Local 1 (Independence)

Teachers at Independence use the wilderness as an outdoor science lab. Chris French said:

> Prior to coming to Independence, most of our students have never seen the wilderness, much less tried surviving in it. When they're freshmen, right off the bat we take them to Shenandoah National Park in the Blue Ridge Mountains.
>
> As part of their learning they build shelter out of tarps. No tents! They need to go to the bathroom in holes they dig themselves. We don't give much instruction. The goal is to teach them that they *can* figure out how to do things without someone standing over them. Also, that surviving requires contributing to the community so the community will support you in return. These are the frames of mind we want them to have as they grow into the school.
>
> Students are also learning content for credit out there. They examine life cycles as part of their biology learning. They measure stream velocity for physics learning. They are out there *doing it*. They see for themselves how things work. As they grow older they participate in other experiential trips. We

take them to hike forty miles with a forty pound knapsack. For the activities on that trip they earn science and gym credit. As seniors they take a ninety-mile bike ride down the C & O Canal earning U.S. history and gym credit. With discretionary funding, teachers have decided to compensate teachers who spend their time on these trips.

AUTONOMOUS TEACHERS IN TEN OF THE ELEVEN SCHOOLS DIFFERENTIATE LEARNING

When teachers differentiate learning, they provide students in the same school or classroom with different avenues for learning content and skills as well as different avenues for processing, constructing, or making sense of ideas. They also develop or provide different teaching and learning materials so all students within a school or classroom can learn effectively, regardless of their different learning levels (Tomlinson 2001). At ten of the eleven schools, autonomous teachers differentiated learning in varying ways, to varying degrees.

Differentiation through Self-Directed Learning Programs

Teachers in the seven schools offering self-directed learning said they offer the ultimate in differentiation. Jonathan Woloshin at TAGOS Leadership Academy explained that teachers in these schools have the ability to meet students where they are.

"Our goal is to move each individual student to his or her next level of achievement," Woloshin said. Students make choices that match their learning interests and capabilities. Also, students can adjust the learning choices quickly as they learn more about their own learning styles, aptitudes, motivations, and rates of learning. Woloshin's colleague Stephanie Davis said, "Project-based, [self-directed] learning is as differentiated as it gets."

The experiences of siblings Megan and Jacob, who both attend EOC, illustrate this concept. Their teacher Cathy Diaz, as well as their dad, explained that both do well with self-directed, experiential activities at EOC, but teachers' coaching and support need to be different for each. Jacob tends to dive right into the learning, but needs to improve his skills in project planning and reflection. Sometimes he's so into the learning he forgets to complete the documentation needed to get credit, but with coaching he is improving.

Megan has excellent project management skills, but sometimes gets caught up in perfecting project plans and takes too long to get started. She is building her capacity to identify her interests, narrow them, and turn them into projects. EOC's learning program allows each to learn the skills they need for future success.

The learning program also allows both Megan and Jacob to explore their aptitudes and interests. Megan, a junior, is interested in business. She recently created a project in which she helped her mom start a business on eBay. Megan determined she would learn and perform all of the advertising and budget aspects of the work, earning credit in both language arts and math.

Her brother Jacob, a sophomore, is more of an engineer. He designed and built a water ionizer, an in-demand item in today's market that is also very expensive to purchase. He elected to put a do-it-yourself video on YouTube as a public demonstration of his learning, which had been viewed more than 22,500 times as of November 2011.[3] People who are using the video to create their own ionizers post questions and Jacob responds. Learning to track his progress, Jacob documented eighty-five hours of work over seven months and earned .85 units of science credit.

Differentiated Learning via Flexible Grouping at Chrysalis Charter School (Chrysalis)

Chrysalis teachers use flexible grouping which means, as teacher Sara Hoxie frames it, "Every child advances at her own pace." In the areas of math and language arts, students regularly switch classrooms to access learning at their own level. So, for example, some fifth-grade students join a group of mostly eighth-grade students to learn math. At the same time, some eighth-grade students join a group of mostly sixth-grade students to learn math.

Since so many students are regularly moving around, teachers report that there isn't a stigma attached to being at a different learning level than your peers. In fact, students know teachers' desire for each one to be right where he or she is supposed to be. Laura Bowie said, "We do not believe in forcing an eighth-grade student into algebra if he is not ready. We're willing to take the hit in test scores more than we're willing to put a student in a situation where he will fail a course he wasn't ready for in the first place. The individual case is the best way to go. We differentiate because the students' attitude and confidence is most important for their learning."

Differentiated Learning at SFCS Means Providing Extra Attention to Students Who Need It and Less to Students Who Are Doing Well

SFCS teachers have had deep dialogues about the definitions of "equality" and "equity" and what they wish to provide at their school. Nora Houseman said, "We chose to use the lens of equity." Offering equality, SFCS teachers explained, would mean that every student would get the same amount of attention from teachers. Offering equity means that teachers recognize students' diversity and spend more time with the school's lowest-performing students than they do with other students. SFCS teachers make their choice clear to all students and families who attend SFCS.

TEACHERS AT ALBA AND EOC REPORTED THAT THEY DESIGN PROGRAMS THAT INDIVIDUALIZE LEARNING IN WAYS VERY DISTINCTIVE FROM MOST OTHER EXISTING SCHOOLS TODAY

Academia de Lenguaje y Bellas Artes (ALBA): Bilingual, Bicultural Education Focused on Retention of Spanish Knowledge

ALBA teachers said that their learning program is distinctive from most existing schools, including most bilingual schools, for two reasons. First, most bilingual education is seen as transitional and is typically offered for no more than three years. The goal of these learning programs is to ensure students don't fall behind their same-age peers in learning content such as math and science while they learn English. The linguistic goal is English acquisition only.

At ALBA, however, the teachers' goal is to embrace, retain, and build on students' native language. Teachers speak Spanish exclusively to students while they are in three-year-old Head Start through first grade, except for the thirty minutes of English language development a day that is required by Wisconsin law. Students in grades 2–5 learn in bilingual classrooms, with an aim toward acquiring English while continuing to improve their Spanish.

Second, ALBA teachers offer a culturally relevant, arts-heavy curriculum. ALBA's website says, "Acquisition of the English language becomes second nature since it is presented within the context and understanding of the culture of the community [that] ALBA school serves. Children are encouraged to maintain their cultural ties through language and arts while acquiring language and life-long learning skills needed to be successful in a high school."

Brenda Martinez said, "We say, 'Don't lose your Spanish or your culture!' This is what parents here want for their children and for themselves. Language and culture is a barrier for these parents in other schools. But they can be truly involved here, and they know we see them as the main source of students' knowledge, language, identity, and personal development. We're their partners in teaching."

EdVisions Online Campus (EOC): Synchronous and Asynchronous Learning for Self-Directed Learners, in an Online Schooling Community

EOC teachers report that their school is distinctive from most online schools because they offer synchronous *and* asynchronous learning opportunities that are designed to support individualized and self-directed learning. EOC teachers facilitate synchronous learning using software called Elluminate. The software gives students the ability to access real-time coaching from teachers in ways that suit their individual needs. A video conferencing tool, for example, allows students to have "live" discussions about their projects with one or more teachers.

Importantly, EOC students also work asynchronously. This means they can manage their own project work, addressing multiple projects and any seminar work at their own pace and at any time of the day. As necessary, students may exchange e-mails or instant messages with teachers, community members, or peers.

EOC teachers also embrace synchronous learning in order to create a sense of community for their online campus. While students and their teachers are in different places they frequently interact with one another—including peers—in real time, using technology tools. Using Elluminate, teachers can host group chats (for homeroom-style advisory meetings including conversations about school culture) and daily web seminars (for students who choose to take math as a course, for example).

There is also a whiteboard tool for students to share what they are working on, such as a math problem, with teachers and peers. From their personal computers everyone can see and write on the same whiteboard. When the whiteboard tool is combined with audio tools, teachers and students alike can offer explanations and demonstrations to one another at any time.

EOC's program is different from the many online schools offering asynchronous learning in which students take courses whenever they can via prerecorded lectures, completing prescripted worksheets and assignments. These students generally have only limited interaction with others and do not determine and manage their own learning activities.

EOC teachers said they've worked hard to provide students with synchronous and asynchronous learning opportunities that support individualization and community-building rather than using materials designed to "batch process" students through standard coursework.

QUESTIONS AND CHALLENGES

Autonomous teachers reported two primary questions and challenges that arise when they innovate with learning programs.

1. Teachers reported that there seems to be public concern about the potential for flaws in the new and different learning programs they develop. They acknowledged this potential, but suggested that there are flaws in conventional learning programs, too. Teachers suggested that the questions the public should ask are these: Do autonomous teachers recognize flaws? And, if so, how do they develop solutions?

Autonomous teachers boasted that one of the advantages of autonomy is that whenever they recognize a flaw in their school or learning program design they can correct it immediately; they don't need to wait for a decision from anyone else, or navigate "the bureaucracy," before they can make a change. With accountability for school success, teachers said they are more motivated than ever to work collectively to identify and address areas for improvement.

Many autonomous teachers in the five middle and high schools with self-directed learning programs, for example, have moved away from self-directed math learning and now offer direct teacher instruction or asynchronous online courses for math combined with peer-to-peer tutoring. Teachers decided to change course after students and families indicated they were having trouble staying motivated with math-based projects, and when students' math performance was showing they were not grasping the concepts well.

MNCS teachers made a change when they discovered via exit interviews that a good number of students were leaving the school right before their senior year because they were intimidated by the required 300-hour senior project. Teachers amended their curriculum immediately, but didn't back away from the requirement. Instead, they collaborated to "scaffold" the learning program to give younger students an opportunity to acquire the skills and confidence necessary to do their senior project. Students now complete final projects in their sophomore and junior years as well, with increasing responsibility levels and time requirements.

Teachers said that some question whether their learning program designs ought to account better for students' potential need to change schools. Many of the schools that autonomous teachers design require students to learn state-required standards over two or more years, allow for differentiation in pace, and don't necessarily learn content in conventional grade-level sequencing. If parents move out of the area and students must transfer schools, students can be put in a precarious position.

Teachers said they make families aware of this when they are making decisions about whether to attend the school. A few teachers also pointed out that if the nation seeks innovation, then people will need to learn to tolerate new ideas—especially if families are notified and willing to assume the risks.

2. When autonomous teachers in schools affiliated with districts create new and different learning programs, they find themselves spending a lot of time either negotiating workarounds or translating what they do.

Autonomous teachers understand they are pioneers in advancing their craft, and realize that they need to have patience as systems adjust to their innovations. Teachers happily do this in exchange for autonomy. Yet they reported that they face a variety of challenges as they exercise learning program autonomy in school districts that remain largely committed to systems that support conventional notions of school. The following are a few examples:

Autonomous Teachers Must Report Students' Credits as They Apply to Districts' Conventional Course Lists

Autonomous teachers in district-affiliated schools must report students' learning as if it were learned in a conventional course. This is a challenge for teachers who use self-directed and/or experiential learning programs. While students might earn all of the credit hours and learn all of the standards necessary for a conventional civics course over a few years and projects, for example, most school districts will not award students any civic learning credit until they have completed all of the course requirements.

Teachers design their own spreadsheet systems at their schools in order to track students' credits and grades earned toward conventional courses, and eventually merge it all together and report it to the district. Still, it is cumbersome to document students' credits. More insidious, school districts' tracking systems inaccurately assess students' progress-to-date.

Autonomous Teachers Must Report Attendance by Districts' Scheduled Class Periods

At the middle and high school levels, autonomous teachers in district-affiliated schools said they must report attendance by the districts' approved class period schedule, even if they elect to use a different schedule and even if students don't take courses and classes.

The reporting system suits one of the seven middle and high schools well. Everywhere else, however, students are either managing their own learning schedule—with flexibility to leave campus or be in all areas of a school building—or learning in a single classroom with one teacher who varies the schedule daily. Nevertheless, teachers create a procedure for tracking and submitting attendance conventionally.

School Districts Have Contracts with Vendors or Require Schools to Use In-House Suppliers, Obligating Autonomous Teachers to Use the Services Whether or Not They Conflict with the Learning Program and Environment Teachers Are Working to Create

When districts arrange contracts for services, autonomous teachers are obligated to comply with the terms of the agreements. Teachers at Phoenix wanted to purchase city bus passes, for example, so their students could use transportation for experiential learning as freely as the students in chartered schools with similar learning models. But the districts' contract with the bus union had a stipulation that they could not.

Physical plant issues were also of great concern to teachers, as many said they were only able to work with districts' providers, who are not known for their flexibility. One group of teachers reported they wanted to paint the walls bright colors, for example. Physical plant workers denied their request, offering them five shades of white instead.

Teachers said "tech support" is another difficult area. Many teachers have the discretion to make "extra" equipment purchases but they are often told that any "outside" equipment that the district tech department is not trained to service must be serviced elsewhere. Services will be at school's expense, but they must use discretionary funding. They are obligated to pay the entire line item fee for district tech support even if they do not rely on it much.

Moreover, students' computer use is monitored by district tech support. District leaders and technicians design their monitoring policies as if all schools are the same, so sometimes dealing with their monitoring can be time consuming for schools that don't fit the mold.

Ard at Phoenix reported, "One of the tech department's jobs is to police computer use. We get calls from them telling us that a student has been on Wikipedia for a couple of hours. They don't understand that our students aren't in classrooms all day and that our model requires that students do research on their computers, sometimes for hours at a time." The service limitations and regular interruptions cause teachers to wonder if the fee they are paying the district would be better spent on more customized support from an outside vendor.

Teachers sense they are protecting their autonomy by exercising patience in these and other areas, so they comply for now. They expected they would have to plow down old barriers as they navigate new territory. But teachers wonder as they find success and consider scaling up: How long will it be before innovations are accepted and accommodated? Will autonomous teachers always be required to mold their models to conventional expectations? Could shifting to accommodate innovation lead to more efficient use of resources?

NOTES

1. A ninth-grade student could tackle curriculum typically not offered until twelfth grade, for example.

2. At the elementary level, some teachers focus on encouraging students' Habits of Mind, or other similar behaviors, for tackling things they haven't tackled before. The goal is for students to learn an approach for responding to problems they face, and feel confident that they have the tools to respond appropriately.

The original "habits" are a collection of sixteen thinking dispositions identified by Professor Art Costa. They include dispositions such as "persisting," "thinking flexibly," and "taking responsible risks." Mission Hill teachers have adapted them for their students in an effort to encourage depth of knowledge and familiarity with skills that can be used outside of school and for academic learning. Mission Hill's "Habits" are (1) evidence, (2) viewpoint, (3) connections/cause and effect, (4) conjecture, and (5) relevance.

3. Jacob's DIY Water Ionizer video, which he made to demonstrate his science learning at EdVisions Off Campus, on YouTube: www.youtube.com/watch?v=eZDqyAgA8DU.

Minnesota New Country School students are hard at work in their warehouse-style school building. Each has an L-shaped desk and computer for their self-directed learning.

Student Kelsey gives a tour of the Minnesota New Country School greenhouse where students grow food and sell it for profit at farmers' markets, learning and exercising a wide range of skills, from agriculture to sales.

Avalon School student Ruby sits at her personal work space, where she simultaneously pursues her academic and creative interests.

Chrysalis Charter School teacher Sara Hoxie and her kindergarten class sing and dance during morning "circle" time.

EdVisions Off Campus student Jacob meets with his teacher from his rural home. Teacher Gigi Dobosenski works with students from her home work space.

Independence School Local 1 students learn to do DNA testing using micropipettes that their teacher, Jocelyn Virtudes, borrowed from a local university in order to save school financial resources.

Student-created artwork lines some hallways of High School in the Community.
Students earned academic credit for their contributions.

Brenda Martinez teaches fourth grade at the bilingual and bicultural Academia de Lenguaje y Bellas Artes (ALBA). Martinez was also selected by her peers to be the school's lead teacher.

Teacher-advisor Patrick Yecha and students working at their desks at Phoenix High School.

Teacher Melissa Tonachel guides a student one-on-one while other students self-direct their learning at Mission Hill K–8 School.

Students at San Francisco Community School ask their peers about their experiences with bullying on campus for a class project.

TAGOS students and teacher-advisors meet in their daily circle to discuss students' ideas about a possible new graduation requirement. Afterward, they played a game of "soccer" to build community. Students score goals by hitting the ball through another student's chair legs.

Chapter Eight

Practice #5

Address Social and Discipline Problems as Part of Student Learning

Autonomous teachers' decision to put students in a position to be active learners—as described in each of the two prior chapters—influences how they deal with social and discipline problems. Teachers in nine of the eleven schools said that their sense of accountability for school success causes them to give students real responsibilities for co-creating and co-enforcing community norms.

Students participate using various dimensions of Restorative Justice—an approach that shifts schools' emphasis from managing behavior to focusing on the building, nurturing, and repairing of relationships. They also participate via increased opportunities to dialogue with teachers and via student congress, which teachers have opted to make a voting branch of school governance.

Students' involvement is educational, teachers said, even for students who are well behaved. As Tracy Money, a founder of Phoenix High School (Phoenix), said, "Discipline is seen as a part of learning, just like everything else."

Teachers in all eleven schools embrace the idea that it is the job of every teacher (not just a disciplinary leader's) to uphold their collectively determined disciplinary policies. Teachers in all of the schools also act on a principle that addressing social and emotional issues is part of their collective responsibility—their schools' responsibility. In other words, they don't view dealing with these matters as something that is outside of their responsibility.

In fact, when students make strides in addressing their social and emotional issues, teachers in many schools even count it as part of student and school achievement.

A few teachers pointed out that this decision is rooted in conceptual and empirical research. Indeed, books such as *The Foundations of Social and Emotional Learning* make a case "for linking social and emotional learning to improved school attitudes, behavior, [academic] performance [and lifelong learning]" (Bloodworth et. al. 2004, 3).

Autonomous teachers collectively establish policies that comply with states' zero-tolerance laws which mandate school personnel to suspend or expel students for infractions such as bringing drugs or weapons to campus, no matter what the reason.[1] They also comply with due process requirements for students who have been punished under these laws. But for everything else, most autonomous teachers work with students to determine school disciplinary policies and consciously decide against the practice of "dictating" (their word) a lot of blanket rules with specific consequences.

Situations requiring disciplinary action are just not that clear cut, they said, and they find that their chosen approaches are more effective for facilitating individual student progress. There are clearly outlined community norms and expectations in every school, but autonomous teachers anticipate that individuals will respond to them differently.

Jessica Fishman at San Francisco Community School (SFCS) captured the attitude of most autonomous teachers interviewed for this book. "There is no child we shouldn't be able to reach," she said. "How we got good was to consciously, as a whole team, stop blaming students and parents for not fitting into a mold. We stopped looking at what we can't control. We [design approaches] that focus on what we *can* control; what we *can* accomplish with individual students while they are at school with us." Teachers' capacity to take on these approaches, they said, is dependent on their autonomy to set school-level policies regarding discipline, design learning programs, and allocate budget (at least a discretionary amount).

In the conventional settings where some formerly worked, school districts spelled out specific disciplinary approaches and teachers' compliance was expected. In such settings, teachers explained, they only felt accountable for following what they were being told to do. That is, "enforce these rules with these consequences" and "handle social issues in this way."

Many teachers explained their perspective that some of the dictated rules and enforcement protocol actually distracted from learning, and were even ethically questionable. But there wasn't much they could do, they said. Why raise questions about whether the methods were right when there was not any real ability to influence them?

AUTONOMOUS TEACHERS GIVE STUDENTS REAL RESPONSIBILITIES TO CO-CREATE AND CO-ENFORCE COMMUNITY NORMS AND EXPECTATIONS

Autonomous teachers find that giving students real responsibilities for school discipline is not just a great strategy for maintaining a healthy community; it is also a powerful vehicle for learning. Teachers in nine of the eleven schools share with students the responsibility for co-creating and co-enforcing community norms and expectations regarding how they will live, work, and learn together.

Teachers in the remaining two schools—Academia de Lenguaje y Bellas Artes (ALBA) and Independence School Local 1 (Independence)—don't share these responsibilities with students, but do join their colleagues in elevating the importance of dialoguing with students and families in order to effectively discipline individuals and address any social and emotional needs that might be distracting from learning.

In all of these environments, students discover how and why to participate as members of a democratic society and as members of any community they will be a part of in the future. Almost 98 percent of autonomous teachers surveyed said, for example, that they do an excellent (52.8 percent), very good (32.6 percent), or good (12.4 percent) job of cultivating problem solvers more than rule followers. Almost 89 percent of teachers surveyed reported they were excellent (42.7 percent), very good (33.7 percent), or good (12.4 percent) at inviting new ideas from students. Eighty-five percent said they were excellent (34.5 percent), very good (39.1 percent), or good (11.5 percent) at implementing the ideas.

Heather George at High School in the Community (HSC) said, "Our own freedoms and opportunities to influence success overflow into freedoms and opportunities we give our students."

Jill Mulhausen at Phoenix said, "When people see students as the problem, they don't turn to them for solutions. That's a loss for everyone. Discipline works better when students participate in it. Plus students learn a lot of skills that we all want them to graduate knowing. Most importantly, they learn how to deal with things with one another rather than expecting us to police them."

Most teachers said that, with both intrinsic and extrinsic motivation to maintain their freedoms and peace within the community, students do a much better job of enforcing community norms than teachers could ever do.

Cultivation of problem-solvers more than rule-followers

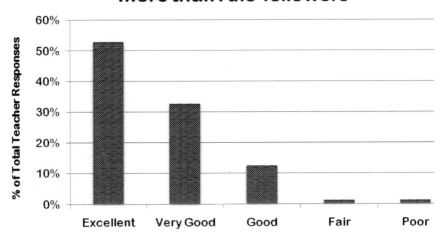

AUTONOMOUS TEACHERS IN ALL ELEVEN SCHOOLS CARRY
OUT RESTORATIVE JUSTICE PRACTICES TO SOME DEGREE

Restorative Justice is a well-established approach to discipline that autonomous teachers in all eleven schools have opted to use to some degree. The
following definition of Restorative Justice and short discussion of its implications for schools is excerpted from *Mediation in Practice*.

> In broad terms Restorative Justice constitutes an innovative approach to of-
> fending and inappropriate behaviour which puts repairing harm done to rela-
> tionships and people over and above the need for assigning blame and dispens-
> ing punishment. A restorative approach in a school shifts the emphasis from
> managing behaviour to focusing on the building, nurturing and repairing of
> relationships. Schools need relationship management policies, which consider
> everyone's needs and responsibilities towards each other, rather than behavi-
> our management policies. Behaviour management policies tend to focus only
> on the behaviour of young people and the imposition of sanctions has the
> potential to harm the crucial adult/student relationships on which good teach-
> ing and learning depend (Hopkins 2003, 4).

According to the website for the National Centre for Restorative Approaches
in Youth Settings, there are seven dimensions of Restorative Justice. In practice, these should be seen by school leaders, "as pieces of a jigsaw, which,
put together, create a congruent whole school approach to relationship building and conflict management" (National Centre for Restorative Approaches

in Youth Settings 2012). These are: restorative enquiry, restorative discussion, mediation, victim/wrongdoer mediation, circles, restorative conference, and family group conference. These dimensions evolve from four key questions: "(1) Who has been affected by what has happened? (2) What can be done to make things better for all concerned? (3) How can we ensure that everyone involved gets a chance to tell their side of the story and hear everyone else's perspective? (4) What can be learnt so something like this can be avoided in the future?" (Hopkins 2003).

Autonomous teachers practice all seven dimensions of Restorative Justice to varying degrees. For simplicity in this discussion, they are collapsed into three dimensions: discussion with students and parents, circles, and mediation.

Restorative Justice Dimension #1: Discussion with Students and Parents

Autonomous teachers in all eleven schools choose to discipline via discussion with students and their families in order to remove barriers to learning. Conversation and coaching help teachers identify when individual students need help and what support students' need to realize their potential to be disciplined, focused learners. Dialogue helps teachers to build trust with students and families, which is important to their success as disciplinarians and facilitators of learning.

Erik Good said HSC teachers were very proud that, in a recent climate survey administered by New Haven Public Schools, over 82 percent of students strongly agreed or agreed that there was at least one adult at the school who they could trust. He explained that the teachers' approach gets students' attention.

"Our students have little trust that adults at school care about them when they first arrive here. They left other environments because their needs weren't being met—they were not learning well, they were bullied, or whatever—and they didn't think anything was being done about it," Good said. "We set out to change their experience. We approach discipline as a dialogue. Rather than, 'I'm the adult, you're the kid, do what I want or else,' we emphasize, 'You're here. You're part of the community and culture. What do you need so you can do the learning you're here to do?'"

Ayla Gavins at Mission Hill K–8 School (Mission Hill) explained the value of the discussion approach.

When students' behavior needs discipline, we open a dialogue. Our approach is not, "You did this, now here's your consequence." We don't assume anything about who was responsible, or have a consequence in mind. Instead we ask, "What happened?" This opens up an opportunity for students to tell us what is going on with them. They don't feel blamed. Instead they know they

will be heard. So they will talk. *Then* we can ask them to take responsibility
and find out if there are other [social problems or learning disorders] affecting
their behavior.

Via dialogue, teachers said, they sometimes find out that students who are
acting out are in need of social services and refer them to a colleague—
sometimes a social worker who they hire with discretionary funds—who is
responsible for helping them access the services. Teachers acknowledge the
achievement when these students then figure out how to get to school and
focus on learning. When teachers are aware of students' social and emotional
issues they sometimes adjust their teaching and learning approaches.

At HSC for example, many students face extreme poverty or issues such
as homelessness, teen parenting, and verbal and sexual abuse. A few teachers
said they consequently don't expect to be able to use homework as a strategy
for getting students to meet graduation standards, so they focus on other
strategies.

HSC teacher Cameo Thorne said, "We see that our students' basic needs
aren't being met. Sixty-five percent of our freshman class is on referral to our
social worker. [That's why we've decided to invest a portion of our discretionary funding to have one on campus more frequently than the district
requires.] As we address basic needs, students become more emotionally
ready for their education. They know we care, and that we aren't going away.
From there we can help individuals meet graduation requirements at a pace
that makes sense for them."

Autonomous teachers also make a point to bring parents into the dialogue.
Parents, they said, offer excellent insights into the strategies that work for
individual students. Monessa Newell at Avalon School (Avalon) said that she
and her colleagues reject the idea that there is a "best practice" or "go to"
strategy that will work for disciplining all students.

"We ask the families for ideas about what works at home," Newell said.
"We know our limits. We don't expect ourselves to be the expert on what
works for everyone." Brenda Martinez said ALBA teachers ask parents to
pick up their children at the classroom door, daily, so there is always an
opportunity to converse with them.

Over 96 percent of autonomous teachers surveyed said they had excellent
(61.8 percent), very good (23.6 percent), or good (11.2 percent) ability to
have authentic, open discussions with parents. Good at HSC said, "Once
teachers realize they are in charge they learn quickly that involving parents
improves outcomes."

Restorative Justice Dimension #2: Circles

Teachers and students in nine schools use circles as a restorative approach. Generally, circles are for team building and problem solving and enable a group to get to know each other and develop mutual respect, trust, and concern. Autonomous teachers also use circles as a space for students to co-create school rules and influence school operations.

Circles sometimes take place as whole-school, town hall–style meetings. Other times they take place with smaller groups such as the teachers and students in individual classrooms or advisories (multiage students advised by the same teacher). Sometimes circles involve only the people most affected by a problem that needs addressing. In all nine schools, circles take place daily, opening—and often closing—the school day. But circles may happen at any time as a need arises. Sometimes they are organized by teachers; sometimes by students.

A few examples from Phoenix illustrate how circles work in practice. Male students were disgusted about someone leaving feces outside the toilet in their bathroom. They knew not to take the problem to teachers, but instead to a circle with male members of the community. Concerned students discussed the effect on the community, including health concerns and what happens when people feel disrespected.

To ensure it wouldn't happen again, the males collectively decided to lock the bathroom. They implemented and managed a process requiring all students to sign for the key. By all reports, this was a successful resolution. Today, students have removed the lock but continue to maintain a sign-out log.

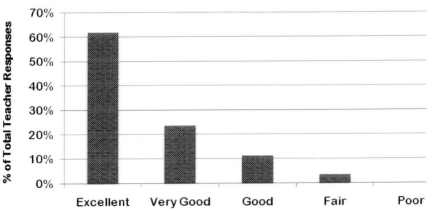

Ability to have open and authentic discussions with parents

Phoenix students also called a circle to discuss the school's daily schedule. The schedule wasn't working well for many students. At Phoenix, students are self-directed learners working in a large, one-room learning space. Scheduled "silent time" was always at the same time of day, but students pointed out that some of them work well in the morning, while others work better in the afternoon. Also, some thrive with background noise while others thrive with silence. They proposed and secured teacher approval for a schedule that would accommodate various needs, switching silent time between morning and afternoon on a daily basis.

In a third example, Phoenix students called a circle when teachers created a rule against drinking at desks. Students learned that the teachers' goal was to protect computer equipment—all Phoenix students have computers on their desks. Students proposed using spill-proof containers and keeping drinks off their main surfaces. Teachers agreed, but emphasized that their openness was contingent on students following the rules themselves. Teachers report that students are careful to enforce the rules among themselves in order to maintain the privilege.

At Mission Hill and SFCS, both K–8 schools, teachers lead students in their classrooms through circle. At the beginning of each year students create community rules and expectations. Students brainstorm ideas, discuss them, vote on them, write out the final rules together, and commit to them.

Janerra Rachko at Mission Hill said, "This is just the first exposure. We give lots of choices and students do lots of voting as the year goes on. We teach democracy. Everyone must participate and support the community decision." Teachers and students said they regularly remind one another of norms. When students need discipline that takes time away from other students, teachers tell them they are being "unfair to the community."

Through circle, teachers report that students learn skills such as self-awareness, empathy, questioning, objectivity, analysis and synthesis, appreciation for differences, self-expression, collaboration, and compromise. At the middle and high school level, some schools provide academic credit in language arts (speech and communication) and civics for circle participation and leadership.

They also learn that their role in creating and following community norms is an important part of maintaining free and peaceful communities. In other words, "discipline" is not something that only adults do. Having a disciplined, safe, learning-focused community requires involvement from all members.

Restorative Justice Dimension #3: Mediation

Tailoring Academics to Guide Our Students (TAGOS Leadership Academy) and Avalon teachers use student-led peer mediation. Students who are trained to be mediators learn skills such as active listening, nonviolent communication, and how to deal with difficult situations. Their job is to conduct mediations between parties who have a conflict. Mediators guide a dialogue to find out the following: What happened? Who has been affected by what has happened? What can be done to make things better for all concerned?

Every member of the community has the right to bring anyone else to mediation. Students can bring adults, adults can bring students, and students can bring other students. In cases of mediation between victims and wrongdoers the dialogue usually starts small but eventually evolves into the wrongdoers acknowledging their behavior and renewing their commitments to the greater community.

Jonathan Woloshin at TAGOS Leadership Academy described how this relates to student learning. "Sometimes [wrongdoers are] aware of the effect they've had on everyone [prior to mediation], but often they're not. If we just punished the problems away no one would learn from the experience."

AUTONOMOUS TEACHERS IN TWO SCHOOLS HAVE CREATED STUDENT CONGRESSES, WHICH ARE A VOTING BRANCH OF SCHOOL GOVERNMENT

Teachers at Avalon and Minnesota New Country School (MNCS) have each established a student congress as a voting branch of school government. Student congresses run a lot like Restorative Justice circles, and students learn similar skills via their participation. A key distinction is that students' authority is formally written into the school constitution, solidifying teachers' commitment to take seriously students' proposals. Via congress, students have the power to write and pass bills affecting school policies. Teachers have veto power, but they generally use it to encourage students to strengthen ideas, not to squash them entirely.

At MNCS, students proposed a bill to use cell phones while on campus without restriction, and teachers vetoed it while at the same time encouraging students to consider when cell phone use is necessary. So students wrote another bill. Again, they proposed to use cell phones, but this time not for socializing. They sought to use them in the same way that adult professionals use them—for communication related to learning and to coordinate daily logistics with their families.

When students got word that teachers were on the fence about vetoing this version of the bill, they stopped school in the middle of the day and checked on how teachers had used their own cell phones during school hours. When teachers realized that they were using phones for the same reasons students were proposing, the two parties struck up a compromise. Students can now make calls during breaks or when standing next to a teacher.

AUTONOMOUS TEACHERS MAKE ALL TEACHERS RESPONSIBLE FOR DAY-TO-DAY DISCIPLINARY MATTERS, WHICH THEY SAY MAKES FOR A POSITIVE SCHOOL CULTURE

Autonomous teachers are clear that their success with addressing social and disciplinary needs depends on everyone's ability to see the work as part of their own realm of responsibility. Most have collectively created a school discipline policy and a cultural expectation that all teachers will handle many day-to-day problems as they see them. Jocelyn Virtudes at Independence said, "For discipline, I'm the [equivalent of] a principal in my classroom. I handle everything here." Teachers also expressed that they handle discipline throughout the school, whenever they notice a problem.

This way of operating is new to most teachers. Teachers admit that when they were new to the schools with autonomy they would send misbehaving students to their principals or lead teachers out of habit, with the expectation that these leaders would handle discipline for them.

When the leaders explained that this is not school policy, and that teachers have decided all are responsible for disciplining students, new teachers said they were at first more skeptical than honored. They worried it would take time away from other students and they were used to letting someone else worry about disciplining in ways that are compliant with state laws. In time, however, they found that the strategy has a positive impact on school culture.

They begin to find that they tolerate more and dictate less, teachers said. Without the ability to send students away, teachers collectively decide that some things might not be worth disciplining at all. In fact, they find that an overabundance of rules for minor infractions, and the requirement to enforce them, can be the real distraction from learning.

Chris French at Independence said, "We offer a lot of leeway here compared to the way most schools in the district are going. We don't send students home for dress code violations. We let them drink coffee, eat at their desks, and we've even let them take naps when we know their urban lifestyles are taking a toll. We avoid allowing them any excuse to sit in 'the office' or go home. We're teaching them real discipline: stay and learn."

George at HSC said, "We're viewed as more lax than [conventional schools]. There is no dictating, and it looks loosey goosey. The point of removal is different. We have an increased level of willingness to deal with things, which helps us to get students learning."

Teachers report that when students realize they are not going to be sent away for minor violations, they know teachers are serious about keeping every student's attention toward learning. They stop trying to disrupt the learning space and come to respect it. The schools aren't immune to discipline problems, but teachers explain that students generally cooperate well. Teachers in a few schools said that they are aware of some students' gang involvement, but have found that the students choose to keep gang activity off campus.

QUESTIONS AND CHALLENGES

Autonomous teachers reported two primary challenges that arise when they address disciplinary and social needs as part of student learning.

1. Many newly autonomous teachers are initially skeptical and even avoidant of addressing discipline as part of learning.

A good number of autonomous teachers interviewed said that while they come to see the benefits of handling discipline themselves, the responsibility is one of the most difficult to adjust to. Conventional schooling has taught them that teachers' efficiency in the classroom—their ability "to teach"—depends on their ability to let serious disciplinary matters be handled somewhere else, by somebody else. This is seen as the best thing for teachers and for all the well-behaved students who are "there to learn."

Good at HSC said,

> There's a safety in being told how to do something. Culturally, people who've grown up [with conventional schooling] have come to expect uniform sets of rules and expectations that apply the same to everyone. The first year people come to teach here they have culture shock [in regard to their new and different responsibilities]. There is no system to fall back on. Your classroom is *your* classroom.
>
> Even when you know what you are getting into [with teacher autonomy], this can be hard to accept. Things are so different and, while people who have been here for a while encourage you, share ideas, and explain the benefits, you don't know the value of doing it a new way until you try it for a while. We sometimes have to say, "If you're looking for us to tell you how to teach and what to say, keep looking. Just be open. Try what we're doing here."

Martinez at ALBA and Carrie Bakken at Avalon echoed Good. As lead teachers they, too, have to help teachers through culture shock by firmly avoiding getting involved when teachers new to their schools try to send students to "the office" or "*the* disciplinarian." Martinez said, "Sometimes I need to repeatedly make clear that I'm not 'in charge' of discipline; every teacher is. You can come to me for ideas, but I'm not going to handle the issue for you. If I did, I'd have to answer to my colleagues who don't want me in that role."

Newer teachers said that, in time, they came to see the wisdom of autonomous teachers' approaches. They now ask the same questions as their colleagues, including: what do the students who need discipline as well as social and emotional interventions learn when teachers can so easily send problems away?

Moreover, what skills are students failing to learn, useful both now and in future life and work, when schools convey that discipline is separate from everything else going on? Most students will eventually become professionals and parents who will need to know effective disciplinary strategies, how to work with difficult people, and how to be responsible, respectful members of their communities.

2. State and school district disciplinary requirements and support systems are often designed assuming conventional rules and consequences, which can be in conflict with the approaches autonomous teachers embrace.

Autonomous teachers appreciate states' zero-tolerance policies, and can see a need for them. But they also wonder if zero-tolerance policies create a fear of liability which leads to mandated disciplinary approaches. Higher-than-average teacher tolerance in a zero-tolerance environment can seem at odds.

Even though autonomous teachers believe it is possible to honor both approaches at the same time, they worry that people immersed in conventional culture see higher-than-average tolerance as too "loosey goosey." They further worry that school districts and school authorizers will view their approaches as ineffective and mandate more conventional approaches. School districts and school authorizers might also fail to adjust disciplinary support services to accommodate teachers' innovative approaches, teachers said.

A security guard at HSC, for example, said that he uses methods designed around conventional assumptions, even though HSC is an unconventional school. Still relatively new to his assignment at HSC, the guard said the "completely different" nature of HSC makes him nervous. Most schools in New Haven don't allow former students on campus just to visit, he said. Also, most students in New Haven don't call teachers by their first names as students at HSC do.

The security guard fears that the informality diminishes the line of respect between students and adults. But HSC teachers sense they get more respect, and more information useful for keeping the school safe, by removing the hierarchical "Mr. and Ms." language. One teacher suggested that perhaps the security guard should be nervous because he is expected to apply conventional methods in an unconventional environment.

Autonomous teachers ask these questions: Where should adaptation take place? Should teachers' approaches adapt to conventional security strategies? Or should security strategies adapt to teachers' unconventional disciplinary approaches?

Autonomous teachers hope that when education leaders grant them the ability to innovate with discipline and other aspects of schooling, they will also be open to the idea that policies and support services designed for conventional schools may need to be redesigned to accommodate innovation. Teachers fear that if leaders are not open to redesign then "the way things have always been" will be used as a reason to prevent them from taking on new approaches that work well for their students.

NOTE

1. Documented cases of students punished according to states' zero-tolerance laws include a kindergartener from Ionia, Michigan, who, in March 2010, was suspended for making a finger gun and a six-year-old Cub Scout who was suspended and sent to a "reform school" for bringing a camping utensil that is a knife, fork, and spoon in his school lunch (McVicar 2010; Urbina 2009).

Chapter Nine

Practice #6

Broaden the Definition and Scope of Student Achievement and Assessment

States and school districts use assessments as a means of holding school leaders accountable for student achievement. The desired results are that all students will be proficient in a "common" set of standards when they complete each grade level and graduate from high schools. Most of the time "proficiency"[1] is measured by aggregate scores on standardized tests.

None of the teachers in the eleven schools were granted autonomy from state and school district requirements that teachers will design learning programs so students will meet a set of "common" academic standards. None were exempt from the federal No Child Left Behind Act (NCLB) of 2001 requirement that all students take standardized assessments so states can measure schools' adequate yearly progress (AYP).[2]

Teachers in two schools affiliated with school districts had some autonomy regarding district-level assessments. Mission Hill K–8 School (Mission Hill) teachers had autonomy to decide if and when students would participate in district-level assessments. And teachers at High School in the Community (HSC) were able to decide—as leaders in all schools in their district do—how much they would count students' scores on district assessments toward their final course grades.

But autonomous teachers[3] ask these questions: Is "proficiency" all they, or any school leaders, should be held accountable for? Are the desired results an accurate reflection of what we, as a nation, want our students to know and be able to do? And why are we solely measuring academic achievement, when so many additional areas of achievement, beyond academia, are being defined as important by our business and community leaders?

119

Autonomous teachers take students' academic achievement and performance on standardized tests seriously, and are not opposed to being accountable for it. Yet few, if any of them, found state and school district assessments to be the best measure of the achievements of their students. Furthermore, many lamented that the results of these tests are not very useful for figuring out how to improve learning programs to increase student achievement.

The tests that state leaders generally choose aren't designed to measure students' individual academic progress and nonacademic achievements, the teachers explained. Instead the tests measure how students in each school perform in specific subject areas—mainly math, reading, writing, and science—in aggregate. Teachers don't question whether students' proficiency in these core areas is important. They just wonder if that's *all* we want students to be proficient in.

Autonomous teachers also point out that most students learn from teachers who are required to use standard curriculum guides designed to keep students on pace to score "proficient" on state tests when they reach a particular grade level. Flexibility to help students who are "off pace"—ahead or behind—or for schools largely serving "off pace" students, is limited.

In Minnesota, for example, even if a student enters high school doing fifth-grade level math and progresses to Algebra I by eleventh grade, he or she will take the same Minnesota Comprehensive Assessment (MCA) that all other students take in eleventh grade. This test will measure whether the student has learned math at an Algebra II level, even though she will not yet have been exposed to Algebra II.

Teachers emphasized that the results will capture little to nothing about the student's four years' worth of learning growth in mathematics while attending the school. Yet, teachers explained, schools—and, given 2011 and 2012 gubernatorial proposals,[4] now teachers—will be held accountable for her not having passed.

Teachers described their situation as very difficult. They see three options: (1) make learning program choices that are best for raising AYP; (2) make program choices that are best for their students' individual learning growth in both standard academic areas and additional areas necessary for life and work; or (3) figure out a way to do both without overspending, overtesting, or creating too much work for themselves and their students.

Autonomous teachers usually make the third choice—complying with assessment requirements *and* doing more than what is required. In doing so, they broaden the scope and definition of achievement and assessment.

THE MAJORITY OF AUTONOMOUS TEACHERS MEASURE WHAT STATE STANDARDIZED ASSESSMENTS DO NOT — INDIVIDUAL LEARNING GROWTH

Autonomous teachers have found that, when it comes to improving learning programs and working with individual students, assessment tools that measure growth in student learning are far more effective than the assessments used by most states and school districts. So in addition to state assessments, teachers in the three Minnesota schools—all chartered—have elected to use their budget autonomy to allocate funds for formal growth assessment using the Northwest Evaluation Association (NWEA) tests. Teachers at other sites, who have less discretionary funding, have chosen to add internally developed tests and observations to monitor growth.

Teachers in all schools feel responsible for students' individual progress toward goals. Eighty-six percent of teachers rated themselves as excellent (36.0 percent), very good (31.4 percent), or good (18.6 percent) at their commitment to setting specific, measurable goals for individual students. Just over 87 percent indicated they do the same for the school as a whole (excellent [34.9 percent], very good [34.9 percent], or good [17.4 percent]).

When assessments show that students' learning growth is slow, autonomous teachers know they need to make changes and seek ways to improve. "We have no fear about test scores," said Gigi Dobosenski from EdVisions Off Campus (EOC). "We use them to test if what we're doing is working."

Growth assessments prompted teachers at Avalon School (Avalon), EOC, and Minnesota New Country School (MNCS) to move away from self-directed learning in math for all students, for example. EOC and Avalon students now have the choice to take math courses with direct instruction from a teacher, and most take advantage.

Students at MNCS now take courses with direct instruction through prealgebra. After that students learn math with asynchronous software programs such as Accelerated Math and ALEKS (Assessment and Learning in Knowledge Spaces). When MNCS students struggle to understand a concept using the software, they get together with same-level peer groups to teach one another. Mission Hill teachers also made school-wide changes to their math learning program based on their own analysis of students' growth, deciding to spend an extra hour on math weekly.

Stephanie Davis at Tailoring Academics to Guide Our Students (TAGOS Leadership Academy) echoed the view of many other autonomous teachers that assessing growth keeps teachers focused on helping each student get to their next level of achievement. "Students might be aware that the person next to them is not at their level of achievement, but they have no idea if they are making as much progress as the person next to them.

"My job as a teacher is to help students identify and remove barriers to *their own* progress. I had the tools to do that when I worked in a traditional school. But the school structures didn't allow for me to use them well. People need to recognize that 'proficient' [state-defined], for some, is a reach while for others it is far too low."

AUTONOMOUS TEACHERS THINK CAREFULLY ABOUT MAKING CHANGES TO THE STRATEGIES THAT WORK WELL FOR THE STUDENTS THEY SERVE IN ORDER TO RAISE AYP

Ninety-three percent of autonomous teachers surveyed indicated they are excellent (16.3 percent), very good (43.0 percent), or good (33.7 percent) at assessing student performance using state and school district tools. Nobie Camarena at San Francisco Community School (SFCS) said, "I can't say we don't value [state standardized] tests. We look at results and take them seriously."

Few autonomous teachers would disagree. Most said the threats of school closure and loss of students serve as extrinsic motivators for teachers to do what is necessary for their students to do well on state and district assessments. Teachers are concerned about students scoring well enough to keep their school "off the radar," so many make adjustments so their schools will make AYP. At the same time, teachers try not to compromise strategies that work well for the students they serve just to satisfy AYP.

Teachers at Academia de Lenguaje y Bellas Artes (ALBA), for example, used their scheduling autonomy to change the school calendar. Students attend school for the same total number of days as most students in Milwaukee Public Schools; however, they start two weeks earlier and end two weeks earlier. Teachers say this allows students more time for preparation before state assessments measuring AYP are given. ALBA teachers have also tried extending daily school hours for students in grades 3 to 5 (the years in which students are tested), but later decided the strategy was burning out teachers.

ALBA teachers have been consistently tempted to drop a couple of their key learning strategies to raise AYP, but they haven't yet done so. Based on research about how students grasp academic language, and their own experiences with students, ALBA teachers have continually renewed their decision not to introduce English language into the classroom—except for the minimum amount of time required by the state of Wisconsin—until grade 2.

ALBA teachers also continue to place a large emphasis on bicultural education—including bicultural fine arts—which they believe is important to both retaining families and encouraging them to invest in student learning.

ALBA teachers and families believe bilingual and bicultural knowledge is a valuable, marketable skill that they don't want to "rid" students of, even though other learning emphases might be better for making AYP.

Sue Rodahl, ALBA's assessment coordinator, said,

> Every year the pressure [of making AYP] makes us wrestle with our decision to stick with how we do bilingual and bicultural education. We ask ourselves, "*Are* we doing a better job doing things differently? *Should* we lose art for academics? *Should* we teach English earlier?" Then we look at the research that says it takes five to seven years to grasp academic language and once again realize that our model is designed well for the students who come here.

So, ALBA teachers continue to seek out and maintain methods that balance staying "off the radar" and innovating with their learning program.

A good majority of the teachers interviewed said that, like ALBA, they are continually managing the balance. But teachers at TAGOS Leadership Academy have run into what many fear—being "on the radar" and consequently losing some learning program autonomy.

Students' relatively low scores—which might show real improvement for individuals at TAGOS Leadership Academy but are low in comparison to students in other schools—have prompted Janesville Public Schools to require specific, paper-and-pencil preparation for Wisconsin standardized assessments. This means that students must take practice tests for a certain amount of time per day, at the same time of the day.

TAGOS Leadership Academy teachers report that one effect they have observed has been a diminishment in students' once growing confidence in their overall learning progress, as well as a diminishment in students' ability to "show what they know" on standardized assessments in general. The material being covered in the prep is not necessarily in line with where students are in their learning.

Teachers explained that when students engage in the TAGOS Leadership Academy learning program they typically gain pride in moving forward even if they are not on pace with *most* students in the state. This leads to students' motivation to take on new learning challenges and move toward graduation. Yet the daily, standard-paced prep for state assessments only reminds students of what they have not achieved. "TAGOS staff members see a loss of confidence in many students after they participate in mandated district preparation for the Wisconsin Knowledge and Concepts Exam (WKCE)," said Jonathan Woloshin.

AUTONOMOUS TEACHERS CREATE CULTURES THAT INTERPRET TEST SCORES, GRADES, AND EVEN TEACHER EVALUATIONS AS FEEDBACK AND NOT A LABEL

Autonomous teachers said again and again that they create cultures in which people see assessment outcomes, grades, and even teacher evaluations as feedback that helps individuals and schools understand where they are at a point in time. Scores, they realize, have little to do with what students and schools have the *potential* to do.

Autonomous teachers encourage students and one another to use scores as a source of information about how to improve and achieve more, rather than as a label saying "good enough" or "needs improvement." These cultures, teachers said, help students and teachers maintain their pride in what *has* been achieved as well as their motivation to continue achieving. Proficiency doesn't mean "done." Below proficiency doesn't mean "hasn't been making progress."

Cameo Thorne at HSC said, "Our students enter this school behind standard pace. [Due to that] and their life circumstances . . . many won't be ready for the CAPT (Connecticut Academic Performance Test) the first time they have to take it. If we're to succeed in motivating them and motivating ourselves to continue achieving here, we can't let these scores tell them who they are. If we started to do that, what would be the point?"

"Deprogramming" students from conventional ideas about scores is not easy and requires specific attention, teachers said. Chrysalis Charter School teachers help students learn to sing a song in chorus, repeating the phrase, "Feedback is our friend." Some teachers have decided to avoid grading all together. SFCS teachers, for example, created a report card that indicates when students have mastered specific standards on a path toward total completion. The school district has since adopted this report card for use in other schools, they said.

AUTONOMOUS TEACHERS EXPECT THAT STUDENTS WILL DEMONSTRATE ACHIEVEMENT IN AREAS BEYOND ACADEMICS

Autonomous teachers seek to prepare students for life, work, and civic participation. They believe that students' "beyond-academic" achievements, as well as students' attitudes toward learning and working, are at least as important to students' success as academic achievements. So they design learning programs and other school structures to support beyond-academic achievement. In some cases, teachers require students to achieve in beyond-academic areas in order to earn credits toward graduation.

Areas for beyond-academic achievement include, but are not limited to, the following: character development; students' belief in their own abilities; students' ability to take responsibility for their own ongoing learning and failure; students' learning of twenty-first century skills such as critical thinking, problem solving, communication, and collaboration; and students' acceptance of increased, serious responsibilities such that they'll be able to navigate life as an adult.

Chapters 4–8 described in detail a number of ways in which teachers put students in a position to achieve in nonacademic areas, including:

Giving Students the Opportunity to Direct Some or All of Their Learning

Students and teachers in about half of the eleven schools said that they frequently quote the superhero Spiderman's language when discussing students' higher-than-average levels of autonomy. That is, "With great power comes great responsibility." Students in a position to direct their own learning come to understand that their level of voice and choice both inside and outside of school has to do with their willingness to be responsible and accountable for their successes and failures, their attitude, and their ability to work collaboratively with peers and authority figures. Many students practice these skills regularly and are evaluated for their progress.

Giving Students the Opportunity to Develop Habits of Mind[5]

At the elementary level, some teachers focus on encouraging students' Habits of Mind, or other similar behaviors. The goal is for students to learn an approach for responding to problems they face, and to develop a sense of confidence in their ability to respond appropriately. The "habits" are a collection of sixteen thinking dispositions identified by Professor Art Costa. They include dispositions such as "persisting," "thinking flexibly," and "taking responsible risks."

Granting Students Freedom of Movement and Encouraging Use of Teachers' First Names

When teachers establish learning cultures that remove hierarchical boundaries, students learn new skills simply by being a part of the environment. With freedom of movement, for example, teachers report that students learn how to self-correct when off task. And teachers report that giving students the ability to call teachers by their first names provides students the opportunity to learn how to communicate, negotiate, and work effectively with people who are in positions of authority but who are also a part of their team.

Giving Students a Real Opportunity to Fail and Start Again

HSC teachers report that students' complacency about poor performance is a real problem when they first arrive at the school. For years, many students who now attend HSC passed classes in their previous schools without mastering material, despite teachers' threats that they would fail. Students who experienced this have come to believe that little is required, and they are astonished to learn that their academic achievement is far behind.

Erik Good reported of HSC ninth graders, "Twenty-seven percent of our students are at or below third-grade level in reading. Seventy percent are at or below sixth-grade level. Few of them believe us, and understand the potential consequences, when we tell them this truth. 'It can't be,' they think. 'We've made it to ninth grade!' So we have to start by getting them to recognize the truth while still seeing their potential to succeed."

Autonomous teachers allow time for students to realize they are responsible for their own graduation. A student at TAGOS Leadership Academy reported, for example, that during his first semester he earned a very small amount of credit compared to what he was supposed to earn. The teachers explained the potential consequences of his actions, and suggested pathways to completion, but he didn't listen.

The teachers refused to give him credits he didn't earn. But, to his surprise, they also didn't kick him out. He's grateful for both. The student now realizes that *he* is responsible for his learning. He'll graduate later than a standard student, but for the first time he was put into a position to figure out how and, more importantly, why *he* wanted to graduate.

Expecting Students to Self-Govern Their Behavior; Providing Students with Real Roles in School Governance, Hiring, and Discipline

Teachers reported that when students have real responsibilities—instead of empty opportunities to practice responsibility—they learn how their behavior affects the functioning of their communities. Students experience that they have an important role in defining and solving community problems. They also learn how to participate in collaborative decision making, gaining the capacity to identify common ground and negotiate compromises.

SOME AUTONOMOUS TEACHERS TAKE UP AND DEVELOP INNOVATIVE TOOLS FOR ASSESSING BOTH ACADEMIC *AND* BEYOND-ACADEMIC ACHIEVEMENT

Autonomous teachers who have chosen self-directed learning programs for middle and high school students (at Avalon, EOC, MNCS, Phoenix High School [Phoenix], and TAGOS Leadership Academy) take up and develop innovative processes and tools to assess students' academic and beyond-academic achievement. Autonomous teachers in four of the eleven schools visited (ALBA, Independence School Local 1 [Independence], Mission Hill, and SFCS) take up better-known assessment strategies, including portfolio assessments and public demonstrations of learning, for this purpose.

Teachers use the results of these assessments the same way that they use growth assessment outcomes; that is, to determine how to help individuals learn and how to improve their schools. Patrick Yecha at Phoenix said that the assessments' outcomes have taught him, "Our students might not know everything students in traditional schools know. But they know a lot that students in traditional schools don't."

Teachers' assessment designs and choices include:

The Hope Survey

The Hope Survey, developed and repeatedly tested by researchers at major universities with a variety of student populations, determines students' psychological adjustment in a school environment over time. The assessment tool measures "agency"—whether or not a person feels motivated to obtain goals. It also measures "pathways"—whether or not a person sees workable routes to goal attainment.

High "hope scale" scores correlate positively with dispositional optimism, self-esteem, and problem-solving ability and correlate negatively with depression and hopelessness. High scores are also positively correlated with success in college, physical health, and self-actualization. Beyond using scores to evaluate individual student outcomes, teachers can use scores to consider how well they are doing overall in addressing students' sense of autonomy, belongingness and goal orientation. See appendix D for more information about the Hope Survey.

Project Evaluation Rubrics

In self-directed, project-based learning environments, teachers have developed rubrics to measure students' academic and nonacademic achievement per project. The rubrics score students' academic learning as well as their skills in public presentation, writing, problem solving, time management, analysis, team work, information retention, self advocacy, community inter-action, and critical thinking. Students assess themselves (teachers report they are usually harder on themselves than teachers would be), and are also as-sessed by two teachers and a community member.

"A project assessment is like a thesis defense," Dobosenski at EOC said. "Students must communicate why they should earn credit for their work and what level of mastery they attained." Karen Locke at EOC added, "It's not about scope and sequence. Instead, we ask if students reach the goals they set out for themselves. We also consider how much they grow as individuals during every project, and project-to-project."

Monessa Newell at Avalon said, "Our students have a rubric they use to assess their own projects. They are learning to advocate for themselves and own their work." See appendix E for a sample project rubric from Avalon.

Rounding with Students

TAGOS Leadership Academy teachers reported that they were the first in Janesville Public Schools to take up a district-recommended strategy to round with students at thirty and ninety days after entry, just as medical doctors round with patients. The main purpose of any rounding is to find out what's going well and determine what modifications can be made and then to use that information in collaborative discussions aimed at school improve-ment.

At TAGOS Leadership Academy, rounding is a quick assessment process (two to five questions) that teachers said gives them the information they need to diagnose problems before they occur and also reinforces teachers' positive behaviors that students find useful for their learning. Teachers find the process especially useful early on in a student's attendance so they can identify and work with students who need help adjusting to self-directed learning and beyond-academic requirements they have never been exposed to in the past.

Raised Responsibility Rubric

TAGOS Leadership Academy teachers developed the Raised Responsibility Rubric to assess students' intrinsic motivation, which they believe is related to the students' ability to take on increased responsibility and autonomy during different blocks of the school day: project time, math-learning time, silent reading, and advisory circle. Students use the rubric to assess their own behavior every six weeks and, along with their teachers, track their progress over time.

Students understand that the goal is to move forward along four possible stages: Anarchy (noisy, out-of-control or unsafe behavior), Bossing Others (bothering and bullying others by not following identified school standards

and expectations for behavior), Cooperation and Conformity (
others and extrinsically behaving according to the standards and e
for behavior), and Democracy (listening to others and intrinsical:, ...
to the standards and expectations for behavior with self-rule rather than extrinsic forces). See the Raised Responsibility Rubric in appendix F.

Portfolio Assessments

Teachers at Mission Hill and SFCS create student portfolios—a systematic
collection of work that depicts a student's activities, accomplishments and
achievements in one or more school subjects. Mission Hill and SFCS teachers use what are known as process portfolios, which document students'
stages of learning and provide a progressive record of student growth (Venn
2000, 530–31; 533).

At Mission Hill, for example, teachers keep an archive of student work
and records of accomplishments. In addition, they track growth via written
teacher observations and video tapes. They tape second- and third-grade
students as they read and write in the fall and then again in the spring.
Teachers also use video to track students' self-reflection and public demonstration abilities. A panel of teachers examines full portfolios to assess
growth twice yearly, in the fall and spring.

Public Demonstrations of Learning

Teachers require students to regularly demonstrate what they know during
public learning exhibitions. Sometimes students present their learning to
members of the greater community. Other times they present to their whole
school or to smaller groups of teachers and peers. Teachers evaluate students
for their ability and growth in describing their learning reflectively and con-
versationally.

QUESTIONS AND CHALLENGES

This chapter has already described autonomous teachers' sense that the national focus on AYP and "common" standards hinders their ability to implement strategies that will advance students' individual learning growth in both
academic and nonacademic areas. This chapter also included teachers' ideas
about what happens to students' confidence and motivation when conventional assessments fail to capture their learning progress. Related to these
concerns, teachers mentioned two additional questions and challenges.

1. Will autonomous teachers' innovative approaches to achievement and assessment eventually influence the federal government, states, and school districts to change course?

The teachers interviewed for this book are willing to take on new approaches to achievement and assessment in addition to meeting their obligations with required conventional approaches, but they hold out hope that they won't have to do both forever. Doing both extends scarce fiscal resources, they said, and is generally very taxing on both teachers and students' time and energy. Yet teachers know that meeting conventional obligations alone will not give them the information they need to continuously improve their schools.

Generally speaking, many teachers were cynical about the potential for large-scale change in the areas of achievement and assessment—conventional culture runs deep and, as one teacher put it, the country seems to be struggling in its effort to find better approaches. Most teachers understand that state and school district assessments are necessary to hold schools accountable for student learning. They hope, however, for a change in course.

Many want states and school districts to focus on meaningful assessments that eliminate the need to do additional assessments at the school level. In that vein, a few teachers wondered if their choices and innovations will eventually influence the federal government, states, and school districts to at least open a conversation about what new approaches to achievement and assessment ought to accommodate, such as individualized student learning and nonacademic areas of achievement.

2. To what extent might conventional approaches to achievement and assessment threaten teachers' autonomy?

States and school districts, as a whole, must make AYP. This can cause state and district leaders to micromanage schools with students who have low test scores. Such is the case with Janesville Public Schools' requirement that TAGOS Leadership Academy students engage in conventional preparation for standardized state assessments, despite TAGOS teachers' de facto, informal autonomy to determine their learning program.

A question some teachers who are affiliated with school districts wonder about is, to what extent will district leaders try and micromanage schools in which teachers have autonomy? Or, to flip the question, to what extent will district leaders tolerate the trial of new and different approaches? Some teachers also wonder, on a grander scale, do some autonomy arrangements work better than others to avoid micromanagement or are all arrangements equally susceptible to infringement?

Teachers realize that if they are not meeting expectations, it makes sense for those who are granting the autonomy to intervene at some point. But, some wonder, what is the appropriate point of intervention? Some teachers were clear that if it's too easy for state and district leaders to intervene then teachers will not be very willing to innovate. They are not opposed to being held accountable for what results from their choices in school design, yet they fear that state and district leaders will too loosely use "accountability" as an excuse for intervention.

NOTES

1. Each state can set its own definition of "proficiency," and definitions vary. See the next footnote for further information about what states are required to do by the federal No Child Left Behind Act (NCLB) of 2001. The Thomas B. Fordham Institute published a graphic in 2007 that illustrated the variance.

"To compare what states define as 'proficient,' the scores students must get on state tests for NCLB proficiency—called 'cut scores'—were correlated to the national Measures of Academic Progress (MAP) test," the graphic said. Estimated reading proficiency scores for selected states ranged from 11 in Colorado to 65 in Massachusetts, with a median cut score of 26 (twenty-six states were examined). Estimated math proficiency scores ranged from 16 in Colorado to a 67 in Massachusetts, with a median cut score of 40 (twenty-five states were examined). The graphic also suggested that there is variance in the difficulty of the tests, with Colorado's being easier than Massachusetts's."

2. NCLB allows state education agencies to develop target starting goals for AYP. After those are developed, states must increase aggregate student achievement in gradual increments in order for 100 percent of the students to become proficient on state assessments by the 2013–2014 school year. Those who accomplish the incremental goals "make AYP." If they do not "make AYP," there are layered consequences.

In the first year, schools are given an opportunity to turn things around. If the school does not make AYP for a second year, then it enters "Program Improvement" status and has to create a plan for improvement and students must be given the opportunity to attend a different school. If the school continues not making AYP in years three to five, then federal funds are used to provide supplemental educational services to students and corrective actions ensue (such as new curriculum, extended school years, and new leaders). After six years of not making AYP, the school must implement an "alternative governance" plan in year seven. The "alternate governance" plan must include one of the following:

- Reopen the school as a public charter school, or
- Replace all or most of the staff responsible for the lack of progress, or
- Enter into a contract with a private company to operate the school, or
- Turn over operation and management of the school to the state, or
- Implement any other fundamental reforms approved by the state.

For more information, please refer to *Making Sense of State AYP Lists* by Ross Wiener of The Education Trust (2003).

3. While teachers generally do not have autonomy in the area of assessment, teachers report that it is their sense of autonomy and accountability that pushes them to raise questions and to broaden the definition of achievement and assessment at their schools. Thus, the term "autonomous teachers" will continue to be used in this chapter.

4. The National Council on Teacher Quality reports that nearly two-thirds of states have overhauled policies in the last two years to tighten oversight of teachers, using techniques including tying teacher evaluations to student test scores, linking their pay to performance, or making it tougher to earn tenure. At least twenty-three states and the District of Columbia now evaluate public school teachers in part by student standardized tests, while fourteen allow districts to use this data to dismiss ineffective teachers, according to the report from the National Council on Teacher Quality, an advocacy group.

5. See chapter 7, note 2 in this volume.

Chapter Ten

Practice #7

Encourage Teacher Improvement Using 360-Degree, Peer-, and Self-Evaluation Methods as Well as Peer Coaching and Mentoring

Teachers in nine schools have some degree of autonomy in the area of teacher evaluation. Almost all reported that they are willing to be evaluated, and hold themselves and one another accountable, for their individual and collective performance in the areas in which they have autonomy to make decisions related to school success. Further, most asserted that the people with whom they share accountability should have the ability to participate in evaluation of their individual performance.

With these ideas in mind, teachers in seven of the nine schools have elected to use 360-degree, peer-, and/or self-evaluation methods. The teachers said these processes enable them to hold one another accountable for setting and reaching individual improvement goals.

Teachers in these seven schools said that they have decided to evaluate themselves in areas extending beyond what most school districts and authorizers require. Their teacher evaluations cover teachers' expanded roles, including their performance as collaborators, leaders, advisors, and managers. Also, many teachers collectively require themselves to be evaluated more frequently than once a year and even after earning tenure. That is, if they have decided that tenure can be earned. Teachers in four of these schools have one-year, at-will contracts for employment.

Finally, teachers said their evaluation processes open people up to receiving coaching and mentoring from their peers in areas needing improvement—something they said was taboo in the conventional settings where they had previously worked.

Teachers in the eighth school have de jure autonomy in the area of teacher evaluation but have elected not to do formal evaluation of teachers. These teachers also have one-year, at-will contracts, which they believe nullifies the need to conduct formal evaluation—there is no need to document progress toward tenure or to document poor behavior that could lead to dismissal. Teachers at this school view student and parent satisfaction, as well as daily informal evaluation from their colleagues, as their gauge of how well they're performing.

Finally, teachers in the remaining three of the eleven schools do not have autonomy in the area of teacher evaluation and are using conventional evaluation methods.

Even with the variances in autonomy and approaches to evaluation, 76.1 percent of all teachers surveyed for this book rated themselves as excellent (19.6 percent), very good (38.0 percent), or good (18.5 percent) at holding one another accountable. Almost 73.7 percent rated the quality of their performance review as excellent (12.1 percent), very good (42.9 percent), or good (18.7 percent). And 78.1 percent rated the speed of addressing problems with teachers' performance as excellent (13.2 percent), very good (31.9 percent), or good (33.0 percent).

AUTONOMOUS TEACHERS IN THREE SCHOOLS VISITED USE 360-DEGREE, MULTISOURCE EVALUATION

- Avalon School (Avalon)
- EdVisions Off Campus (EOC)
- Minnesota New Country School (MNCS)

With complete autonomy over evaluation methods, teachers in the three Minnesota chartered schools—Avalon, EOC, and MNCS—invite feedback from multiple sources including peers, students, and parents; and all of it is considered.

Teachers reported that three factors contribute to the success of this evaluation method, the first two cultural and last one structural. First, teachers in these environments see themselves as unfinished learners who must always use feedback to improve their teaching and their schools. Second, these teachers are open to be coached and mentored, and each look to 360-degree evaluation outcomes as a guide for the areas in which they need to be coached. Third, these teachers have elected to have one year, at-will employment contracts, so their job security depends highly on the outcomes of their evaluations.

"There's a real 'loss of job' consequence for a poor evaluation and failure to correct yourself. So accountability for performance is high," said Carrie Bakken at Avalon. Bakken went on to explain that one-year commitments also mean that any teacher could choose to leave annually. This provides the incentive for teachers to conduct evaluations respectfully, especially to prevent the loss of quality colleagues.

Teachers at EOC and MNCS conduct the peer aspect of 360-degree evaluation annually (MNCS) or biannually (EOC) using rubrics they designed to gauge and improve performance. The rubrics measure skills and abilities necessary to implement their schools' distinctive learning programs, as well as every teacher's individual value-added. On a four-point scale, peers rate peers' content knowledge, evaluation skills, ability to assist students in developing project proposals, reflective practice, coaching and advising ability, and organization.

Avalon teachers have a different system. Using an online platform called SurveyMonkey, peers annually evaluate peers on three questions: (1) What is going well? (2) What suggestions do you have for improvement? (3) Should this person return next year? First, peers answer this last question on a four-point scale: strongly confident, confident, have some reservations, have strong reservations. Then, in an open-ended space, peers offer feedback.

Comments are to be respectful and constructive in nature, but Avalon teachers said they've struggled in this area and have experimented with different methods to ensure people take care with their criticism while still feeling comfortable to state concerns.

At all three schools, student and parent evaluations weigh heavily in the areas of parent communication, relationship building, and ability to create a strong learning environment.

Since reviewing the results of these processes is a large undertaking, autonomous teachers in these schools delegate the task to a personnel team that is made up of teachers. Personnel teams usually find that no corrective action is necessary for most teachers. On the rare occasions when corrective action *is* needed, personnel teams appoint a group of their colleagues to help teachers who are having difficulty to set personal goals and map how to accomplish them. The appointed colleagues are expected to frequently work with each individual to assess progress toward goals and report progress to the personnel team.

Individual teachers in all three schools use evaluation results to set challenging goals for themselves for the coming year. Personnel teams are responsible for holding teachers accountable for accomplishing these goals.

Monessa Newell at Avalon said, "We've found that having your own goals, and being accountable to your peers for accomplishing them, is the best way to make teacher evaluation productive."

PARTIALLY AUTONOMOUS TEACHERS IN FOUR OF THE DISTRICT-AFFILIATED SCHOOLS VISITED USE PEER EVALUATION IN ADDITION TO WHAT IS REQUIRED BY THEIR COLLECTIVE BARGAINING AGREEMENTS

* Academia de Lenguaje y Bellas Artes (ALBA)
* High School in the Community (HSC)
* Independence School Local 1 (Independence)
* Mission Hill K–8 School (Mission Hill)

In three district-affiliated school environments—ALBA, Independence, and Mission Hill—teachers have autonomy to conduct peer evaluation in addition to the more conventional evaluation required by collective bargaining agreements. They do not have autonomy to forgo conventional evaluation or to document poor performance indicated from peer review.

Conventional evaluation requires that someone with an administrative credential be a part of evaluation, and these three schools have someone with such a credential on their team (Mission Hill must have an administrator on site; ALBA and Independence teachers have the option to use an off-site administrator, but do not use the option as they currently have administrators on site).

At a fourth district-affiliated school—HSC—teachers are embracing a city-wide break from convention. All New Haven Public Schools have been moving to peer evaluation since 2009. HSC teachers have customized the requirements for their own governance model. They do not have autonomy, however, to do anything but peer evaluation.

Why do these teachers pursue their own, additional evaluation when they are also required to use district- and union-required methods? They reported that evaluation is an essential tool for their governance models, because they are collectively responsible for whole school success.

As with the 360-degree model, teachers chose peer evaluation to open the opportunity and expectation for coaching and mentoring from one another—something they reported was too often missing when they worked in more conventional settings. Also, teachers indicated that peer evaluation for both new and veteran teachers reinforces individual responsibility to improve performance as part of accountability to the whole team.

Partially Autonomous Teachers Find a Balance between Administrator-Conducted and Peer-Conducted Evaluation, as Required by the Nature of Their Autonomy Arrangements

The ways in which these teachers balance administrator-conducted and peer-conducted evaluations vary. The pilot school agreement between Mission Hill and Boston Public Schools requires that a principal conduct district- and union-required evaluations for nonpermanent teachers—who are in their first three years in the school district—in order to maintain confidentiality and avoid liability. The pilot agreement allows for the school's governing board to give teachers the ability to determine what happens after that, and Mission Hill's governing board has granted teachers this authority.

At Mission Hill, teachers determined that teachers who have permanent employment with the district will be peer reviewed every other school year. Teachers chose to use the phrase "permanent employment with the district," and not tenured, because no teacher at Mission Hill has tenure within the context of the school. Every teacher has a one-year, at-will contract for employment. Principal Ayla Gavins said, "So, a teacher at Mission Hill could be permanent and not be invited back to the school. The same is true in reverse. A teacher who is not permanent yet can be invited back repeatedly."

Teachers have decided that Principal Gavins should participate in some of these evaluations, but in the role of peer/teacher. The principal only gets involved in her principal role on rare occasions; mainly when legal documentation of a teacher's poor performance is necessary. School districts typically require a lot of formal documentation from a trained administrator for a teacher to be removed from a school, so these teachers must use that route when they are concerned that a colleague might not be a good fit.

Teachers find a similar balance at ALBA and Independence. In these schools, however, there is more flexibility regarding principal or other administrator involvement. ALBA teachers have a modification from their collective bargaining agreement allowing for peer evaluation teams to conduct teachers' final reviews in the first and second years of their employment with Milwaukee Public Schools, while a district-appointed administrator (on or off site) completes one observation during each of those years. In year three, when tenure is granted, the district-appointed administrator must conduct the final evaluation.

The collective bargaining agreement requires that tenured teachers will be evaluated in years four and five, and then every five years thereafter, by two peers and a parent. Teachers have the authority to evaluate teachers more often, but ALBA teachers rarely exercise that authority.

As is the case with Mission Hill, an administrator must handle documentation of poor performance. Until fall 2010, ALBA did not have an administrator on site. Instead, an assigned administrator from the district would visit campus to observe and evaluate. But this arrangement made documentation too long a process, ALBA teachers said. Teachers needed to schedule the off-site administrator to witness poor performers, and the administrator would not necessarily see poor performance upon arrival.

To speed up documentation and removal processes, ALBA teachers requested that the district assign them a part-time, onsite assistant principal who would have more familiarity with poor performers.

Independence's codirector (who is seen as an "assistant principal" by Baltimore Public Schools) conducts one full observation of teachers each year of their first three years of employment as required by the school district. In addition, the chartering agreement between Independence and Baltimore City Schools allows for every teacher to work with a peer review team to set and accomplish individual goals throughout the year. The codirector gets involved in the peer review process only when documentation is necessary.

At HSC, where schools throughout the entire city are moving toward a peer-evaluation model, peer groups meet monthly for discussions and give district-required formal ratings to individuals twice a year. Most schools conducting peer evaluation in New Haven must have an Instructional Manager (an administrator trained in evaluation) complete teachers' ratings based on peer-evaluation outcomes, but HSC has used its informal autonomy arrangement with New Haven Public Schools to customize the process and allow peer groups to complete the ratings themselves. HSC is still determining how to deal with documentation requirements.

Teachers in all four schools reported that, rather than risk removal, anyone who is not showing improvement during a documentation process typically seeks to leave the school. When teachers leave, they go back into their district's selection pool to be considered for other schools.

Partially autonomous teachers create formal peer evaluation processes to enhance individuals' commitment to self-reflection and continuous improvement

In all four schools with peer evaluation, autonomous teachers seek to create an expectation that individuals must continuously work to improve their craft. At ALBA, Independence and Mission Hill, peers hold one another accountable for setting and accomplishing teaching-related goals that individuals develop themselves.

At Mission Hill, teachers who are permanently employed by Boston Public Schools are peer reviewed every other year by a peer review team, which is made up of one peer of the teacher's choice and one peer of the principal's choice. Twice a year, all teachers being evaluated assess their own performance against a collection of teaching standards[1] and write-up a self-reflective, journalistic paper. After that, each teacher's peer review team conducts an observation, reviews the teacher's self-assessments, and dialogues with the teacher to encourage continued progress.

Teachers at Independence developed a similar process. Every teacher identifies three individual goals to accomplish by the end of the year: one instructional, one related to teachers' work in comanaging the school, and one in any area the teacher chooses. Teachers pick two colleagues to serve on their peer evaluation teams. Teachers are observed by their team every two weeks. They also meet with their team after each observation to discuss progress toward goals as well as strategies for achieving them.

At ALBA, teachers are peer reviewed by two colleagues and a parent. The teacher being reviewed picks one of their colleagues, and the other is chosen by peers. The three observe the teacher using a district- and union-approved rubric and consider the teacher's progress toward his or her own, preidentified goals. The three then have a dialogue with the teacher to discuss their observations and suggestions for growth.

Mission Hill, Independence, and ALBA focus on individuals setting their own goals as a means to self-reflection and continuous improvement, teachers reported. Jennera Williams at Mission Hill said, "Having to set goals, and evaluate others' accomplishments, encourages a lot of personal growth. I think deeply about my progress toward my goals, and I am really self-reflective about how I can improve." Elissa Guarnaro at ALBA said, "People seem more accountable for getting better when they set their own goals. Conventional evaluation can clump everyone together and let individuals off the hook."

While HSC teachers do not formally set personal goals, their process focuses them on continuous individual improvement. At HSC every teacher is evaluated by a peer-evaluation group made up of four randomly drawn, certified teachers, including one of two elected school leaders (the lead facilitator or student membership coordinator who, in the eyes of New Haven Public Schools, are the principal and assistant principal).

Every month, starting at the beginning of the school year, one group member observes the teacher for progress toward district-required benchmarks and then the full group meets to discuss the outcomes of the observation, identifying strengths and areas for development. Mid-year, the group meets to fill out district-required ratings and to discuss second semester goals. The lead facilitator and student membership coordinator must sign off on the midyear ratings and goals and submit them to the district central office. Then, the teacher gets a new peer-evaluation team.

By the end of the year every teacher has been observed, evaluated, and mentored by seven to eight certified teachers.

AUTONOMOUS TEACHERS IN ONE SCHOOL USE INFORMAL, IMPROMPTU FEEDBACK PROCESSES

• Chrysalis Charter School (Chrysalis)

Chrysalis teachers choose not to have a formal evaluation process even though they have autonomy to do so. Like the Minnesota teachers who opted for a 360-degree evaluation process, Chrysalis teachers in California have one-year, at-will contracts for employment. Chrysalis teachers decided that the contract nullifies the need for formal evaluation because there is no need to document progress toward tenure or to document poor behavior that could lead to dismissal.

Some teachers have questioned, however, whether this decision was made based on conventional ideas about the nature of evaluation. A veteran in the group has initiated a discussion about how a formalized peer-evaluation process, or other similar processes, might be used as a tool for discussion and improvement.

All Chrysalis teachers interviewed made clear that the lack of formal evaluation does not mean that they are trying to avoid evaluation. In fact, teachers can and do walk into any classroom, observe, and offer informal feedback at any time. One teacher wondered if formalization might end this practice, creating a "culture of paranoia."

Chrysalis teachers also stressed their strong belief that the marketplace is the best source of individual and group evaluation. Sara Hoxie said, "Parents leave if the product isn't good, so we make sure it is good. We are constantly thinking about areas for improvement based on feedback from families." To ensure quality feedback, and to provide a means for families to express when they perceive a teacher is not responding well to concerns, teachers formed a parent advisory board that is responsible for acting as a liaison between families and teachers when necessary.

Laura Bowie said, "If I'm doing something badly, I hear about it from the students and parents directly first. I'm responsible for improving things myself. If I don't, parents will make sure it is addressed by taking it to the parent advisory board. And if I still don't address it, my peers will consider whether the problem calls for them not to renew my contract."

TEACHERS IN THREE SCHOOLS PRACTICE CONVENTIONAL EVALUATION METHODS

• Phoenix High School (Phoenix)

- Tailoring Academics to Guide Our Students (TAGOS Leadership Academy)
- San Francisco Community School (SFCS)

In three of the schools visited—Phoenix, TAGOS Leadership Academy, and SFCS—teachers were practicing conventional evaluation. Phoenix teachers do not have any agreement formalizing their autonomy. District-appointed administrators, who are supportive of the teaching arrangement at Phoenix, come to the school to conduct conventional evaluations two or three times per year.

TAGOS Leadership Academy teachers emphasized that they do not evaluate one another formally, as they do not have this authority from their collective bargaining agreement: the agreement does not allow teachers to conduct evaluations. The school has an off-site principal who is also the director of special education for Janesville Public Schools. The principal supervises teachers and conducts evaluations, and is generally supportive of the teaching and learning arrangements.

TAGOS Leadership Academy teachers reported that in the past, however, off-site administrators assigned to conduct evaluations seemed to grasp at straws, offering feedback that wasn't meaningful. Teaching and learning is so different at TAGOS Leadership Academy that conventional evaluation practices don't work well to evaluate teachers' work, they said.

The district- and union-approved observation rubric assumes teachers will be instructing students in a conventional classroom, for example, whereas at TAGOS, teachers' role is to guide and advise self-directed learners. According to TAGOS Leadership Academy teachers, administrators who didn't understand their learning program, yet didn't have an alternative rubric, started tracking odd issues. One teacher said that an administrator noted in a teacher's evaluation how many adults in the school were wearing black on the day of observation, for example.

TAGOS Leadership Academy teacher Jonathan Woloshin said he began to think about creating more appropriate tools, but given teachers' lack of authority in this area he wondered if it would be worth the investment. He said, "The best tool would get honest feedback about how teachers work in the TAGOS model. How are teachers making the shift from being an instructor to guiding students as they direct their own learning? Where are they on the scale from being imposing on students? Are they offering mandates or offering ideas? Does the teacher see himself as a learner?"

SFCS teachers have developed such a tool over forty years of operation. Unlike TAGOS Leadership Academy, teachers there have always—until recently—had informal autonomy in the area of evaluation. SFCS teachers established a peer evaluation model which was overseen by their own personnel committee.

FINDING MEANINGFUL EVALUATION

I was nervous the first time I was officially evaluated by my principal. She was a supportive, kind, experienced educator and never gave me reason to stress, but the process was intimidating for me. I prepared my lesson carefully, made sure my pre-evaluation form was filled out correctly, and warned my students that the principal was coming to visit that day so they had better be on their best behavior. The observation itself was simple: my principal came in, sat down at an empty desk, took notes, walked around the room, and twenty minutes later was gone. I breathed a sigh of relief and finished the day.

A few days later I met with the principal in her office to go over and sign my evaluation. She was very positive and I had check marks in all the right boxes. Her comments were helpful and she offered a couple areas I could work on. We both signed the page and it was over. As a new teacher I completed this process two more times that year.

When I became an administrator and took on the role of evaluating, it was eye opening. I always thought other teachers taught the same way I did, but it turned out I was wrong. I loved visiting teachers' classrooms because I was able to learn so much from these teachers—creative lessons, new classroom management strategies, and ways to engage reluctant learners, for example. I wish I had the chance to observe other teachers and learn these things while I was still in the classroom.

At schools where teachers are part of the union, evaluation is part of the collective bargaining agreement. The rules established in the agreements are meant to protect teachers and ensure competency in the classroom. Sadly, evaluation has often become more of a checklist than a meaningful tool to improve instruction, whether the teacher is brand new or a twenty-year veteran. The process rarely lends itself to real reflection and improvement for most teachers. While most involved in education agree that evaluation should change, it is a controversial subject because teachers' jobs are on the line.

I was interested in learning about evaluation at the schools we visited. I expected some peer evaluation from teachers who chose these collaborative environments. It made sense to me that teachers who lead together would prioritize knowing how each other taught in their classrooms, but I didn't expect they would have such formally organized systems. I walked away very impressed by the depth of evaluation many of these autonomous teachers participate in.

These teachers take evaluation seriously and make it a priority to have evaluation be a meaningful tool to improve their skills. They aren't checking off boxes on a mandated form. They are making goals for themselves and being held accountable by and supported by their fellow colleagues for reaching them.

Learning about 360-degree evaluation was the most exciting for me. I had never heard of it before and the more I considered it, the more it made perfect sense. Including students, parents, and other teachers' impressions and observations in an evaluation creates an accurate picture of a teacher's skills, inside and outside the classroom because it allows feedback from all the people impacted by the teacher. This type of evaluation gives teachers feedback from all angles. It especially makes sense at schools that prioritize a teacher's contributions to the whole school community as well as inside the classroom.

I think the innovations autonomous teachers create in the area of evaluation could be very useful to all schools. Being part of this type of evaluation system would have made me a more reflective and continuously improving teacher. And a more reflective growth environment would be good for all educators.

According to SFCS teachers, their local teachers' union and school district were supportive of their evaluation practices because it was working well given the models for teaching and learning at the school, despite the fact that evaluation was conducted by many teachers and not a single administrator. The arrangement compromised confidentiality under the collective bargaining agreement, but in some thirty-five years there were not any complaints.

In recent years, however, after a teacher who was unhappy with peer evaluation outcomes filed a grievance against SFCS's former elected head teacher, the fragility of the informal arrangement was exposed. The head teacher hadn't conducted the evaluation. Instead, a team of teachers did.

Technically, confidentiality was breached and SFCS teachers did not have any formal agreement backing up their ability to use peer review. According to SFCS teachers, the local administrators' union stepped in and insisted that all SFCS teacher evaluations and personnel issues be conducted conventionally—by one administrator who would ensure confidentiality.

Given SFCS's positive history with their informal arrangement, the district and teachers' union were supportive of SFCS teachers retaining their de facto authority. But the teachers' union had a lot on its plate and decided that helping SFCS with this matter wasn't their priority that year. SFCS teachers decided that without help from their teachers' union they could not take on the fight. They dismantled the personnel committee and the head teacher now handles all personnel and evaluation matters.

According to current head teacher, Jessica Fishman, the new arrangement almost immediately brought negative change in teachers' sense of collective accountability, and she fears the situation may worsen. "I can tell the culture is shifting," she said.

> This new arrangement undermines trust we used to have between all teachers. There is less accountability to the entire team when one person is in charge of evaluations. We're struggling to redefine everything. People used to take personnel concerns to the personnel team. Now people are unsure how to address concerns. On one hand we're all saying, "Everyone is accountable to everyone," while on the other hand our new structure conveys that the buck stops with me. This changes the whole dynamic of what we've been doing here.

ACROSS ALL ELEVEN SCHOOLS, TEACHERS COMMONLY PRACTICE INFORMAL MENTORING AND COACHING

Many of the teachers with formal processes for 360-degree evaluation, as well as Chrysalis teachers, said that they embrace informal mentoring and coaching to help identify and address both individual and collective areas for improvement. At Avalon and MNCS there are very few physical areas not visible to all teachers and students. Teachers call these environments "fish bowls." Teachers literally observe one another, and both seek out and offer feedback, all day long.

Teachers who join these environments after having worked in conventional arrangements said the constant, informal observation and dialogue takes some getting used to. Crystal Simons from Chrysalis reported, "At first I couldn't believe it when teachers would just walk into my classroom, have a seat, and watch me teach. That just never would have happened at [the conventional school where she previously worked]. Now I know it's just how we do things here. When our school is managed by all of the teachers, of course other teachers want to know if I'm doing a good job."

Teachers in the four schools with peer evaluation mentioned informal mentoring and coaching less frequently than those who do 360-degree evaluation and conventional evaluation. Perhaps this is partially related to the set-up of the schools. Most teachers using peer evaluation methods teach in classrooms, while most teachers using conventional evaluation work in more open, "fish bowl" spaces.

In general, teachers from all eleven schools said that informal mentoring and coaching is important to making collective accountability work. "We're always informally evaluating one another," said Stephanie Davis at TAGOS Leadership Academy. "This is not something that is inappropriate or that makes me nervous. It's out of love for the school. We all want the school to be the best and to fix weaknesses. We all feel safe to discuss our concerns."

Fishman at SFCS said, "Coaching and mentoring creates accountability on another level—more than what comes about from conventional evaluation." Jill Mulhausen at Phoenix said, "Our informal evaluation is much more authentic than the district and union-approved evaluation, which is pretty cookie-cutter. Our processes are more helpful."

QUESTIONS AND CHALLENGES

Teachers reported two primary questions and challenges in the area of evaluation.

1. To what degree are teachers able to give honest and thorough evaluation to peers they must work closely with?

When teachers are collectively accountable for their schools' success, they must extensively rely on one another on a daily, even hourly, basis. Teachers said that the high degree of collaboration described in chapter 5 builds trust and fosters personal relationships that few are willing to risk. This can have both a positive and negative impact on evaluation.

Positively speaking, any desire to be an "overzealous nitpicker"—a term one teacher used—stays in check. Another positive is that in these environments the culture allows teachers to constantly give and receive informal coaching and mentoring. Teachers suggested that since feedback is more public, and isn't reserved for evaluation, improvement can happen quickly.

On the negative side, a few teachers in four schools said they did a fair or poor job of assessing teacher performance, in part, as it relates to students' performance (72.3 percent of all surveyed said they did an excellent [14.9 percent], very good [33.3 percent], or good [24.1 percent] job). The reasons? In one-on-one interviews, teachers openly questioned if they are addressing evaluation thoroughly enough. They worried that they are collectively pushing evaluation down the list of priorities and not spending enough time on it.

To address their own concerns, teachers in the three Minnesota schools using 360-degree evaluation applied for and received Q Comp funds from the State Department of Education. Q Comp stands for "Quality Compensation for Teachers" and allows the schools to provide performance pay to teachers who receive positive peer evaluations on an objective rubric and whose students' state test scores improve. Several teachers mentioned this was just the incentive they needed to focus more intently on evaluation.

Teachers also wondered if they are realizing the full potential of their evaluation processes. Some questioned their own ability to be honest with their peers about areas for improvement, and wondered if their peers were being honest with them. Conversely, some teachers communicated that honesty is *not* an issue. Melissa Tonachel at Mission Hill said, for example. "It's a demanding responsibility. We are tough on one another. People are not apologetic about what they say, and we all still work together well for the most part."

But teachers in other environments were not as certain. Nichole Kotasek at MNCS said, for example, "It's a better process [than conventional evaluation models], but it's not perfect. The tone is constructive for the most part, but our relationships are too close to honestly fill out rubrics and have necessary conversations at times. I don't want to destroy relationships with people I need to work so closely with."

Erik Good said of HSC teachers' transition to peer review, "There have been some hiccups. There has also been substantially more conversation among the faculty about teaching. The ratings are likely to come back a little high—it's dangerous and tricky to have to evaluate your equals. But given the nature of our administrative structure it seems best to have the process be as public as possible. We want to avoid [internal] perceptions of hidden agendas or being 'out to get' anyone."

Indeed, autonomous teachers who have experimented with anonymous evaluation in other environments said that it did not work as well as other peer review processes in the areas of avoiding negatives and enhancing positives.

Like Kotasek and Good, nearly all of the teachers with concerns clearly communicated that—despite any problems—the evaluation processes they use now lead to outcomes superior to those they were aware of in their prior working environments, particularly in the area of helpful individual feedback for continuous improvement.

The issues teachers reported here are not uncommon to worker owned and operated organizations. In their 1984 publication, *Worker Cooperatives in America*, Robert Jackall and Henry M. Levin wrote of the opportunities and problems for workers in these environments.

> [T]he affective ties which are the basis for selection into collectives bind workers to one another and to their groups in very intense ways. On one hand, such ties provide collectives with a resiliency that is necessary to cope with their marginality; on the other, they personalize and thus intensify even routine disputes, often producing tangled emotional situations that are very difficult to reconcile. Many cooperatives flounder on the very intensity that is their hallmark. (Jackall and Levin 1984, 95–96)

2. To what extent does having partial or informal autonomy in the area of evaluation allow for conventional culture to reassert itself, despite teachers' intense work to create new models that bring about new outcomes?

Teachers with partial or informal autonomy in the area of evaluation said they face several situations that pose real challenges to their ability to carry out new models. Some teachers ask these questions: Do these challenges and limitations need to exist? Can we imagine ways of overcoming them without needing to insist on the status quo?

First, where teachers do not have any real waiver from collective bargaining agreements they wonder and worry about what will happen if their peer evaluation results are contested. As discussed earlier, neither SFCS teachers' successful thirty-five-year history with peer evaluation nor their support from the district and teacher union could protect them from losing their chosen evaluation structure when a grievance was filed. Stories like this discourage teachers with informal autonomy from innovating in the area of evaluation.

Second, some teachers who faced dilemmas regarding documentation questioned whether formal training for conducting evaluation needs to be limited to administrators. ALBA's teachers asked Milwaukee Public Schools to assign them an on-site administrator to help document poor performance. To be clear, they didn't seek an administrator because of a lack of confidence in their ability to conduct documentation themselves but because the district and union require that someone with an administrative license must perform this function, primarily to maintain confidentiality and avoid liability.

Could teachers "specialize" or get an emphasis in teacher evaluation as part of their pre-service schooling or continuing education, they wonder? Or could everyone receive training to participate in evaluation? They predicted that such training would make them a valuable asset to their communities.

Third, teachers in at least two of the schools reported that in today's economy the district hiring pools are full of candidates who have been laid off under the "last hired, first fired" agreements. These teachers must be hired back first if there are positions available in district schools. In schools where teachers do not have waivers from honoring this requirement (in other words, where they do not have de jure, formal hiring autonomy) they often must hire candidates who want a job but don't necessarily buy in to the idea of "collective accountability for school success."

Teachers reported that on occasion these new hires have intentionally abstained from participation in informal coaching and informal peer evaluation, for example, citing that teacher-to-teacher evaluation is inappropriate according to union rules. As one put it, "These are excellent teachers! But their decisions not to do what works here are gradually eroding our culture of collective accountability."

NOTE

1. Mission Hill K–8 School teachers evaluate themselves for their performance against a collection of teaching standards, including Boston Public Schools standards as indicated on the district's teacher evaluation document, the California Professional Teaching Standards, and the National Teaching Certification standards.

Chapter Eleven

Practice #8

Make Budget Trade-Offs to Meet the Needs of Students They Serve

Teachers in four of the eleven schools, all chartered, have autonomy to allocate their entire school budgets. Teachers in the remaining seven schools, all affiliated with school districts, have autonomy to allocate a discretionary portion of their school budgets that is leftover after district leaders allocate the majority of the funds.

Teachers from all eleven schools, even those who have limited autonomy, pointed out that their budgetary discretion opens up the opportunity for them to make decisions—albeit to different extents—to better meet the needs of students they serve. Teachers also reported that they are willing to accept accountability for their spending choices. Just over 80 percent of teachers surveyed from all eleven schools said their collective willingness to accept accountability for their school's financial outcomes is excellent (25.3 percent), very good (36.3 percent), or good (18.7 percent).

Teachers who have autonomy to allocate their entire school budgets said their strong sense of accountability for school success causes them to pay close attention to how they distribute and manage all of their schools' resources. One of their goals is to make fiscally responsible decisions so their schools will remain open. They also seek to retain students and teachers, and to improve student learning. Sometimes meeting these goals requires them to participate in the difficult process of prioritizing some areas of expenditure over others. With so much at stake, these teachers have even frozen their salaries to spend on other needs.

Teachers who have partial autonomy to allocate their school budgets indicated that they feel accountable for schools' fiscal outcomes, but only to the extent that they can influence them. Like their fully autonomous peers, these teachers also seek to retain students and teachers, and to improve student learning.

Yet they sensed that their ability to reach these goals is constrained by their partial budget autonomy. They are not able to support their innovations in school design by reallocating their budgets, for example. Fearing that pointing out the limitations of their arrangements might jeopardize their innovation and autonomy in other areas, many teachers do not express their frustration with limited budget autonomy to those who granted it.

TEACHERS WITH FULL-BUDGET AUTONOMY CAREFULLY WEIGH SALARY AND WAGE EXPENDITURES AGAINST OTHER SPENDING OPPORTUNITIES

Teachers at Avalon School (Avalon), Chrysalis Charter School (Chrysalis), EdVisions Off Campus (EOC), and Minnesota New Country School (MNCS) have autonomy to allocate their entire school budgets. In this position, they have come to understand that raising salaries and wages requires cuts in other areas of their school budgets—especially when there are not increases in revenue. Their sense of accountability for school success causes them to take their decisions about when and what to cut very seriously.

They collectively decided that teachers' jobs and raises simply cannot be guaranteed each year. All four schools offer teachers one-year, at-will contracts for employment. None guarantee annual salary adjustments for cost of living or years of experience. None guarantee automatic adjustments to teachers who receive continuing education.

Dee Thomas at MNCS said,

> Around 60–65 percent of our school budget goes toward salaries. Surrounding schools spend around 70 percent. We tinker with the idea of moving to 70 percent to stay competitive. Usually that leads us into a discussion about what we'd have to cut to be able to do that. Every year we revisit: Do we have to cut the things that make this school great, like [students' access to digital technology for learning]? And if we do cut those things, then would we lose students and [associated] per-pupil funding? With these questions in mind, we usually keep salaries level. And everyone is really clear on why. No one is complaining.

Gigi Dobosenski at EOC said, "We don't have steps-and-lanes, and we have at-will contracts. Nothing is set in stone. If necessary, we can change things month to month. Currently, we've elected to freeze all our salaries so we can retain as many jobs as possible during this recession." Teachers at Chrysalis also decided to forgo pay increases for the 2010–2011 school year. Alysia Krafel reported, "Teachers prioritized keeping aides in every classroom over their own raises. They know aides make their daily jobs easier and keep the program here strong for the students, so they decided the trade-off was well worth it."

Sometimes autonomous teachers must make tough choices, such as whom to layoff or who among them *will* get a raise. Teachers in all four schools reported that they make decisions based on individuals' value to the school. To them, "value" can have something to do with education and experience level, but these aren't the only factors influencing their decisions. They noted that, in order to make these choices, their autonomy to set their staff pattern as well as their autonomy to hire and dismiss colleagues is as essential as their budget autonomy.

Avalon teachers use steps-and-lanes, but teachers' progression through them is not automatic. At MNCS and EOC, every teacher's salary is reset to a base amount each year. In all three schools, if the budget allows for some pay raises or increases from the base salary, then teachers must explain their value to their colleagues. Teachers reported that the main question each must answer is this: how much effort would it take for your colleagues to replace your value-added to the team? Teachers said that knowing that this is the question that will determine their salary, they make an effort to contribute their talents well throughout the year.

Teachers also described how they've come up with creative ideas to avoid layoffs altogether. Thomas at MNCS said,

> Last year when our finance team looked at the state funding, [it] determined that we needed to cut our expenses. Because 60 percent of our budget was based on salaries, that would be the focus. While it appeared that we needed to cut a position, every staff member played a key role in the day-to-day running of the school. We didn't want to lose any individual.
>
> The personnel team discussed the option of asking everyone to consider volunteering to reduce their hours or go part-time. Four staff members came forward with proposals to work part-time; two were parents needing more time with their children and two artists wanted time to work on their "second" passions. Three staff went to 80 percent time, and one staff went to 60 percent time. The cumulative total reduction in hours was comparable to one mid-level position, so we were able to maintain all staff. We will revisit this plan each year in relation to the budget.

THE IMPORTANCE OF BUDGET AUTONOMY

As a teacher I never really thought about budget autonomy. I was given a small classroom budget, and although it was never enough to cover the cost of basic student supplies, I knew school funds were limited and did the best I could. As an administrator, I found the budget process interesting, yet our discretionary spending money was still quite limited. Even when we had larger pots of money they always had to be spent in specific areas, for example on technology.

The district controlled a lot of the money; our principal created a plan to use all the categorical money (restricted funds) and our school site council—a group of teachers, parents, students, and the principal—approved the plan, as required by California law. Any general fund money (unrestricted funds) was left for the principal to distribute.

When we visited the four schools with complete budget and salary autonomy I was blown away by the thoughtful, purposeful, strategic way the autonomous teachers chose to spend their financial resources. Just like all schools, the budgets are limited. But with full budget and salary autonomy the teachers have the freedom to make trade-offs between possible expenditures to prioritize what is important for their students.

The serious thinking and debate that went into their final budgets impressed me. I didn't hear any complaining about how money was being spent, but rather a real understanding of the financial data and why certain choices had been made that year.

I respect the teachers for staying true to their mission and goals in their budgeting decisions. For example, at Chrysalis their purpose focuses on nature. So the teachers chose to spend money to buy a school bus to take students on weekly field studies instead of spending money on computers. Where I worked we would have never had the opportunity to make that choice. The staffs I was part of certainly had the capacity and talent to have those types of discussions and make smart financial choices, but it was never an option.

Autonomy to determine salaries was another area I never considered or questioned. "Steps-and-lanes" was the way the system worked. When I started at a district, I had a salary schedule in my welcome packet; it was clear and upfront. But at Minnesota New Country School (MNCS) I learned that not only did teachers decide not to have steps-and-lanes, they had to negotiate for their own salaries and prove their value to the school on an annual basis!

This is a big, and probably scary, step for a lot of teachers, but MNCS teachers took it on in an open and professional way. The teachers were willing to keep their salaries level and spend in other areas that were necessary for student success. When budget cuts came from the state they were able to find creative ways, through part-time contracts, to not layoff a teacher.

Even many of the teachers without formal budget autonomy had fewer spending/ budget restrictions than the schools where I have worked. Again, their budgeting process really impressed me. Although they weren't able to make the same level of choices as the schools with full autonomy in this area, they were able to make impactful trade-offs to best meet the needs of their students.

High School in the Community's (HSC) choice to hire a social worker for more hours than the district provides makes perfect sense when you understand the needs of their students. That they have the power to make this choice is important to the success of their students.

I walked away from these schools with a better understanding of the power of budget in the hands of teachers. That is, to make responsible, creative choices to best meet the needs of the students at their schools.

TEACHERS WITH FULL- AND PARTIAL-BUDGET AUTONOMY REPORTED THAT THEY TAKE ON EXTRA DUTIES AND USE MATERIALS EFFICIENTLY TO FREE UP FUNDING FOR USE IN OTHER AREAS, BUT TO DIFFERENT EXTENTS

Teachers at Avalon, Chrysalis, EOC, and MNCS said that they willingly take on extra duties to reduce costs. Rather than hire substitute teachers, for example, teachers in all four schools decide to divide the absent teacher's students among other teachers. At MNCS, teachers eliminated the custodian position, giving teachers and students the responsibility for keeping the learning environment clean. (Teachers report the school stays quite clean when everyone is in this position!)

MNCS and Avalon teachers also save on technology maintenance by training student volunteers to be tech leaders. These leaders solve most problems, teachers said, and teachers solve almost all the rest. So teachers only occasionally need to seek costly tech support from an outside service provider.

Teachers in these four schools pitch in to do administrative work, too. As explained in chapter 5, some teachers dedicate a significant portion of their time to administrative duties, often for a stipend paid in addition to their salary. But some tasks are just part of their job, teachers said. Teachers who have chosen self-directed learning programs said that adding basic administrative tasks to their day doesn't take them away from teaching. Jo Sullivan at Avalon said, "We're not doing direct instruction all day long, so we can find time to fit in nonteaching tasks and still advise our students."

Teachers with partial budget autonomy at Mission Hill K–8 School (Mission Hill), Phoenix High School (Phoenix), San Francisco Community School (SFCS), and Tailoring Academics to Guide Our Students (TAGOS Leadership Academy) make similar decisions to take on administrative and support duties in order to free up funding.

Yet it is not always possible to make these trade-offs. Some have the option to reallocate funding saved from not using substitute teachers, for example, so they are willing to take on extra students in order to save. Others are not able to reallocate the funding, so there isn't a reason or opportunity to consider saving money in this way.

Teachers in all schools reported that their autonomy led them to change their perspectives about the value of their schools' material resources. While most believe that funding for K–12 public schooling is too limited in general, their autonomy has helped them see better where there are opportunities to use resources wisely.

Thomas at MNCS said, "Before I came here, as a principal and teacher in [conventional schools], I never even thought about where the toilet paper came from. Now I know exactly how much it costs and I try to make everyone here aware of what we can lose by overusing it or switching to [more expensive brands]." Thomas and her colleagues at MNCS limit their spending on other materials as well. They buy their school furniture, such as tables and chairs, at auction rather than new. They even worked with students to assemble the furniture themselves.

Jill Mulhausen at Phoenix said, "I used to think supplies like paper and ink for photocopying and printing were just provided; whatever amount we needed should just be there. But I didn't really think about how much was *needed*. Here, everyone conserves. We ask students to develop strategies to keep the costs down, and we all do our best to abide by them."

Jocelyn Virtudes at Independence School Local 1 found a way to get the equipment she needed in her classroom without needing to use up school discretionary funds. She formed a relationship with folks from the University of Maryland–Baltimore Campus, who allow her to borrow, rather than purchase, the most up-to-date science-learning equipment. Like Virtudes, teachers in almost all of the eleven schools used resources freely available at local libraries, colleges, parks, and historical spaces, opting not to purchase these resources at their schools.

Chrysalis teachers said they sacrificed new equipment purchases for some time in order to save the money necessary to buy their own school bus. They made the bus purchase a priority so they could attract students from a broader geographic area to attend the school. They also wanted the ability to better achieve their shared purpose by bringing students to the local nature reserve more frequently.

Teachers reported that their decisions about how and where to spend, as well as how and where to make cuts, can be difficult. Individuals are not always on the same page. While a good number of teachers expressed their disappointment when one or two of their expenditure proposals were not approved by their colleagues, they said they were assuaged by knowing the reasons why. They also had the sense that they might be able to persuade their colleagues in time.

In conventional settings where they previously worked, the same teachers said, they didn't have much, if any, opportunity to propose expenditures. They didn't have any knowledge of what was being funded in lieu of what they would have liked to have funded.

Thomas at MNCS explained,

> At our school if you want $2,000 for something, you take it to the finance committee. There you'll probably right away hear, "There's not the money for that [given our current budget allocations]." Then you learn you must propose

a trade-off. The committee *will* consider trade-offs. If your proposal is rejected after that, it's still a disappointment. But there's a difference from how things operate elsewhere. Here you know why the priority was to spend elsewhere, and often that priority makes sense.

PARTIALLY AUTONOMOUS TEACHERS IN SOME DISTRICT-AFFILIATED SCHOOLS PERCEIVE THAT THEIR DISTRICT LEADERS ARE PLEASED WITH FINANCIAL REWARDS ASSOCIATED WITH THEIR AUTONOMY ARRANGEMENTS

Teachers in some schools affiliated with school districts communicated their perception that district leaders are interested in the potential cost savings and revenue gains associated with teacher autonomy. These teachers explained that since the learning programs they choose appeal to students who might not otherwise be enrolled in school at all, or who might have enrolled in a different district or a chartered school, they are "recapturing" for their school district the per-pupil revenue that follows the students. What's more, many students who might have been counted toward the quit rates are now attending and graduating.

Mulhausen at Phoenix said, "For the district, there is not much risk and a lot of reward. With Phoenix, the district gets more revenue. They also get higher retention and improved graduation rates."

Some teachers perceive that district leaders see their shared leadership model as an opportunity to "save a principal's salary." TAGOS Leadership Academy teachers reported that district leaders look favorably on their "lean staff model." Some questioned, though, whether these cost savings should be passed through to the schools for the needs of the students instead of retained by school districts.

QUESTIONS AND CHALLENGES

Autonomous teachers reported two primary challenges associated with their budget autonomy.

1. Teachers in district-affiliated schools said that controlling school's budgets with fixed line items doesn't accommodate for innovation. They are afraid that asking for increased budgetary discretion will jeopardize their overall autonomy, so they remain silent.

Some teachers with partial budget autonomy explained that because they cannot reallocate nondiscretionary portions of their school budgets, they are unable to make spending trade-offs to support innovation. School districts' line-item budgeting is often "use it or lose it," they said.

If they innovate to eliminate academic departments, for example, they lose the district budget allotment for department funds. If they decide not to use textbooks in favor of software or outdoor learning, they lose the district budget allotment for textbooks. Teachers said that in many areas unused line-item funds go back into the districts' general funds. In these cases, staying as conventional as possible has fiscal advantages for schools and students.

These teachers frequently said they are afraid to ask their district leaders to better accommodate their innovation by giving teachers the opportunity to retain any unused line-item funding and spend it on other school needs for the benefit of their students. Teachers worry that asking for this authority will put their unconventional modes of operation under a microscope and invite unwanted infringement on their autonomy in other areas. So they remain silent.

Some hold on to the hope that in time, once they have shown their schools to be assets to their school districts, leaders will gradually offer increased budget autonomy. This just happened for teachers in one school, who said that their superintendent recently, without being asked, offered them a way to get more discretionary funding by loosening up line-item requirements. "I'm not sure why we weren't getting access to this funding before, or why we are now," one teacher remarked. "[The superintendent] is acting like we should have been getting this all along. At any rate, we're happy to get it!"

Teachers in district-affiliated schools consistently wonder this: How can they work together with school district leaders to find ways to secure more budget autonomy than they currently have?

2. When teachers know their schools' success—including their own jobs and salaries—is dependent on their own wise budget decisions, some can be risk averse.

A few autonomous teachers mentioned their sense that their colleagues can be risk averse when it comes to making decisions that could potentially have a serious impact on schools' overall financial situations. Krafel at Chrysalis, for example, explained that as a local school closed she saw real potential for Chrysalis to secure more revenue. She pitched to her colleagues that they should grow the school so it could absorb some of the students.

"It was a calculated risk," Krafel said. "I was willing to risk my salary to invest in school improvements that would allow us to do this, but others weren't willing to do the same. So we made the decision that only my salary would be at risk." According to Krafel, the risk paid off very well, and she was willing to share the rewards with everyone. Other teachers who were interviewed spoke of similar missed opportunities, but no one else was willing to assume personal risk as Krafel was.

Krafel and others wonder this: what cultural changes are necessary to increase teachers' risk tolerance and willingness to try creative new approaches?

3

Implementation Strategies for Those Who Want to Support Teacher Autonomy

Chapter Twelve

It's Time to Trust Teachers

Lately, a major national strategy for improving our schools has been to hold teachers accountable for school success while at the same time telling them what to teach and how to teach it. We attempt to control teachers' behaviors and school operations with mandates in both policy and practice. This book has explored whether we could get high-performing schools with a dramatically different strategy: trusting teachers, the professionals who are closest to the students, to make decisions that influence whole school success.

If we trusted teachers to call the shots, the responsibility of education managers who are working outside of the schools—school boards, chartered school authorizers,[1] superintendents, state commissioners, and state governors—would be to negotiate mutually agreed-upon objectives with teachers; then measure results and, when warranted, enforce consequences. Teachers who want autonomy would be granted authority to collectively determine how to achieve the objectives inside their schools.

This arrangement would not be mandated. Those who want to would be welcome to continue working toward improvement within conventional schools. Anyone granting and accepting teacher autonomy would simply be trying a parallel strategy at improvement.

The idea of teacher autonomy is at once simple, and exceedingly complex. We're so accustomed to the way things have always been that it is hard to imagine teachers having enlarged professional roles, even though some already have them. It's also difficult to speculate about the kinds of schools teachers would create. This book has helped lessen the need to imagine or speculate.

We sought out to answer two essential questions:

1. What would teachers do if they had the autonomy to collectively make the decisions influencing whole school success?
2. Can we trust autonomous teachers to make good decisions?

In chapter 1 we established that autonomous teachers' choices are "good" if they emulate the nine cultural characteristics of high-performing organizations. Chapter 3 made the case that autonomous teachers in the eleven schools do, for the most part, emulate the characteristics, which include accepting accountability and acting on the opportunity to innovate. Chapters 4–11 demonstrated that autonomous teachers' most prominent practices flow from their cultivation of those cultural characteristics.

Teachers made clear that their work isn't easy. They face many challenges, they make mistakes, and they sometimes miss important opportunities. Yet teachers also reported that their decisions have resulted in many positive improvements for teachers and students. Autonomous teachers asserted over and over again that autonomy heightens their sense of accountability to their colleagues, students, and schools. The mix of autonomy and accountability mobilizes their energy toward change and improvement.

As a result of their efforts, many students are taking an active role in their learning. Students who might have dropped out are now staying in school. Learning is individualized, and learning growth is acknowledged. In addition to reading, writing, and math, students are expected to develop life, career, technology, and media skills as well as learning and innovating skills. Teachers say they have more satisfying jobs. Resources are used efficiently and to meet the needs of students.

In chapter 1 we conveyed quality-improvement experts' findings that the design of every system determines the results it gets. So if the results are not the desired results, then the system needs to be redesigned to achieve what is desired (Deming 2000; Wehling and Schneider 2007; Berwick, Godfrey, and Roessner 1990; Hanna 1988). The outcomes emerging from the eleven schools suggest that if we want high-performing schools then the fundamentally different incentive structure of teacher autonomy is the design change we need. It's time to trust teachers with professional authority in return for their acceptance of accountability for school success.

But teachers can't do this alone. Teachers who want to succeed in their pursuit of autonomy and in their creation of high-performing schools will need support from various potential change agents, including education managers at all levels of government, teachers' unions, employers, leaders of teacher training institutions, and researchers. In the remainder of this chapter we will suggest a number of ways in which those who support teachers can encourage successful implementation of teacher autonomy. This is not an exhaustive list of implementation strategies, and is offered with the expectation that others will add more to the discussion.

EDUCATION MANAGERS WHO ARE OUTSIDE OF SCHOOLS CAN CHOOSE TO HOLD TEACHERS ACCOUNTABLE VIA FORMAL AGREEMENTS FOR SERVICE INSTEAD OF VIA MANDATES AND OTHER ATTEMPTS AT CONTROL

Literature suggests that managers in high-performing organizations give workers autonomy to practice their craft and hold them accountable for meeting objectives. Yet some education managers hesitate to grant teachers authority to make decisions influencing school success because they have difficulty letting go of the idea that their management role can be different from "telling people what to do and how to do it."

Afraid of failing to meet the requirements set by the No Child Left Behind Act of 2001, managers have tightened the reins from the top down. Each layer of management imposes controls on the next, and they keep on tightening. These actions represent education managers' narrow view of how they can realize successful outcomes.

In the summer of 1998 the Minnesota School Board Association's lobbyist said to its membership that if boards let teachers control professional issues, they would have no role left.[2] The United Administrators of San Francisco, a union representing administrators, acted on a similar fear when they recently asserted that autonomous teachers at the San Francisco Community School (SFCS) could not conduct peer evaluation because evaluation is something that people with administrative credentials do.

Since SFCS teachers' Small Schools By Design agreement did not grant them de jure, formal autonomy in the area of evaluation, the administrators effectively forced teachers to stop doing peer evaluation at the school. Teachers there reported that this has eroded many aspects of their high-performing culture.

Researchers conclude that managers have imposed tight restrictions in even the major attempts at autonomy to date. The Thomas B. Fordham Institute and Public Impact reported in *Charter School Autonomy: A Half-Broken Promise* that a good portion of chartered school authorizers see themselves as needing to control people working in the schools. Sixty percent of chartering contracts imposed restrictions on autonomy beyond state requirements. School districts and institutions of higher education serving as authorizers typically imposed the most additional constraints, while nonprofit organizations and state boards of education imposed the least, the study said (Brinson and Rosch 2010).

The Fordham Institute and Public Impact study theorized that district school boards and superintendents who charter schools may have an especially hard time loosening controls over in-school professionals because district-authorized schools legally remain part of the district. "If these charters fail to develop legally sound discipline policies or fail to provide special education services in accordance with the law, responsibility ultimately rests with the district," the study said (Brinson and Rosch 2010).

"Interviews revealed that district authorizers may choose to protect themselves by reducing charter freedoms in specific areas as a preemptive means of avoiding legal problems later. The other types of authorizers—[who typically state in charter contracts that they are not legally liable for charter school actions]—may not feel as directly responsible for charter failures, and therefore may be in a position to grant greater autonomy to schools" (Brinson and Rosch 2010, 17).

Decentralization strategies have also failed to realize their potential due to local managers' inability to let go of control. Most school board members and district administrators who have tried decentralization granted only partial decision-making authority to in-school administrators. When this proved unsuccessful the managers blamed principals and teachers, and vice versa. Decentralization advocates argue, however, that since there was not a real delegation of authority in all of the necessary areas, the strategy was never really tried in the first place (Hansen and Roza 2005).

While these examples point to local managers, it's important to understand that school district leaders and chartered school authorizers might put restrictions in place because state policymakers do not give *them* the authority to make the decisions affecting school outcomes. State policymakers create an additional sphere of mandates and controls. In 2011, for example, governors across the nation proposed to limit school districts' choices in the areas of teacher evaluation, tenure, and pay.

According to The Fordham Institute and Public Impact, state laws are the primary source of constraints on chartered school autonomy, accounting for nearly three quarters of all infringements. Policymakers' most common restrictions on chartered schools were in the areas of teacher hiring, renegotiating contracts to make midcourse changes to their programs, establishing governance boards, choosing special education service providers, and determining whether or not teachers would participate in state retirement systems (Brinson and Rosch 2010).

State policymakers, in turn, can point to mandates from federal policymakers as a reason for their choices. In the name of accountability, for example, the No Child Left Behind (NCLB) Act of 2001 mandated that by 2014 all students in every state must be proficient in reading and math while showing adequate yearly progress (AYP) toward that goal in the previous years. AYP is demonstrated by aggregate standardized test scores.

NCLB also mandated that all teachers must be "highly qualified," meaning they have obtained full state certification or passed a teacher licensing examination and demonstrated specific content area competence. State policymakers say these requirements have restricted their ability to individualize learning, more broadly define "highly qualified," and innovate in the ways necessary to bring forth success.

Granting teachers autonomy offers a way out of this continuous ratcheting up of controls. Federal policymakers could grant more autonomy to states, and state policymakers could use it to create state laws that specifically enable school boards and chartered school authorizers to contract—or make other formal arrangements—for teachers' services.

Local education managers, such as school boards and chartered school authorizers, can lobby for these provisions, and willingly use the options provided. They can grant formal autonomy arrangements—contracts and/or other documents—that entrust teachers who request it with the authority to make decisions influencing school success. Then they can hold teachers accountable for meeting clear, mutually agreed-upon expectations, or objectives. They can also enforce consequences for teachers who do not meet expectations.

While autonomy plus accountability is not a foolproof strategy, autonomous teachers' practices in the eleven schools suggest that education managers can expect teachers in their jurisdictions to design "good" schools that meet many of K–12's unmet demands.

When Setting Agreements, Managers Should Understand That Teachers' Emulation of High-Performing Cultures Is Related to the Degree of Autonomy Granted to Them

Teachers in the eleven schools suggested that their motivation to accept accountability and emulate the other eight characteristics of high-performing organizations is partially intrinsic; they get a thrill out of succeeding in their jobs and helping their students succeed. Their motivation is also heightened by extrinsic influences, such as potential school closure due to loss of contracts or loss of students. But in addition to motivational factors, teachers made clear that the extent to which they emulate high-performing cultures is related to the degree of autonomy granted to them.

Chapter 2 outlined various arrangements by which local education managers currently grant teachers autonomy. Some arrangements are de jure, formalized via contracts and waivers, while other arrangements are entirely or partially de facto, or informal. In some arrangements managers grant teachers full autonomy while in other arrangements managers grant only partial autonomy.

According to teachers, a consequence of informal and partial autonomy is that they have a limited ability to do everything they think necessary for school success. Although their sense of accountability is amplified with even a limited amount of autonomy, ultimately they are not interested in accepting accountability for results in the areas in which they do not have control.

Moreover, teachers sense that full autonomy sets them up better for success. Informal and partial autonomy arrangements limit their capacity to be entrepreneurs and innovators, and they sometimes feel forced to act like renegades. They feel they must stay "under the radar" by remaining "conventional enough."

They spend time on tasks that would be unnecessary if they had full autonomy, such as attending professional development seminars that assume they work in conventional settings. They are constantly nervous about suffering consequences for bucking convention, no matter how well they are performing. This is not how we want our teachers to be spending their time and our resources. Managers could get more of what we *do* want from teachers by trusting them; by providing formal and full autonomy to make the decisions influencing school success, and holding teachers accountable.

EDUCATION MANAGERS WHO ARE OUTSIDE OF SCHOOLS CAN CHOOSE TO WORK WITH AUTONOMOUS TEACHERS TO CONTINUOUSLY IDENTIFY AND REMOVE THE BARRIERS TO CULTIVATING HIGH-PERFORMING CULTURES

Education managers will not be able to anticipate everything autonomous teachers will need to be successful. Autonomous teachers are likely to try a lot of new ideas with teaching and learning that will require new kinds of support. Education managers who are outside of schools must recognize this and continuously work with autonomous teachers to find out what is limiting teachers' ability to emulate high-performing cultures.

They might even start out by piloting the teacher autonomy strategy, giving themselves time to learn the ropes. But even as managers get deeper into implementation, their attitude should be, "If it is not illegal, immoral, or inane, you can propose it. We are open to your ideas. We'll work things out as we go along."

If teachers' experiences offer us a preview of things to come, then district managers might find that providing more autonomy requires more than a contract. It might require a restructuring of district operations.

Physical plant departments, for example, might only be willing to help teachers create new learning spaces, for example, if autonomous teachers are allowed to hire them *or* off-site service providers. Managers might need to be open to leasing new kinds of buildings, instead of requiring that teachers must set up schools in buildings designed for traditional learning. District transportation contracts might need to allow for students to travel into the community for learning activities throughout the day. Transportation won't be just about getting to and from a single building.

For inspiration and guidance, managers can look to sources examining how school leaders have dealt with the challenges associated with fundamental change. One such source is William G. Ouchi's *The Secret of TSL*. Ouchi studied three generations of attempts at decentralization or school empowerment.[3]

Examining Ouchi's work, it's notable that the early adopters of "school empowerment" acted without guidelines, a master plan, or even a clear vision for where they wanted to end up. For the most part, policymakers, school boards, other school district leaders, and principals were willing to work together through trial and error to identify and remove structural barriers to success and to advance what works. Managers who did not formally and continuously commit to improving their arrangements found their reforms either disappeared or were easily undermined within dominant conventional cultures.

The lessons from earlier experiences suggest education managers will do well to see themselves as learners rather than prescriptive planners who already know what works. Both managers and teachers should expect that their first arrangements for teacher autonomy might not be good enough, and that they will need to continuously refine the arrangements. Expecting perfection from the start would be a major misstep.

As Ouchi put it, changing school management structures "is more like building a marriage [than building a house]: it's a living being that never stops changing and evolving and you have to attend to it all of the time" (Ouchi 2009, 292).

THE BUSINESS COMMUNITY SHOULD SUPPORT THE TEACHER AUTONOMY STRATEGY FOR IMPROVEMENT BECAUSE IT EMBRACES A MANAGEMENT PERSPECTIVE THAT IS EFFECTIVE WITHIN THEIR OWN ORGANIZATIONS.

The business community is an active participant in the efforts to improve education. Autonomous teachers' emulation of the characteristics of high-performing organizations suggests that members of the business community should support the teacher autonomy strategy because it reflects what they know to be effective within their own organizations.

They could also oppose approaches to "mandate-our-way" to high-performing schools, just as they oppose such approaches for their own enterprises. Or, they could diversify their portfolio. They could support attempts to fix conventional schooling while at the same time being open to teacher autonomy.

The high-performing organizations' framework for measuring whether autonomous teachers make "good" choices comes primarily from the business community. The literature said that one characteristic of high-performing organizations is that managers and workers welcome authority and responsibility for making decisions and accept accountability for the outcomes. Another is that they assess their progress toward goals and act upon results to improve performance.

Moreover, autonomous teachers create schools in which students learn the skills they need when they become workers. They design schools in which students learn reading, writing, and math, *and* learn self-direction, community responsibility, collaboration and communication skills, technology and media literacy, and many more desirable soft skills. And these are just the early results. If well supported, the teacher autonomy strategy has real potential to create the kind of workforce the business community has so frequently communicated it really wants.

TEACHERS' UNIONS CAN CHOOSE TO SUPPORT AUTONOMOUS TEACHERS BY ACTING AS ADVOCATES FOR INCREASED PROFESSIONAL ROLES

In 1988 Albert Shanker, then president of the American Federation of Teachers (AFT), addressed the National Press Club and floated the idea of teachers setting up new autonomous schools. The best name for these schools, he said, came from an educator in Massachusetts named Ray Budde: charter schools (Education|Evolving 2011). That same year Shanker told Ted Kolderie of the Center for Policy Studies that collective bargaining needn't be an essential function of teachers' unions (Kolderie 1988). Almost twenty-five years later, teacher autonomy may bring Shanker's vision to fruition.

Autonomous teachers need unions to serve a new and different function. When teachers have autonomy to allocate their school budgets, choose their colleagues and determine their compensation, schedule, means of evaluation, and more, there simply isn't a need for the union to represent those particular interests to their employer. Their employer doesn't make the decisions; autonomous teachers do, as a group.

Autonomous teachers will, however, need a strong advocate for their profession, their collective autonomy, and, importantly, for adequate funding for public education, which will impact their school budgets and affect their ability to be successful.

Other professionals form associations (such as the American Bar Association for attorneys and the American Medical Association for physicians) to perform functions such as developing and maintaining retirement programs as well as other fringe benefits, providing relevant professional development, and arranging for licensure that suits their evolving profession. Autonomous teachers will need an association, or union, to help them with these functions. The association would provide such support functions to autonomous teachers and the advocacy services to secure autonomy and other support.

Teachers' Unions Could Create a Separate, Autonomous Entity to Figure Out the Best Ways of Supporting Autonomous Teachers

Teachers' unions need not reinvent themselves from within. Organizational theory suggests that they would do well to pursue a new role by creating a subsidiary organization that reports directly to top union leadership but is not obliged to conventional union culture and modes-of-operation (Christensen 2003). The purpose of the entity—in many ways autonomous itself—would be to figure out all of the ways to best support autonomous teachers.

The Dayton Hudson Corporation employed this strategy in the 1950s when it saw that department stores were, as Bruce Dayton said, "a dying breed of cat" (Johnson 2010). The Dayton brothers knew they needed to find a way to continue attracting customers who were moving to suburbs and who increasingly owned automobiles. But their corporate culture and ways of doing business centered on department stores. So they created a subsidiary company responsible for dealing with the changing marketplace, with leaders who reported directly to the corporate board.

The leaders came up with an upscale discount retailing chain called Target. Target grew and eventually became the largest division of Dayton Hudson Corporation, culminating in the company being renamed as Target Corporation in August 2000 (Rowley 2003).

Some organizations are already popping up to serve autonomous teachers, which new union entities could learn from as they establish their purposes. Most autonomous teachers in Minnesota are members of EdVisions Cooperative, which provides business and advocacy services such as payroll, start-up coaching, professional development that is relevant to new and different learning programs, and education for state policymakers about how policy design can evolve to support autonomous teachers and the schools they create.

EdVisions Cooperative also helps its membership to translate the impact of federal and state requirements on their schools. It further provides research and evaluation to help teachers learn what works and what doesn't as they use their autonomy.

The Center for Collaborative Education supports Boston and Los Angeles Pilot Schools as well as other innovative schools, some of which offer teachers autonomy, by coordinating school reform networks, relevant principal and teacher preparation programs, research, and other initiatives. Within each network and initiative, the Center provides coaching, technical assistance, professional development, political advocacy, and networking opportunities.

Teachers' Unions Could Pursue Management Rights through Teacher Autonomy, Instead of via Collective Bargaining

For decades unions have been trying to expand the scope of collective bargaining to include professional issues to no avail. But what if, as Shanker suggested in 1988, teachers' unions could reach their goal by advocating and supporting teacher autonomy instead? Union leaders' external focus could be to seek teacher autonomy in their school districts and states. Internally they could remove barriers to autonomy by providing waivers to their own agreements. Again, unions could create new and separate entities that might be best suited for this job.

Like education managers, teachers unions will need to be open to understanding the ways in which current collective bargaining activities act as barriers to securing meaningful professional discretion for their members. In this book, we reported numerous examples of teachers' disappointment that their own union rules were hindering their ability to work in new and different ways and secure greater autonomy.

Teachers sought more flexibility with hours worked, role differentiation (what they would and would not do, especially in the area of evaluation), and selecting their colleagues and leaders. Some teachers expressed interest in having the ability to determine tenure and pay policies, too. Chapter 11 showed that teachers could bring forth innovative approaches in those areas if trusted by their unions to do so.

As Shanker also suggested, teachers' unions should be open to the idea that they might best secure professional authority via chartering. This book found that teachers working in chartered schools have the most areas of autonomy.

Chartering is an area of contentious debate, and union leaders have often come down on the side of working for change within school districts. Yet some union leaders report that they have found the conditions for innovation within school districts to be deteriorating over the last twenty years. These leaders say that in the meantime their members have been increasingly demanding professional roles. Unable to meet these needs within districts, they've been left with no choice but to turn to chartering (Nordgren 2011).

The Minneapolis Federation of Teachers (MFT), for example, was a strong advocate for Minnesota's 2009 Site-Governed Schools law that allows for the creation of schools inside districts that enjoy the same autonomy and exemption from state regulation as schools in the chartering sector. Yet MFT leaders have been very public in stating that even with the new state law they have received little support from the Minneapolis Public Schools Board of Education to advance teacher autonomy through site-governed schools. Their members also expressed little confidence that their efforts to start site-governed schools would be worth their time, believing the school board would not approve their proposals (Nordgren 2010).

So in 2010 MFT leaders sought and secured an innovation grant from the American Federation of Teachers to fund the development of a new 501(c)(3) nonprofit organization called Minnesota Guild of Public Charter Schools (Guild) that would be run as a separate legal entity with its own governing board. In late November 2011, the Guild received approval from the Minnesota Department of Education to serve as an authorizer of chartered schools throughout the state. Teachers can now seek to start chartered schools with teacher autonomy through this authorizer.

In an op-ed piece published in the *Minneapolis Star Tribune* on December 11, 2011, MFT President Lynn Nordgren explained the union's motivation for supporting establishment of the Guild. "Conventional wisdom suggests that the interests of teacher unions and charter schools are at odds. I believe that's wrong," she said.

"As professional educators and union members, we want and need to be part of the charter school conversation. By becoming a public charter school authorizer, the Guild will approve new, high-quality charter schools and ensure that they meet high standards and help students achieve. We will also ensure that teachers are respected and have a voice in the schools where they work" (*Star Tribune*, December 11, 2011).

The National Education Association (NEA), also appears to be exploring such options, although not yet via chartering. Former NEA executive director John Wilson and NEA senior policy analyst-strategic intent John Wright, both visited schools with teacher autonomy and met with Milwaukee Teacher Education Association leaders in fall 2009.

In 2010, the NEA also created a Commission on Effective Teachers and Teaching—a group of twenty-one accomplished autonomous teachers and educational leaders from around the country—to "craft a new vision of a teaching profession that is led by teachers and ensures teacher and teaching effectiveness" among other things.

After working with dozens of education experts and thousands of teachers from every kind of school and community, the Commission's December 2011 report concluded,

> We envision a teaching profession that embraces collective accountability for student learning balanced with collaborative autonomy that allows educators to do what is best for students. . . .
>
> In the system we envision: School leadership is a joint endeavor with highly effective classroom teachers. In a collaborative school culture where all teachers share responsibility for student learning and well-being, shared decision-making models utilize classroom expertise in advancing the effectiveness of schools and the mission of public education. Administrators and teachers have a collaborative relationship characterized by joint decision-making and accountability. Teachers assume hybrid roles that involve both teaching and leading; effective principals spend some time teaching and welcome opportunities to work with teacher leaders. (NEA 2011)

In line with this vision, the NEA has made small grants to groups of teachers who wish to explore converting existing schools to a teacher autonomy governance model. Reiche Community School in Portland, Maine, secured one of these grants and received support from their school district to convert to a teacher autonomy model in 2011. More NEA teacher-members are exploring the same at Jere Baxter Middle School in Nashville, Tennessee.

LEADERS OF TEACHER TRAINING INSTITUTIONS CAN CHOOSE TO SUPPORT TEACHERS' MIGRATION TO WORKING WITH AUTONOMY AND ACCOUNTABILITY

Generally speaking, teachers in training don't learn how to manage schools in colleges of education. But that needn't be a reason to refrain from granting teachers autonomy. Medical schools don't do much to train physicians to run their office practice either. That's because physicians can hire outside professionals or elect people among themselves to guide them in carrying out that work, just as the teachers interviewed for this book do.

It is likely that few teachers have thought about the full range of professional opportunities they might have with teacher autonomy. But given the experiences of the autonomous teachers, it is also fair to say that a good number of them have the competency and personal characteristics to work within and manage organizations. Additionally, it's fair to speculate that there are many more people with that competency who steer clear now but might enter teaching if teachers' professional roles were expanded.

For the time being, like most early adaptors of innovative opportunities, autonomous teachers tend to develop their own coaching and mentoring to facilitate teachers' professional development, as is described in chapters 4–11. Still, it will be necessary for leaders of at least some teacher training institutions to support both new and veteran teachers who might seek teacher autonomy.

Existing training in the areas of developmental psychology, experimental pedagogy, and best practices will still be important and relevant for autonomous teachers. The training to-be-developed will prepare teachers for working in unconventional ways, within unconventional learning programs and environments. Although a clear path for development is not yet known, that's incumbent with any innovation. Teachers' ideas throughout this book suggest some places to start:

• Develop training that embraces a whole-school management perspective, as opposed to only a classroom management perspective.
• Explain and practice teachers' responsibilities when the traditional leadership hierarchy is inverted and managers are accountable to the collective group of teachers at the school.
• Explain and practice teachers' responsibilities when they are collectively accountable to school districts and school authorizers.
• Teach organizational development theory and practice.
• Teach entrepreneurship, including the ability to recognize opportunities for innovation and manage risk.
• Offer survey courses in the following areas: building a high-performing culture, understanding learning programs and associated teacher roles (e.g., guides instead of instructors), whole-school disciplinary strategies, whole-school assessment, and improvement strategies; 360-degree and peer evaluation methods.
• Offer specialized training and licensure for particular learning programs (e.g., project-based learning or self-directed learning emphases) or for particular areas of management that might make them appealing to a group of autonomous teachers (e.g., finance, evaluation, assessment, culture, organizational development).

RESEARCHERS, FOUNDATIONS, TEACHERS, AND OTHERS
COULD ESTABLISH AN INFRASTRUCTURE OF INFORMATION
THAT IS NECESSARY FOR UNDERSTANDING AND
SUPPORTING INNOVATION THROUGH TEACHER AUTONOMY

Autonomous teachers interviewed for this book, as well as many others who were interviewed during this project's national search for schools with teacher autonomy, were unaware of others' existence. It's easy to assume, then, that many more teachers, teachers' unions and education managers are not aware of the opportunity at all. With such limited awareness there is little potential for autonomous teachers to collaborate as they navigate the opportunities and challenges that come with calling the shots.

Moreover, teachers who are just learning about teacher autonomy express that there is no central place to turn to for information and support. In fact, many voiced that they don't know how to begin. As one potentially autonomous teacher put it, "We don't know what we don't know. We started in right away on designing the school, but didn't think about the need to secure [a formal autonomy arrangement, such as a contract] first."

If teacher autonomy is to get to scale *and* realize its potential to bring forth real innovation in teaching and learning then researchers, foundations, teachers, and others must contribute to the creation of a well-developed infrastructure of information for people seeking to understand, support and practice it. Charles Taylor Kerchner made a similar recommendation in his report called "Can Teachers Run Their Own Schools?" published in October 2010 after he visited Avalon School and some Milwaukee schools with teacher autonomy.

Kerchner called for "a text" that would be a vision and guide for collectively autonomous teachers as they develop and improve their practice. The "text" would be comprised of an organizing manual (conveying organizing mechanisms and processes), a training manual (conveying how to train teachers to create, work in and sustain schools with teacher autonomy), and routines (teachers in a variety of school settings would establish a common understanding of how they approach numerous aspects of their work, and why they choose these approaches).

"As Thomas Kuhn wrote 40 years ago," Kerchner wrote, "one way of telling whether a paradigm shift has taken place is to see if anyone has written a text about the new idea" (Kerchner 2010, 31). A text, Kerchner clarified, is not a book—which is hardbound and can therefore not evolve with teacher autonomy—but a collection of evolving materials, or infrastructure, that provide guidance for putting ideas into practice (Kerchner 2010).

Autonomous teachers need this infrastructure as they struggle through the difficult work of advancing their own craft. They need it in order to identify their strengths and weaknesses and also to recognize and replicate innovation that emerges from the arrangements. Teachers who wish to become autonomous need an infrastructure both for practical guidance through the start-up process and for navigating the politics of negotiating contracts for autonomy.

School authorizers and school district leaders need an infrastructure for ensuring accountability via contracts and to help them learn new ways of supporting the teacher autonomy strategy. Teachers' unions and other professional associations need it to help them with the creation of new entities and other strategies for supporting teacher autonomy. Teacher training institutions need it to figure out the kinds of skills and knowledge that autonomous teachers need to be successful, and to design new preparation programs accordingly.

The national media would benefit from an infrastructure of information as well. Journalists have begun covering teacher autonomy but tout each new school with teacher autonomy as "the first" although some fifty already exist.

Furthermore, journalists have set the teacher autonomy story as "schools without principals" just as early reporting on the automobile industry described cars as "carriages without horses" (Sennett 1896). They focus little on the stories of teachers in expanded professional roles or of teachers developing innovations in teaching and learning.

Infrastructure might help journalists see better what *is* happening, instead of what they think isn't. (As chapter 5 makes clear, some autonomous teachers *do* collectively select principals, lead teachers, and committee members who are accountable to the teacher group!) Moreover, an infrastructure of information could help prevent journalists from creating unrealistic public expectations by helping the public understand the rewards as well as the challenges.

Some worry that a failure to develop an infrastructure will put teacher autonomy in the same category of other promising education reform ideas that have not lived up to unrealistic expectations of success. For example, Larry Cuban, professor of education at Stanford University and former fourteen-year urban high school teacher and seven-year district superintendent, warned that autonomy structures don't innovate—they just provide the opportunity to innovate.

In a blog post he titled, "Please Don't Hype Teacher-Led Schools," Cuban wrote, "One doesn't need exaggerated claims to believe that groups of teachers founding charters, taking over failing schools, or simply creating different ones is a smart idea . . . Nonetheless, there are some facts that cannot be ignored. . . . Some teacher-run schools will flop. . . . [Also] designing new schools and running them is as complicated and risky as starting any new venture as edupreneurs say repeatedly" (Cuban 2010). A well-developed infrastructure of information won't prevent failures, but it could help lessen them.

This book can serve as a launching pad for creating the infrastructure of information needed for understanding and supporting teacher autonomy. Researchers can begin to acknowledge and explore, now, the various autonomy arrangements identified in chapter 2 and the potential for teachers to bring forth innovation in each arrangement. Researchers can also acknowledge and explore the ten potential areas of autonomy, and, if warranted, add and subtract from the list.

Researchers can measure autonomous teachers' success, including how well they emulate the cultural characteristics of high-performing organizations and how well they innovate and replicate their successes. Measuring teacher autonomy's success will likely require researchers to build new assessment tools, like those developed by teachers (see chapter 9). Researchers can conduct investigations to test if the findings in this book can be validated, contradicted, or refined. Certainly this book has raised a lot of new questions.

Researchers and teachers can also build, support, and participate in information-sharing networks. Such networks would be designed to create a common language among autonomous teachers, to learn what teachers do with their autonomy and to identify best practices for replication. The networks could also become resource libraries full of sample autonomy agreements, sample evaluation and assessment rubrics, sample discipline policies, and anything else that can help spur on success.

All of this work would be the basis for the development of organizing manuals, training manuals, and routines as Kerchner suggested. Researchers and teachers will need financial support from foundations, unions and professional associations to do this well.

These ideas are just a start. Teacher autonomy will evolve. Much more work will need to be done.

Is it worthwhile to commit to these large undertakings? Yes. Teachers' choices described throughout this book suggest that if we want high-performing schools then granting teachers the autonomy to call the shots is a promising strategy to pursue. To seize opportunities to improve K–12, and especially to fulfill unmet demands, we need to stop blaming teachers for K–12's problems. It's time to trust teachers with professional authority in return for their acceptance of accountability for school success.

You might be thinking that since the teacher autonomy strategy is currently operating at a small scale; why should anyone consider replicating it at this point? But don't let that stop you from taking on and supporting the idea. It's best not to ignore small beginnings.

The Wright Brothers set off a dramatic period of innovation in flight at Kitty Hawk in 1903. Yet their plane was nowhere close to what we fly today. And many failures in aircraft design have blemished the path to innovation. In this light, it seems short sighted not to give this idea the support it needs because of questions about scalability and imperfections that can be ironed out over time. You never know, today's autonomous teachers might be early movers and shakers in what could be a dramatic period of innovation in K–12.

NOTES

1. A chartered school authorizer is the entity that chartered school boards enter into contract with for permission to operate and oversight. Chartered school authorizers, also called sponsors (in some states), determine who should be entrusted with public funds and teaching students (Piper 2009).

2. This statement was made in response to the previous years' collective bargaining agreement between the Minneapolis Federation of Teachers and the Minneapolis school board, which was supposed to grant district teachers professional roles but ultimately did not (Kolderie 2005).

3. Ouchi cites the school-based management efforts of Michael Strembitsky, superintendent of schools in Edmonton, Alberta, from 1973 to 1995, as the foundation for three generations of later efforts at school empowerment. Generation one includes Boston, Houston, and Seattle. Generation two includes St. Paul and San Francisco. Generation three includes Chicago, Oakland, and New York City (Ouchi 2009, 28; 146–266).

Ouchi says school empowerment occurred when school principals were granted the autonomy to determine school budgets, staffing, curriculum, and schedule in school districts. These efforts succeed when there is:

- "real" choice for families,
- a system of accountability, and
- Weighted Student Formula budgeting, an innovation in which money is not allocated to schools, but to students. Students choose their schools and the money follows students to the schools (Ouchi 2009, 269).

Ouchi wrote, "A web of accountability . . . must be simultaneously loose enough to give each principal lots of elbow room but tight enough to keep them focused on student performance, budget performance, and communication with teachers, parents, and the community" (Ouchi 59).

Appendix A: Evolution of K–12 Public Schools with Teacher Autonomy[1]

Asking "Where does teacher autonomy start?" is like asking where a river starts. You have to go upstream, where you will find no single source, but several little streams flowing together.

Efforts to create "professional communities of practice" and to advance "site-based management" suggested that teachers ought to have larger roles, but never fully contemplated teacher autonomy as it is defined in this book. Ruth Anne Olson's concept of teacher ownership of professional practices in the 1980s made a real impact on the notion of what would be possible if teachers were granted the autonomy needed to accept accountability for their schools' outcomes.

This timeline documents Olson's efforts as well as the critical roles states, school districts, unions, and chartering laws have since had in developing teacher autonomy and greater professional roles for teachers.

1970, 1972: Two district schools with teacher autonomy open on opposite coasts.

Two district schools, San Francisco Community School (SFCS, K–8) and High School in the Community (HSC, 9–12) in New Haven open on opposite coasts. Both are district schools. Both offer students new, different learning models, with SFCS offering project-based learning to at-risk students and HSC offering service-learning in community settings. The teaching groups were not aware of one another. Throughout the 1970s a number of schools with teacher autonomy appear in the independent school sector, but not much happens in public school settings.

1980s: Ruth Anne Olson begins to develop "teacher ownership" ideas.

Ruth Anne Olson develops the idea of teacher ownership of professional practices as a consultant to a Minnesota project entitled Public School Incentives. Her work is supported by several foundations including Northwest Area Foundation, First Bank System Foundation (now US Bancorp), F.R. Bigelow Foundation, Medtronic Foundation, and Fingerhut Corporation Foundation.

1983, 1986: Two reports, "A Nation at Risk" and "A Nation Prepared," stimulate a cultural shift.

Two reports, "A Nation at Risk" (National Commission on Excellence in Education 1983) and "A Nation Prepared: Teachers for the 21st Century" (Carnegie Corporation 1986), stimulate a cultural shift. "Restructuring" seems more possible. The Carnegie Forum foresees schools with teacher autonomy being in operation by the twenty-first century and becoming increasingly common over time.

1986: Foundations support the development of two reports on teacher autonomy.

Medtronic Foundation, Fingerhut Corporation Foundation, and Public School Incentives support the development and production of two 1986 reports: "Private Practice in Public School Teaching. Book I: The Concept, Need and Design," by Ted Kolderie, a champion of public service options and structural reform and innovation in public education, and "Private Practice in Public School Teaching. Book II: The Experiences of Teachers and School Administrators," by Ruth Anne Olson.

Olson works as a consultant, locating teachers willing to work with a new model and showing them how to do it. She finds there is no market for teachers in K–12 education wanting to work on contract.

Late 1980s: Wisconsin educators explore contracting their services to school districts.

Senn Brown, Chris Yelich, and a small group of enterprising educators in Wisconsin get interested in Olson's ideas and begin to form a network for like-minded teachers who want to contract with Wisconsin school districts.

1990: Wisconsin educators formalize their network, influencing the state's 1993 chartering law.

The network formed by Brown and Yelich formalizes as the American Association of Educators in Private Practice (AAEPP), with a key goal of changing the way teachers think about their careers. AAEPP advances the idea that teachers can go into business for themselves. The Wisconsin Association of School Boards (Brown being its director of legislative services) is also involved, and their interest in contracting to receive instructional services in schools influences the design of the Wisconsin chartering law first passed in 1993.

For several years, AAEPP draws increasingly large groups to meetings. At first the interest is in teachers forming professional practices, but eventually the group's focus changes to business firms and entrepreneurs getting contracts with districts.

1992: Minnesota Le Sueur–Henderson school district concludes it "needs options."

Minnesota's Le Sueur–Henderson District Superintendent Harold Larson and School Board Chair Virginia Miller lead a strategic planning process, which concludes that the district needs more innovation and freedom of choice.

1992–1993: Teachers from Le Sueur–Henderson develop Minnesota New Country School.

Encouraged by the strategic planning outcomes and Minnesota's 1991 Chartering Law (the first in the nation), a group of entrepreneurial individuals from Le Sueur–Henderson develop and propose Minnesota New Country School (MNCS), a chartered school with a project-based learning model for students in grades 6–12. The group includes a school board member, three teachers and parents. This group also determines they want more satisfying, professional roles for teachers.

At the suggestion of Ted Kolderie and attorney Daniel Mott, they decide to form a workers' cooperative called EdVisions. Members of the cooperative—teachers—would be accountable for running the school. In winter 1993, Le Sueur–Henderson School District voted to authorize MNCS knowing it would be run by teachers.

1994: EdVisions, a cooperative of teachers, contracts with the MNCS Board.

EdVisions Cooperative contracts with the MNCS school board, accepting accountability for school success in exchange for authority to make decisions about the school. The school and cooperative open to the public. The MNCS school board transfers a lump sum to EdVisions to carry out its contract. With their authority the teachers determine curriculum, set the budget, choose the level of technology available to students, determine their own salaries, select their colleagues, and monitor performance.

1994: Boston district forms "pilot schools" to retain teachers after chartering law passed.

Also in 1994, Boston Public Schools (BPS) designs "pilot schools" in an effort to retain teachers and students after the Massachusetts Legislature passed a state chartering law in 1993. Under the pilot agreement, the BPS superintendent delegates authority to pilot schools' governing boards to try new and different means of improving teaching and learning in order to better serve at-risk urban students. The potential now exists for the boards to put more decision-making in teachers' hands. Some do, some don't.

Pilot schools are overseen by the district's chief academic officer. All take part in a city-wide network facilitated by Daniel French at the nonprofit Center for Collaborative Education (CCE). CCE provides schools with coordination support and assistance, including coaching services, professional development, advocacy, and research and evaluation. As part of this work, CCE later develops Five Conditions of Autonomy for schools (Center for Collaborative Education 2009).

1996: Boston Pilot School governing boards augment teachers' authority.

A handful of Boston Pilot School governing boards use the authority vested in them to augment teachers' authority and accountability to varying degrees (at Boston Day and Evening Academy and Fenway in 1996; later Mission Hill K–8 School, Boston Arts Academy [9–12], Another Course to College [9–12], Boston Teachers Union [BTU] School [K–7]). Note: Other Boston Pilot Schools try different arrangements. Those named here are specifically providing some autonomy to teachers.

2000: Gates Foundation invests $4.3 million in EdVisions, to replicate the model.

Thomas Vander Ark, then head of the education program for the Bill & Melinda Gates Foundation, visits EdVisions Cooperative and MNCS in Henderson, Minnesota. Ted Kolderie, now with Hamline University's Center for Policy Studies, arranges a follow-up meeting in St. Paul with Vander Ark, EdVisions cooperative cofounder Douglas Thomas, and other Minnesota education leaders. Vander Ark invites Thomas to submit a proposal for EdVisions Cooperative to replicate the model it created at MNCS. In June, the foundation invests $4.3 million for replication in fifteen Midwest schools.

The effort came to be known as the Gates-EdVisions Project, run by EdVisions Schools, Avalon School (St. Paul, 7–12) opens in 2001. As expansion rolls out some of these schools use the MNCS-brand of teacher autonomy while others adopt arrangements where teachers have less authority.

As part of the expansion, Avalon teachers use the authority to do everything teachers at MNCS do, and they decide to hire administrators who work for/are accountable, to them. Teachers also pass along their autonomy to students, giving them a voting branch of governance and the ability to direct their own learning.

In summer 2000, John Parr, a twenty-plus-year officer of American Federation of State, County and Municipal Employees (AFSCME) and his daughter Cris Parr, a thirteen-year building representative for the Milwaukee Teachers' Education Association (MTEA), visit MNCS. Driving back to Milwaukee, they come up with the idea for a union-compatible model.

Observing all this national movement, Center for Policy Studies senior associate Edward J. Dirkswager assembles a team of experts from education, health care, and law to prepare a book and start-up guide that asks, "What if teachers were owners, not employees?" and demonstrates how being an owner rather than an employee can give teachers control of their professional activity, including full responsibility and accountability for creating and sustaining high-performing learning communities.

2001: Teachers create first Milwaukee union-compatible teacher autonomy model.

John and Cris Parr approach the MTEA with their concept. MTEA was supportive of them moving forward to develop and open Individualized Developmental Educational Approaches to Learning (I.D.E.A.L.), a K–8 school instrumentality-chartered by Milwaukee Public Schools. The Parrs had a number of subsequent meetings with MTEA on the details.

In the Milwaukee arrangement, teachers keep their economic life with district employment via a memorandum of understanding with the district and union that provides waivers from the master contract. Much of the autonomy for teachers is arranged via the chartered school contract between the school board and the school.

I.D.E.A.L. opens in September 2001. Its success paves the way for twelve additional schools run by teacher cooperatives to be instrumentality-chartered by Milwaukee Public Schools between 2002 and 2009, with assistance from John Parr. As of November 2011, three of these schools have since closed.

September 2001: Center for Policy Studies hosts national meeting on teacher ownership.

Also in September 2001, the Center for Policy Studies (CPS) holds a national meeting to get feedback on the idea of teacher ownership, as it had been laid out in the initial drafts of *Teachers as Owners*, and to bring the idea into the national discussion about the future of public education. Hamline University and Wallace-Reader's Digest Fund cosponsor the event held in St. Paul.

Teachers as Owners and CPS coin the term Teacher Professional Partnerships (TPPs), advancing the idea of teachers being in charge of their schools the way other professionals are in charge of their law firms, medical groups, and architectural or engineering practices. A teacher autonomy arrangement is a TPP if there is the following: (1) a group of teachers working in partnership (collectively as a group) at the school, and (2) real delegation of authority to the partnership to manage or arrange for the management of the school.

2002: Gates Foundation invests another $4.5 million in EdVisions.
Seeing that EdVisions Schools was able to successfully scale its model using the grant made in 2000, the Gates Foundation makes an additional $4.5 million investment for EdVisions to replicate its Design Principles in twenty new high schools nationwide. EdVisions Schools eventually include in-district schools with unionized teachers such as Phoenix High School (9–12) in Kennewick, Washington, and Tailoring Academics to Guide Our Students (TAGOS Leadership Academy, 7–12) in Janesville, Wisconsin.

Separately, EdVisions Cooperative evolves to serve varying models of schools with teacher autonomy. By 2004, EdVisions Cooperative has 144 members serving nine schools and it continues to expand.

Joseph P. Graba, a former school teacher, state union leader, Minnesota state legislator, director of the Minnesota Technical College System, and dean of Hamline University's Graduate School of Education first introduces the idea to the Teacher Union Reform Network (TURN). Graba remains active with the network today.

June 2002: Edward J. Dirkswager publishes Teachers as Owners.
Edward J. Dirkswager, editor, publishes *Teachers as Owners* (Scarecrow Press), having incorporated feedback from the September 2001 meeting.

2003: Public Agenda survey: 58 percent of teachers interested in schools run by teachers.
Public Agenda tests a national sample of teachers' attitudes for new arrangements as reported in "Stand By Me: What Teachers Really Think About Unions, Merit Pay and Other Professional Matters."

Findings are that 58 percent of teachers were somewhat or very interested "in working in a [chartered] school run and managed by teachers"; this included 65 percent of teachers surveyed who had worked less than five years and 50 percent of teachers surveyed who had worked more than twenty years (Farkas, Johnson, and Duffett 2003).

2003: Center for Policy Studies and Hamline University form Education|Evolving.
The Center for Policy Studies and Hamline University formalize a joint venture called Education|Evolving (E|E), co-founded by Ted Kolderie and Joseph P. Graba in part to advance the notion of TPPs and significantly expand awareness of the possibilities associated with enlarging teachers' professional roles.

Aware of the growing number of schools with teacher autonomy appearing nationally, E|E associate Kim Farris-Berg prepares an inventory to describe the emerging arrangements' organizational structures.

Graba introduces the idea to the National Board for Professional Teaching Standards and Teach for America, which take interest but don't advance the idea.

2005: Minneapolis Federation of Teachers advocates legislation allowing for a school to become self-governed.

The Minneapolis Federation of Teachers (MFT) forms the Site-governed School (SGS) Committee and includes union-friendly district administrators, E|E and the Minnesota Business Partnership to develop legislation that would allow teacher autonomy in district schools. The Minnesota Legislature passes a bill saying if 60 percent of the teaching staff wants to transition to become a SGS, they can go forward and apply to the state.

A $50,000 planning grant is made available to the first five Minneapolis Public Schools that applied. Only one school takes advantage. According to MFT president Lynn Nordgren, "The problem was that people were hesitant to invest their time in the effort. Even if teachers applied, there was no guarantee that the district would allow it to happen."

2006: Schools with teacher autonomy emerge in California and Baltimore.

Unaware of the other schools with teacher autonomy, Paul and Alysia Krafel and other teachers at the ten-year-old Chrysalis Charter School (K–8) in Palo Cedro, California, form an informally organized teacher cooperative to manage the school. Teachers' authority at Chrysalis is made formal in the school's charter, which is authorized by the Shasta County Office of Education. Once a museum school, Chrysalis now offers hands-on science and nature learning.

Also unaware of other models, the Baltimore Teachers Network moves to start schools with teacher autonomy chartered by Baltimore Public Schools, in which teachers retain their union membership (the ability for teachers to manage the schools is written into the chartering agreements). They start ConneXions Community Leadership Academy (6–12) and Independence School Local 1 (9–12, formerly a district pilot program) in 2006 and 2007, respectively. The schools serve students who might have otherwise dropped out of school.

Expansion and development of Minnesota and Milwaukee schools with teacher autonomy, as well as growing national interest, inspires E|E associate Kim Farris-Berg to produce a second edition of the national inventory describing the emerging organizational structures and learning programs teachers put in place when they are in charge.

December 2006: Teacher autonomy appears in "Tough Choices or Tough Times" report.

The 1986 Carnegie Forum vision of schools with teacher autonomy reappears in a December report of The New Commission on The Skills of the American Workforce, "Tough Choices or Tough Times," by Marc Tucker.

2007: Los Angeles teachers union launches "Belmont Zone of Choice."

United Teachers of Los Angeles (UTLA) and the surrounding community launch the Belmont Zone of Choice, modeled after Boston Pilot Schools. After initial success, UTLA "overwhelmingly" votes to expand the number of schools in 2009. By 2010 there are eleven schools, and a new Kennedy Zone of Choice emerges.

2009: Minnesota Legislature passes a new Site-governed Schools law.

To improve Minneapolis teachers' willingness to start Site-governed Schools, the Minneapolis Federation of Teachers and E|E join forces again to expand the 2005 legislation (see above). The Minnesota Legislature passes the 2009 Site-governed Schools law, allowing for the creation of schools inside districts that enjoy the same autonomy and exemption from state regulation as schools in the chartering sector.

School and teacher autonomy is spelled out explicitly in the law, leaving little to doubt and dispute. The teachers in schools created under the law may have significant control over who works there, what learning model is used, how the budget is allocated, and the schedule of the school days and year. These details are arranged through districts' agreements with applicants who wish to start and run a site-governed school, and the schools are judged on results.

School districts and teachers' unions in Minneapolis, St. Paul, Staples-Motley, and Rochester begin investigating the SGS opportunity. (Note: SGS have the opportunity to give teachers autonomy, but do not have to.) St. Paul teachers include a commitment to design a site-governed schools development process in their contract. After some delay/hesitation, the Minneapolis Public Schools Board of Education approves the first Minneapolis SGS with teacher autonomy. The French Immersion School, Pierre Bottineau (K–5), is set to officially open in fall 2012.

2009: More teachers' unions move to professionalize teaching.

More teachers' unions move to professionalize their members' roles. Denver Classroom Teachers Association proposes the start-up of the district school with teacher autonomy, the Math and Science Leadership Academy (MSLA, K–3). Boston Teachers Union (BTU, K–7) starts the BTU School, a pilot school with teacher autonomy.

Also in 2009, E|E advances the teacher autonomy concept further, releasing videos of teachers and students who work in teacher professional partnerships and also videos that introduce the concept.

Center for Policy Studies senior fellows Kim Farris-Berg and Edward J. Dirkswager, and E|E associate Amy Junge embark on a research project examining what teachers do when they are granted the autonomy needed to accept accountability for their schools' outcomes. The project begins with an effort to identify schools with teacher autonomy nationwide and assesses their areas of autonomy as well as the arrangements securing autonomy. In fall 2010 Farris-Berg and Junge visit eleven schools nationally to investigate the research question.

Fall 2009: John Wilson, NEA executive director, visits Milwaukee teacher cooperatives.

Having become interested in the Milwaukee union-compatible teacher autonomy arrangement, John Wilson, executive director of the National Education Association (NEA) and John Wright, president of the Arizona Education Association make a fall trip to see the schools with teacher autonomy and visit with the MTEA. Marc Tucker, author of the 2006 report "Tough Choices or Tough Times," joins them.

2010: Teachers meet with Arne Duncan to explain "teacher professional partnerships."

On April 27, Carrie Bakken, teacher at Avalon School in St. Paul and Brenda Martinez, teacher at Academia de Lenguaje y Bellas Artes (ALBA, P–5) in Milwaukee meet with U.S. secretary of education, Arne Duncan, and many of his senior staff to explain teacher professional partnerships. In the meeting Bakken and Martinez describe how the TPP arrangement fundamentally changes and improves school conditions for teachers and students. They explain that when teachers have autonomy very different types of schools emerge, and today's issues around tenure, compensation, and teacher evaluation can be resolved.

July 2010: Minnesota Federation of Teachers receives grant to develop independent chartered school authorizer.

The American Federation of Teachers announces it is making an innovation fund grant to the Minneapolis Federation of Teachers to develop a new independent 501(c)(3) nonprofit organization which, if approved by the Minnesota Department of Education, will serve as an authorizer of chartered schools throughout the state. This new organization, called "Minnesota Guild of Public Charter Schools" opens later in 2010 as a separate legal entity from the MFT, with its own governing board.

MFT leaders say they are considering the chartering route to seek greater professional roles for its teacher-members after receiving little support from the Minneapolis Public Schools Board of Education to advance teacher autonomy using the Site-governed Schools model (see 2005 and 2009, above).

Fall 2010: Front page New York Times *story on teacher autonomy; national news coverage begins.*

In August and September, the national media begins to report on schools with teacher autonomy appearing in Denver and other areas around the nation. A front page story in the *New York Times* on September 6, 2010 further fuels journalistic interest (Hu 2010). E|E tracks the ongoing national coverage on its website.

On the *National Journal's Education Experts Blog* on October 18, 2010, Ted Kolderie describes collegial teacher autonomy as central to the national discussion about teachers and teacher unions spurred by the film *Waiting for Superman.*

2011: E|E releases a new inventory of schools with teacher autonomy.

In April, E|E releases a new, online National Inventory of Schools with Teacher Autonomy that includes a list and map of schools along with a discussion of their areas of autonomy, an overview of how teachers secure autonomy, and photographs from visits to eleven school sites.

Fall 2011: Minnesota DOE approves Guild as first union-affiliated authorizer of chartered schools.

In November, the Minnesota Department of Education approves the Guild's (see 2010) application to become an authorizer of chartered schools throughout the state. It is the first union-affiliated authorizer of chartered schools. Lynn Nordgren, president of the Minneapolis Federation of Teachers, said the Guild will tap into teachers' desire to create high-performing schools where they can work collaboratively as professionals.

"We want to authorize schools that rely on teacher expertise to identify and use effective teaching strategies, promote engaged student learning, create educational autonomy, ensure effective organization and develop shared management," Nordgren said (American Federation of Teachers 2).

December 2011: NEA Commission calls for autonomy and accountability for teachers.

In December 2011 the National Education Association (NEA) publishes a report from its Commission on Effective Teachers and Teaching. In 2010 the NEA had charged the Commission—a group of twenty-one accomplished autonomous teachers and educational leaders from around the country—to "craft a new vision of a teaching profession that is led by teachers and ensures teacher and teaching effectiveness" among other things. The December report concluded,

> We envision a teaching profession that embraces collective accountability for student learning balanced with collaborative autonomy that allows educators to do what is best for students. . . . In the system we envision: School leadership is a joint endeavor with highly effective classroom teachers. In a collaborative school culture where all teachers share responsibility for student learning and well-being, shared decision-making models utilize classroom expertise in advancing the effectiveness of schools and the mission of public education.
>
> Administrators and teachers have a collaborative relationship characterized by joint decision-making and accountability. Teachers assume hybrid roles that involve both teaching and leading; effective principals spend some time teaching and welcome opportunities to work with teacher leaders. (NEA 2011)

The NEA also makes small grants to groups of teachers who wish to explore converting existing schools to a teacher autonomy governance model.

NOTE

1. A hyperlinked version of appendix A is available on the Education|Evolving website www.educationevolving.org.

Appendix B: Demographics at the Eleven Schools

Academia de Lenguaje y Bellas Artes ALBA www.2.milwaukee.k12.wi.us/alba/ Milwaukee, WI	Avalon School Avalon www.avalonschool.org St. Paul, MN	Chrysalis Charter School Chrysalis www.chrysalischarter.com Palo Cedro, CA
Type: Instrumentality chartered	**Type:** Chartered	**Type:** Chartered
District: Milwaukee Public Schools	**Authorizer:** Novation Education Opportunities[2]	**Authorizer:** Shasta County Board of Education
Environment: Urban	**Environment:** Urban	**Environment:** Rural
Year opened: 2004	**Year opened:** 2001	**Year opened:** 1996
Grades: Preschool–5	**Grades:** 7–12	**Grades:** K–8
Certificated teachers: 18.5	**Certificated teachers:** 19	**Certificated teachers:** 7
Classified staff[1]: 14	**Classified staff:** 4	**Classified staff:** 13
School enrollment: 355	**School enrollment:** 174	**School enrollment:** 145
Male: 49%	**Male:** 53%	**Male:** 55%
Female: 51%	**Female:** 47%	**Female:** 45%
African American: 0%	**African American:** 18%	**African American:** 1%
Caucasian: 0%	**Caucasian:** 71%	**Caucasian:** 83%
Asian: 0%	**Asian:** 5%	**Asian:** 0%
Hispanic: 99%	**Hispanic:** 4%	**Hispanic:** 9%
Native American: 0%	**Native American:** 2%	**Native American:** 3%
Free or reduce-priced lunch: 97%	**Free or reduce-priced lunch:** 33%	**Free or reduce-priced lunch:** 59%
Special education: 11%	**Special education:** 26%	**Special education:** 6%
Limited English: 88%	**Limited English:** 1%	**Limited English:** 0%
Attendance rate: 95%	**Attendance rate:** 92%	**Attendance rate:** 95%
Mobility: 2.8%	**Graduation rate**[3]: 87%	**Mobility:** 24%

EdVisions Off Campus EOC http://edvisionshighschool.com Minnesota	High School in the Community HSC http://schools.nhps.net/hsc New Haven, CT	Independence School, Local 1 Independence www.independenceschool.org Baltimore, MD
Type: Chartered Authorizer: Volunteers of America Environment: Online Year opened: 2005 Grades: 7–12 Certificated teachers: 8 Classified staff: 0	Type: District magnet District: New Haven Public Schools and City of New Haven Environment: Urban Year opened: 1970 Grades: 9–12 Certificated teachers: 28 Classified staff: 6	Type: Chartered Authorizer: Baltimore City Schools and Baltimore Teachers Network Environment: Urban Year opened: 2007 Grades: 9–12 Certificated teachers: 12 Classified staff: 1
School enrollment: 57 Male: 51% Female: 49%	School enrollment: 307 Male: 40% Female: 60%	School enrollment: 121 Male: 55% Female: 45%
African American: 0% Caucasian: 95% Asian: 0% Hispanic: 4% Native American: 1%	African American: 48% Caucasian: 24% Asian: 1% Hispanic: 27% Native American: 0%	African American: 60% Caucasian: 33% Asian: 0% Hispanic: 0% Native American: 0%
Free or reduce-priced lunch: 49% Special education: 20% Limited English: 0%	Free or reduce-priced lunch: 74% Special education: 15% Limited English: 7%	Free or reduce-priced lunch: 72% Special education: 28% Limited English: 0%
Attendance rate: 85% Graduation rate: 100%	Attendance rate: 91% Graduation rate: 89%	Attendance rate: 93% Graduation rate: 85%

Mission Hill K-8 School
Mission Hill
www.missionhillschool.org
Boston, MA

Type: District pilot school
District: Boston Public Schools
Environment: Urban
Year opened: 1997
Grades: K–8
Certificated teachers: 12
Classified staff: 7

School enrollment: 162
Male: 51%
Female: 49%

African American: 41%
Caucasian: 23%
Asian: 1%
Hispanic: 28%
Native American: 1%

Free or reduce-priced lunch: 48%
Special education: 24%
Limited English: 7%

Attendance rate: 95%
Mobility: 8%

Minnesota New Country School
MNCS
www.newcountryschool.com
Henderson, MN

Type: Chartered
Authorizer: Novation Education
  Opportunities[4]
Environment: Rural
Year opened: 1994
Grades: 6–12
Certificated teachers: 10
Classified staff: 8

School enrollment: 113
Male: 53%
Female: 47%

African American: 3%
Caucasian: 92%
Asian: 1%
Hispanic: 4%
Native American: 1%

Free or reduce-priced lunch: 23%
Special education: 33%
Limited English: 0%

Attendance rate: 94%
Graduation rate: 80%

Phoenix High School
Phoenix
http://school.ksd.org/phoenix
Kennewick, WA

Type: District
District: Kennewick School District
Environment: Suburban
Year opened: 2007
Grades: 9–12
Certificated teachers: 3
Classified staff: 3

School enrollment: 60
Male: 52%
Female: 48%

African American: 2%
Caucasian: 82%
Asian: 3%
Hispanic: 13%
Native American: 0%

Free or reduce-priced lunch: 58%
Special education: 11%
Limited English: 7%

Attendance rate: 83%
Graduation rate: 78%

San Francisco Community School SFCS	Tailoring Academics to Guide Our Students
http://my-sfcs/1.html	TAGOS Leadership Academy
San Francisco, CA	www.tagosleadershipacademy.org
	Janesville, WI
Type: District alternative	Type: Instrumentality chartered
District: San Francisco Unified School District	Authorizer: The School District of Janesville
Environment: Urban/Suburban	Environment: Suburban
Year opened: 1972	Year opened: 2007
Grades: K–8	Grades: 7–12
Certificated teachers: 19	Certificated teachers: 4
Classified staff: 4	Classified staff: 2
School enrollment: 289	School enrollment: 76
Male: 55%	Male: 54%
Female: 45%	Female: 46%
African American: 14%	African American: 1%
Caucasian: 11%	Caucasian: 84%
Asian: 23%	Asian: 1%
Hispanic: 39%	Hispanic: 3%
Native American: 0%	Native American: 4%
Free or reduce-priced lunch: 69%	Free or reduce-priced lunch: 67%
Special education: 11%	Special education: 18%
Limited English: 35%	Limited English: 1%
Attendance rate: 94%	Attendance rate: 88%
Mobility: Unavailable	Graduation rate: 100%

Note: All data is from 2010–2011.
1. Classified staff refers to all school staff other than licensed teachers, for example: classroom aides, administrative support, custodians, etc.
2. Avalon's authorizer at the time of the study was Hamline University.
3. Graduation rates include students who may have taken more than four years to graduate.
4. MNCS's sponsor at the time of the study was Le Sueur–Henderson School Board.
Source: Demographic data was collected from two sources per school: the school's State Department of Education website and the schools' own data on their students.

Appendix C: Online Survey Instrument

The following survey was given online, via a platform called SurveyMonkey, to all teachers at the eleven school sites. Not included below are the demographic questions used for analysis (e.g., Where do you teach?). The survey design is based on the nine cultural characteristics of high-performing organizations gleaned from the review of literature described in chapter 3. Using details from the literature, we sought to examine autonomous teachers' approaches and behaviors in each area.

1. Mission and Purpose
Please note: Some questions below refer to "standards of practice." These include approaches to learning, approaches to decision-making and working together as professionals, parent interaction, academic expectations of students, student voice, discipline, homework, and more.

At our school:
Scale: Yes or no.

1. We have a written statement outlining our purpose (i.e., in the form of a mission and /or vision).
2. We have specific goals for the school.
3. We have commonly understood standards of practice.

Please rate the following based on your experiences at your school:
Scale: Excellent, Very Good, Good, Fair, Poor, N/A

1. Teachers' personal commitment and buy in to our purpose.

2. Teachers' personal commitment and buy in to our standards of practice.
3. Our excitement about our goals.
4. Our record of setting goals.
5. Our record of setting goals that are challenging.
6. Our inclusiveness in which teachers are involved in setting school goals (whether new or veteran).
7. Hiring of teachers based on compatibility with our purpose.
8. Evaluation of teachers based on compatibility with our purpose.
9. Hiring of teachers based on compatibility with our standards of practice.
10. Evaluation of teachers based on compatibility with our standards of practice.
11. Teachers' ability to see connections between the purpose and its implications for teaching.
12. Our school culture's reflection of our purpose.

2. Authority, responsibility, and accountability
At our school:
Scale: Strongly disagree, Disagree, Neither agree nor disagree, Agree, Strongly agree

1. Individuals have all of the authority needed to make the school successful.
2. The collective group of teachers and leaders has all of the authority needed to make the school successful.

Please rate the following based on your experiences at your school:
Scale: Excellent, Very Good, Good, Fair, Poor, N/A

1. Teachers' awareness of their authority to make decisions (whether they're new or veteran).
2. Teachers' willingness to individually accept responsibility for making decisions.
3. Teachers' willingness to collectively accept responsibility for making decisions.
4. Teachers' willingness to individually accept accountability for student performance outcomes.
5. Teachers' willingness to collectively accept accountability for student performance outcomes.
6. Teachers' willingness to collectively accept accountability for the school's financial outcomes.

7. Teachers' access to financial data (whether they're new or veteran).
8. Teachers' trust in other individuals' competence.
9. Teachers' trust in other individuals' honesty.
10. Teachers' clarity about expectations for individual performance.
11. Teachers' clarity about expectations for individual behavior.
12. Speed of addressing any problems with teachers' performance.
13. Speed of addressing any problems with teachers' behavior.
14. Teachers' willingness to hold one another accountable.
15. Quality of our performance review system.

3. Collaboration

Please note: The definition of collaboration is the act of working jointly with one another (it is not necessarily to form consensus).
Please rate the following based on your experiences at your school:
Scale: Excellent, Very Good, Good, Fair, Poor, N/A

1. Our culture's fostering of team work, consultation, and engagement.
2. Our value for differences, as evidenced by a culture of listening to and understanding others regardless of status or function.
3. Teachers' sense of obligation to participate fully.
4. Our interdependence.
5. Open flow of ideas.
6. Our navigation of the distinctions between our norms and values and those of our district and/or authorizer.
7. Collective willingness to invest the time and effort it takes to develop a collaborative community.
8. Our professional growth as fostered by collaboration.

4. Innovation

Please rate the following based on your experiences at your school:
Scale: Excellent, Very Good, Good, Fair, Poor, N/A

1. Our challenging of ourselves to create innovative means to improve performance.
2. Our culture's encouragement of teachers to search out opportunities to change and improve.
3. Our culture's encouragement of trying new things.
4. Cultivation of problem- solvers more than rule followers.
5. Removal of any bureaucratic processes standing in the way of implementing good ideas for improvement.

6. Commitment to continuous improvement and adaptation in the way we work.
7. Acceptance of teachers' innovation in their individual classrooms, or in their work with students.
8. Invitation of and value for creative, new ideas from all teachers.
9. Implementation of creative, new ideas from teachers.
10. Invitation of and value for creative, new ideas from all students.
11. Implementation of creative, new ideas from students.
12. Openness to the possibility that every attempt to improve will not work.

5. Response to the external environment

Please note: The "external environment" we are referring to includes stakeholders, stakeholder's expectations, technology, youth culture, and the economy. Stakeholders might include parents, students, students' future learning institutions, the business community, teacher unions, legislators, and others.

"Political conditions" might include varying goals of districts, agendas of unions and professional associations, and varying levels of acceptance of new and different schools or teacher working models.

"Social conditions" might include the advancement of technology and its implications for student learning, students' increasing exposure to customization, students' varying interests, and families' varying financial ability to pay for future educational opportunities.

Please rate the following based on your experiences at your school:

Scale: Excellent, Very Good, Good, Fair, Poor, N/A

1. Ability to continuously learn from the external environment.
2. Invitation of new ideas from those outside of the school.
3. Value for new ideas from those outside of the school.
4. Ability to adapt when conditions around us have changed.
5. Commitment to seeking opportunities to grow through partnerships with external groups.
6. Commitment to enhancing value for students and their families.
7. Our attitude that students' future employers and/or future educational institutions are stakeholders of our school.
8. Our attitude that we need to learn from others (that we don't necessarily know what's best).
9. Commitment to understanding what our stakeholders desire.
10. Ability to have open and authentic discussions with parents.
11. Sensitivity to political conditions in our decision making.
12. Sensitivity to social conditions in our decision making.

13. Sensitivity to current economic conditions in our decision making, such that student performance is not negatively impacted.

6. Engagement and Motivation
At our school:
Scale: Strongly disagree, Disagree, Neither agree nor disagree, Agree, Strongly agree

1. There is a low level of turnover among teachers.

Please rate the following based on your experiences at your school:
Scale: Excellent, Very Good, Good, Fair, Poor, N/A

1. Teachers' willingness to put in extra effort to meet our goals.
2. Our pride in being part of our team.
3. Our belief that the basic function of a teacher is to motivate students to be learners.
4. Students' freedom to pursue topics of interest to them for academic credit.
5. Our success at motivating students.
6. Availability to students outside of class.
7. Variance of teaching methods according to the needs of the individual student.
8. Variance of teaching methods according to the interests of the individual student.
9. Variance of teaching methods according to the needs of the individual teachers.
10. Variance of teaching methods according to the interests of the individual teachers.
11. Preference for our professional goals over bureaucratic goals.
12. Our commitment to celebrating our collective successes.
13. Recognition of individual contributions to team successes.
14. Students' attitudes about the significance and rewards of learning.
15. Our understanding of the differences among students.
16. Our belief that our students can succeed here at school.
17. Our belief that our students can succeed in their lives.

7. Leadership
Scale: Strongly disagree, Disagree, Neither agree nor disagree, Agree, Strongly agree

1. Leaders are selected by all and accountable to all.

Please rate the following based on your experiences at your school:
Scale: Excellent, Very Good, Good, Fair, Poor, N/A

1. Leaders' commitment to coaching and facilitating.
2. Our commitment to expecting that all are leaders.
3. Intentional cultivation of leadership skills.
4. Diverse and complimentary distribution of leaders.
5. Leaders' empowerment of others.
6. Inclusiveness in defining who is an important decision-maker.
7. Leaders' stimulation of change and improvement.
8. Leaders' commitment to being in service to all.
9. Leaders' integrity and example.
10. Teachers' trust and confidence in our leaders.
11. Teachers' understanding of leadership roles.

8. The Learning Culture, for Teachers and Students
Please rate the following based on your experiences at your school:
Scale: Excellent, Very Good, Good, Fair, Poor, N/A

1. Our culture's encouragement of curiosity and exploration.
2. Our attitude that we are not experts whose role is to impart information to our students.
3. Engagement in reflective dialogue.
4. Commitment to continuous learning and improvement.
5. Value for knowing students as whole persons.
6. Value for knowing colleagues as whole persons.
7. Our commitment to do what is necessary to transform policies and structures that limit students' learning.
8. Support for high quality teaching.
9. Support for teacher learning.
10. Teachers' ability to admit difficulty without social costs.
11. Our culture's reinforcement of central school values.
12. Personalization of student learning.
13. Students' desire to learn.
14. Our culture's support of asking for and receiving help.

9. Performance Assessment
Please rate the following based on your experiences at your school:
Scale: Excellent, Very Good, Good, Fair, Poor, N/A

1. Assessment of student performance using district and state standards.
2. Assessment of student performance using our own standards (in addition to district and state standards).
3. Assessment of teacher performance, in part, as it relates to their students' performance.
4. Assessment of teachers' strengths and weaknesses, in part, as they relate to the school's overall performance.
5. Assessment of teacher's collective/group performance as it relates to school success.
6. Assessment of student satisfaction.
7. Assessment of parent satisfaction.
8. Use of information gathered from assessments to improve our performance.
9. Commitment to setting specific, measurable goals for individual students.
10. Commitment to setting specific, measurable goals for the school as a whole.
11. Commitment to measuring progress toward our success in achieving our purpose.
12. Teachers' access to assessment data (whether new or veteran).
13. Our inclusiveness regarding which teachers can contribute to interpretation of data.
14. Our commitment to acting upon results to improve performance.
15. Our inclusiveness regarding which teachers can participate in deciding how to use data to improve performance.
16. Our commitment to being performance driven.
17. Commitment to understanding reasons for success.
18. Use of technology to monitor students' progress.

10. Share Your Thoughts (optional)
If the questions in this survey spurred any thoughts or ideas you would like to share with us, please do so here:

Appendix D: Hope Survey Assessment Tool (www.hopesurvey.org)

The Hope Survey assesses student perceptions of school and personal growth in six areas: hope, engagement, sense of academic press (their sense of teachers' level of expectation for their performance), goal orientation, belongingness, and autonomy. Teachers and other school leaders use the tool to understand the effect of their learning program and environment on students' overall engagement. Teachers also use the tool to assess students' nonacademic abilities such as optimism and problem solving.

In the fall, teachers and other school leaders give the Hope Survey to all students to establish a baseline. They give the survey again in the spring to assess growth. According to the Hope Survey website, outcomes "provide an indication of how a learning environment affects adolescents and have been shown to correlate positively with success in college, physical health, and self-actualization. With the Hope Survey, schools can build a strong data driven decision-making model which ties together relationships, relevance, and rigor through continuous school improvement."

Below is a sample of questions as well as students' rating scales for each area of questioning. The survey requires students to give some opinion on their perceptions. In other words, indifference isn't an option.

Students' rating scales for each area of questioning

Hope (up to 64)	Engagement (-10 - +10)	Academic Press (1–5)
Belongingness (1–5)	Goal Orientation (1–5)	Autonomy (1–7)

Sample of Hope Survey questions

Autonomy:

- I feel that my teachers provide me choices and options.
- My teachers encourage me to ask questions.

Teachers' Academic Press:

- My teachers like to help me learn.
- My teachers care about how much I learn.

Peer Personal Support:

- In this school, other students like me the way I am.
- In this school, other students really care about me.

Mastery Goal Orientation:

- Teachers in this school want students to really understand their work, not just memorize it.
- In this school, mistakes are okay as long as we are learning.

Performance Goal Orientation:

- In this school, teachers only care about the smart kids.
- This school has given up on some of its students.

Behavioral Engagement:

- I try hard to do well in school.
- In school, I do just enough to get by.

Emotional Engagement:

- I enjoy learning new things in school.
- When I'm in school, I feel bad.

Hope:

- I energetically pursue my goals.
- Even when others get discouraged, I know I can find a way to solve the problem.

HOPE SURVEY RESULTS FROM EDVISIONS SCHOOLS

The following charts show Hope and academic progress at EdVisions Schools from 2007 to 2009. EdVisions Schools is a nonprofit organization that supports a network of small innovative high schools, some of which have teacher autonomy. These schools have self-directed, project-based learning environments, and focus on empowering students, parents, and staff.

The first chart reports findings from two EdVisions Schools, 150 total students. The second chart reports findings from six EdVisions Schools, 450 total students. According to Mark Van Ryzin, one of The Hope Survey founders and designers, these charts demonstrate a link between school climate and school success (Mark Van Ryzin, pers. comm., April 23, 2010).

More information about the Hope Survey is available at www. hopesurvey.org and in the book *Assessing What Really Matters in Schools* by Ronald J. Newell and Mark J. Van Ryzin.

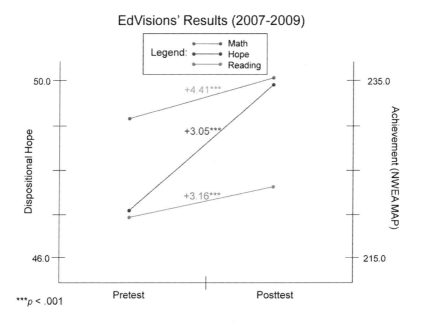

EdVisions' Results (2007-2009)

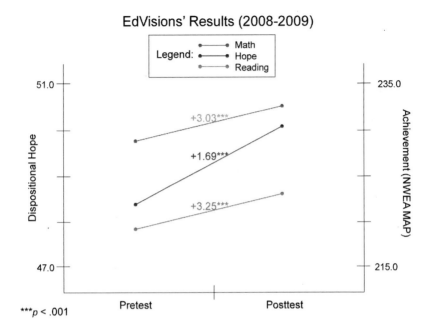

Appendix E: Sample Project Evaluation Rubric

AVALON SCHOOL

Name_____

Project Title:_____

Adapt this rubric to describe *your* project.

Expectations	Exceeded (Professional Work or Work that Surpassed Student Expectations)	Achieved (A/B High School Work)	Met (B/C High School Work)	Attempted (Low/Poor Quality Work)
Goals	• Student addressed all areas of project proposal thoroughly, specifically meeting stated goals. • All standards mentioned in proposal, well addressed in project. • Project purpose made very clear. • Student exceeded goals of project	• Student mostly addressed areas of project proposal, specifically meeting stated goals. • Standards mentioned in proposal addressed.	• Student somewhat addressed most areas of project proposal. • Student addressed some parts of standards mentioned in proposal.	• Project is loosely related to project proposal. • Standards mentioned in proposal not addressed or not well addressed.
Research	• All resources are properly documented with both citations and bibliography; notes are present. • Attention to quality of resources is apparent. • There is a variety of sources • People resources are a main part of the work produced. • The most recent and valuable sources used. • Student goes outside the Avalon environment to do research.	• Student documented most sources with citations and bibliography; kept notes. • Student demonstrated some attention given to quality of sources. • Bibliography showed variety of sources (with a limited use of internet sources). • Student connects with an expert (not including advisor or family).	• Bibliography of all sources and notes are present. • Quality of sources is acceptable. • Project shows a limited variety of sources. • Only internet sources are used.	• Student documented a few sources used and kept some notes. • The quality of sources is not addressed.

AVALON SCHOOL
Passion for Learning

Name _____

Project Title: _____

Adapt this rubric to describe *your* project.

Expectations	Exceeded (Professional Quality)	Achieved (A/B High School Work)	Met (B/C High School Work)	Attempted (Low/Poor Quality Work)
Quality of Product	• Professional quality product shows originality, creativity, and in-depth study. • Student generated own idea. • There is proof of feedback from experts. • Product is delivered to specific audience in the real world.	• Student adapted ideas from others for the product. • Student got feedback from a number of students and/or adults as shown through drafts or notes. • Product created for a specific audience. • **Good high school quality** 1) 2) 3)	• Typical High School work. • Student followed someone else's idea for the product. • Product is intended for a specific audience.	• Poor High School work. • No personal interest in final product. • No demonstration of awareness of audience.
Process and Improvement	• All parts of the project process are completed. • Student asked and answered outstanding questions. • Student sought out feedback, made appropriate improvements, and can explain creation process. • Student shows detailed understanding of information, demonstrates significant thoughtfulness (especially in the reflection), and uses information at a high level. • Reflection is thoroughly revised and at least two pages.	• All parts of project process are completed. • Student asked and answered strong questions. • Student sought feedback and made key improvements. • Most appropriate information is present and understood; student demonstrates thoughtfulness through reflection. • Reflection is revised and at least one to two pages.	• Some parts of the project process are completed. • Student asked and answered some questions. • Student recognized some needs for improvement and made some of them. • New information was gathered and some thoughtfulness shown in the reflection. • Reflection is revised.	• A few parts of the project process are completed. • Student asked and answered some questions. • Student did not seek out feedback for work. • Little new information is gathered but no thoughtfulness shown. • Reflection is unrevised and less than a page.
Project Management	• Student always on track, met all deadlines. • Learning and time use are precisely documented. • Student effectively communicated project progress with advisor.	• Student stayed on track most of the time, met most deadlines. • Student finished project within one week of finalization deadline. • Learning and time use are mostly recorded by student.	• Student stayed on track some of the time and met some deadlines. • Some of learning and time use is documented. • Student gave time to most parts of the project process.	• Student is infrequently on track with time but met final deadline. • Learning and time are poorly documented.

Appendix F: TAGOS Leadership Academy's Raised Responsibility Rubric

	Anarchy	Bossing/bullying	Cooperation/conformity	Democracy
Reading	* Student not practicing reading at all * Deliberately misbehaving and causing a disturbance * Unsafe (Advisor must step in)	* Students would not be doing much reading * Annoying/distracting others * Flip thru the pages but not reading (Advisor must step in)	* Students reading only when an advisor is watching or working with them * When unsupervised not disturbing others but not much effort *External motivation	* Student is reading whether advisor present or not * Read for self-pleasure, knowledge, achievement *Internal motivation
Math	*Student not completing math *Deliberately misbehaving and causing a disturbance *Unsafe (Advisor must step in)	* Students would not be doing much math * Annoying/distracting others * Has math work out but not working (Advisor must step in)	* Students completing math only when an advisor is watching or working with them * When unsupervised not disturbing others but not much effort *External motivation	*Student is completing math whether advisor present or not *Math accomplished for self-pleasure, knowledge, achievement *Internal motivation
Project	* Student is out of seat * Loud * Not engaged in any project work. * Logs time for work not accomplished or does not log time * Unsafe (Advisor must step in)	* Not engaged in any project work. * At seat but surfing the web for fun * Annoying/distracting others (Advisor must step in)	* Students completing project work only when an advisor is watching or working with them * When unsupervised not disturbing others but not much effort *External motivation	*Student is completing project work whether advisor present or not *Projects accomplished for self-pleasure, knowledge, achievement *Internal motivation
Leadership	* Sidebar conversation * Inattentive * Disengaged * Consistently chooses not to be on-time * Hands or feet on others * Unsafe (Advisor must intervene)	* Bossing or bullying * Not engaged in conversation * Encouraging others to be off task * Annoying/distracting others (Advisor must intervene)	* Listens and cooperates * Inspires others * Modeling * Reliable * Positive attitude *External motivation	* Listens and cooperates * Inspires others * Modeling * Reliable * Positive attitude * Internal motivation

Bibliography

American Federation of teachers. March/April 2012. "Union-backed Group Given Green Light to Authorize Charter Schools." *American Teacher* 96 (4): 2.

Banard, C. 1938. *The Functions of the Executive.* Cambridge, MA: Harvard University Press. Quoted in: Ouchi, William, and A. Wilkins. 1985. "Organizational Culture." *Annual Review of Sociology* 11: 457–83.

Barnett, Kerry, and John McCormick. 2003. "Vision, Relationships and Teacher Motivation: A Case Study." *Journal of Educational Administration* 41 (1): 55–73.

Becker, Brian E., Mark A. Huselid, and Dave Ulrich. *The HR Scorecard: Linking People, Strategy, and Performance.* Boston: Harvard Business School. Quoted in: Tomer, John. 2001. "Understanding High Performance Work Systems: The Joint Contribution of Economics and Human Resource Management." *Journal of Socio-Economics* 30 (1): 63–73. www.rohan.sdsu.edu/~frantz/docs/Tomer.pdf.

Bennis, W., and B. Nanus. 1985. *Leaders: The Strategies for Taking Charge.* New York: Harper and Row. Quoted in: Spillane, James P., Richard Halverson, and John B. Drummond. 2001. "Investigating School Leadership Practice: A Distributed Perspective." *Educational Researcher* 30: 23–28.

Berwick, Donald M., A. Blonton Godfrey, and Jane Roessner. 1990. *Curing Health Care: New Strategies for Quality Improvement.* San Francisco: Jossey-Bass Publishers.

Bimber, Bruce A. 1993. *School Decentralization: Lessons from the Study of Bureaucracy.* Santa Monica, CA: RAND Corporation.

Bimber, Bruce A. 1994. *The Decentralization Mirage: Comarping Decision-Making Arrangements in Four High Schools.* Santa Monica, CA: RAND Corporation.

Bloodworth, M. R., H. J. Walberg, R. P. Weissberg, and J. E. Zins. 2004. *The Foundations of Social and Emotional Learning.* New York: Teachers College Columbia University.

Bolman, L. G., and T. E. Deal. 1997. *Reframing Organizations: Artistry, Choice, and Leadership.* 2nd ed. San Francisco: Jossey-Bass Publishers.

Brandl, John E., ed. 2006. *Common Good: Ideas from the Humphrey.* Minneapolis, MN: Hubert H. Humphrey Institute of Public Affairs.

Brandt, Ron. 2003. "Is This School a Learning Organization? 10 Ways to Tell." *Journal of Staff Development* 23: 1.

Brinson, Dana, and Jacob Rosch. 2010. *Charter School Autonomy: A Half-Broken Promise.* Washington, DC: The Thomas B. Fordham Institute and Public Impact.

Brodtrick, Otto. 1988. Canada, Office of the Auditor General. *Annual Report,* chap. 4. Ottawa, ON: Supply and Services Canada. Quoted in: Kernaghan, Kenneth, Brian Marson, and Sandford Borins. 2005. *The New Public Organization,* 3rd ed. Toronto, ON: Institute of Public Administration of Canada.

215

Brodtrick, Otto. 2000. "Learning from the Best." In *The Three Pillars of Public Management: Secrets of Sustained Success*, edited by Ole Ingstrup and Paul Crookall, 3–16. Montreal, QC: McGill-Queens University Press.

Brown, J. S., and P. Duguid. 2000. *The Social Life of Information*. Cambridge, MA: Harvard Business School Press. Quoted in: McLaughlin, M. W., and J. E. Talbert. 2006. *Building School-Based Teacher Learning Communities*. New York: Teachers College Press.

Bryk, Anthony S., Valerie E. Lee, and Peter B. Holland. 1993. *Catholic Schools and the Common Good*. Cambridge, MA: Harvard University Press. Quoted in: Ouchi, William G. 2003. *Making Schools Work*. New York: Simon & Schuster.

Bryk, A. S. 1995. "Lessons from Catholic High Schools on Renewing Our Education Institutions." In *Restructuring Schools: Promising Practices and Policies*, edited by M. T. Hallinon, 81–98. New York: Plenum Press. Quoted in: Darling-Hammond, Linda, and Milbrey W. McLaughlin. 1999. *Investing in Teaching as a Learning Profession: Policy Problems and Prospects*. San Francisco: Jossey-Bass Publishers.

Burns, J. M. 1978. *Leadership*. New York: Harper and Row. Quoted in: Spillane, James P., Richard Halverson, and John B. Drummond. 2001. "Investigating School Leadership Practice: A Distributed Perspective." *Educational Researcher* 30: 23–28.

Bushaw, William J., and Shane J. Lopez. 2011. "Betting on Teachers: The 43rd Annual Phi Delta Kappa/Gallup Poll of the Public's Attitudes toward the Public Schools." *Phi Delta Kappan*, September: 8–26.

Butler, Ruth. 2000. "What Learners Want to Know: The Role of Achievement Goals in Shaping Information Seeking, Learning and Interest." In *Intrinsic and Extrinsic Motivation: The Search for Optimal Motivation and Performance*, edited by C. Sansome and J. M. Harackiewicz, 161–94. San Diego, CA: Academic Press. Quoted in: Butler, Ruth. 2007. "Teachers' Achievement Goal Orientations and Associations with Teachers' Help Seeking: Examination of a Novel Approach to Teacher Motivation." *Journal of Educational Psychology* 99 (2): 241–52.

Butler, Ruth. 2007. "Teachers' Achievement Goal Orientations and Associations with Teachers' Help Seeking: Examination of a Novel Approach to Teacher Motivation." *Journal of Educational Psychology* 99 (2): 241–52.

Carnegie Corporation. 1986. *A Nation Prepared: Teachers for the 21st Century. The Report of the Task Force on Teaching as a Profession.*

Center for Collaborative Education. 2009. "Five Pilot School Areas for Autonomy, plus Accountability."

The Centre for Business Performance. Cranfield School of Management for the IDeA and Audit Commission Performance Management, Measurement, and Information (PMMI) Project. *Literature Review on Performance Measurement and Management*. www.idea.gov.uk/idk/aio/306299 .

Christensen, Clayton. 2003. *The Innovator's Dilemma*. New York: First HarperBusiness.

Christensen, Clayton M., Michael B. Horn, and Curtis W. Johnson. 2008. *Disrupting Class: How Disruptive Innovation Will Change the Way the World Learns*. New York: McGraw Hill.

Cochran-Smith, Marilyn, and Susan L. Lytle. 1999. "Relationships of Knowledge and Practice: Teacher Learning in Communities." In *Review of Research in Education*, edited by A. Irannejad and C. D. Pearson. Washington, DC: American Educational Research Association. http://rre.sagepub.com/cgi/reprint/24/1/249.

Cohen, M., J. March, and J. Olsen. 1972. "A Garbage Can Model of Organizational Choice." *Administrative Science Quarterly* 17: 1–25. Quoted in: Ouchi, William, and A. Wilkins. 1985. "Organizational Culture." *Annual Review of Sociology* 11: 457–83.

Collay, Michelle, Diane Dunlap, Walter Enloe, and George Gagnon. 1998. *Learning Circles: Creating Conditions for Professional Development*. Thousand Oaks, CA: Corwin Press.

Collis, David J., and Cynthia A. Montgomery. 1995. "Competing on Resources: Strategy in the 1990s." *Harvard Business Review* 73 (4): 118–28. Quoted in: Tomer, John. 2001. "Understanding High Performance Work Systems: The Joint Contribution of Economics and Human Resource Management." *Journal of Socio-Economics* 30 (1): 63–73. www.rohan.sdsu.edu/~frantz/docs/Tomer.pdf.

Crary, David. 2010. "Suicides: Schools Confront Anti-gay Bullying." *Huffington Post*, October 9.

Cuban, Larry. 2010. "Please Don't Hype Teacher-Led Schools." *Larry Cuban on School Reform and Classroom Practice* (blog), October 9. http://larrycuban.wordpress.com/2010/10/09/please-dont-hype-teacher-run-schools/.

Darling-Hammond, Linda, and Milbrey W. McLaughlin. 1999. *Investing in Teaching as a Learning Profession: Policy Problems and Prospects*. San Francisco: Jossey-Bass Publishers.

Deming, W. Edwards. 1982. *Out of the Crisis*. Cambridge, MA: Massachusetts Institute of Technology, Center for Advanced Engineering Study. Quoted in: Glasser, William M. D. 1998. *The Quality School: Managing Students without Coercion*. New York: Harper Perennial.

Deming, W. Edwards. 2000a. *Out of the Crisis*. 2nd ed. Cambridge, MA: MIT Press.

Deming, W. Edwards. 2000b. *The New Economics*. Cambridge, MA: MIT Press.

Denhardt, Robert B. 1993. *The Pursuit of Significance: Strategies for Managerial Success in Public Organizations*. Belmont, CA: Wadsworth Publishing. Quoted in: Kernaghan, Kenneth, Brian Marson, and Sandford Borins. 2005. *The New Public Organization*. 3rd ed. Toronto, ON: Institute of Public Administration of Canada.

Denison Consulting. 2006. "Denison Overview: Introduction to the Denison Model." *Researchnotes* 1 (1). www.denisonconsulting.com.

de Waal, Andre. 2005. "The Characteristics of a High Performance Organization." Maastricht School of Management. www.managementdevelopment.com/uploads/643/524/Bam2005.pdf.

Dirkswager, Edward J., ed. 2002. *Teachers as Owners*. Lanham, MD: Scarecrow Press.

Dornbush, S., and W. R. Scott. 1975. *Evaluation and Authority*. San Francisco: Jossey-Bass Publishers. Quoted in: Ouchi, William, and A. Wilkins. 1985. "Organizational Culture." *Annual Review of Sociology* 11: 457–83.

Edmonds, Ronald R. 1982. "Programs of School Improvement: An Overview." Washington, DC: National Institute of Education.

Education|Evolving. 2011. "Origins of Chartering." Accessed December 8, 2011.

Elmore, R., P. Peterson, and S. McCarthey. 1996. *Restructuring in the Classroom*. San Francisco: Jossey-Bass Publishers. Quoted in: Barnett, Kerry, and John McCormick. 2003. "Vision, Relationships and Teacher Motivation: A Case Study." *Journal of Educational Administration* 41 (1): 55–73.

Endlsley, M. R. 1997. "The Role of Situation Awareness in Naturalistic Decision Making." In *Naturalistic Decision Making*, edited by C. Zsambok and G. Klein. Mahwah, NJ: Erlbaum. Quoted in: Weick, K. E., K. M. Sutcliffe, and D. Obstfeld. 1999. "Organizing for High Reliability: Processes of Collective Mindfulness." *Research in Organizational Behavior* 21: 81–123.

Farkas, Steve, Jean Johnson, and Ann Duffett (with Leslie Moye and Jackie Vine). 2003. *Stand by Me: What Teachers Really Think about Unions, Merit Pay and Other Professional Matters*. New York: Public Agenda.

Feldman, M. S. 1989. *Order without Design: Information Production and Policy Making*. Stanford, CA: Stanford University Press. Quoted in: Weick, K. E., K. M. Sutcliffe, and D. Obstfeld. 1999. "Organizing for High Reliability: Processes of Collective Mindfulness." *Research in Organizational Behavior* 21: 81–123.

Fogel, Daniel S. 1989. "The Uniqueness of a Professionally Dominated Organization." *Health Care Management Review* 14 (3): 15–24.

Fullan, Michael. 1993. *Change Forces: Probing the Depths of Education Reform*. Bristol, PA: Falmer Press. Quoted in: Darling-Hammond, Linda, and Milbrey W. McLaughlin. 1999. *Investing in Teaching as a Learning Profession: Policy Problems and Prospects*. San Francisco: Jossey-Bass Publishers.

Fullan, Michael. 2006. "Change Theory: A Force for School Improvement." Seminar Series Paper 157. Presented at the Centre for Strategic Education Seminar Series, November, Victoria, Canada.

Fullan, Michael, and A. Hargreaves. 1991. "What's Worth Fighting For? Working Together for Your School." Toronto: Ontario Public School Teachers Federation. Quoted in: Barnett, Kerry, and John McCormick. 2003. "Vision, Relationships and Teacher Motivation: A Case Study." *Journal of Educational Administration* 41 (1): 55–73.

Gerstner, L. 2002. *Who Says Elephants Can't Dance?* New York: Harper Business. Quoted in: Wriston, and Michael J. 2007. "Creating a High-Performance Culture." *Organization Development Journal*, Spring. http://findarticles.com/p/articles/mi_qa5427/is_200704/ai_n21291280/.

Gibbons, Maurice. 1974. "Walkabout: Searching for the Right Passage from Childhood and School." *Phi Delta Kappan*, May.

Gibbons, Maurice. 2002. *The Self-Directed Learning Handbook: Challenging Adolescent Students to Excel.* San Francisco: Jossey-Bass Publishers.

Gibbons, Maurice. 2008. "Empowering Students." *Self-Directed Learning.*

Glasser, William M. D. 1998a. *Choice Theory.* New York: HarperCollins. Quoted in: Glasser, William M. D. 1998. *The Quality School: Managing Students without Coercion.* New York: Harper Perennial.

Glasser, William M. D. 1998b. *The Quality School: Managing Students without Coercion.* New York: Harper Perennial.

Graham, William K. 1970. "A Method for Measuring the Images of Organizations." Paper presented at the Annual Meeting of the Western Psychological Association, in Los Angeles, California.

Hanna, David. 1988. *Designing Organizations for High Performance.* Boston: Addison Wesley.

Hannan, M. T., and J. Freeman. 1984. "Structural Inertia and Organizational Change." *American Sociological Review* 49: 149–64. Quoted in: Weick, K. E., K. M. Sutcliffe, and D. Obstfeld. 1999. "Organizing for High Reliability: Processes of Collective Mindfulness." *Research in Organizational Behavior* 21: 81–123.

Hansen, Janet, and Marguerite Roza. 2005. *Decentralized Decisionmaking for Schools.* Santa Monica, CA: RAND Corporation.

Hanushek, Eric, et al. 1994. *Making Schools Work: Improving Performance and Controlling Costs.* Washington, DC: Brookings Institution. Quoted in: Ouchi, William G. 2003. *Making Schools Work.* New York: Simon & Schuster.

Hawkins, Beth. 2011. "Americans Adore Teachers and Think Schools Are Doing Quite Well." *MinnPost*, September 2.

Heath, D. H. 1994. *Schools of Hope: Developing Mind and Character in Today's Youth.* San Francisco: Jossey-Bass Publishers, 1994. Quoted in: Newell, Ronald J., and Mark J. Van Ryzin. 2009. *Assessing What Really Matters in Schools.* Lanham, MD: Rowman & Littlefield Education.

Hopkins, B. 2003. "Restorative Justice in Schools." *Mediation in Practice*, April: 4–9.

Hu, Winnie. 2012. "In a New Role, Teachers Move to Run Schools." *New York Times*, September 10.

Ingersoll, Richard M. 2003. *Who Controls Teachers' Work?* Cambridge, MA: Harvard University Press.

Ingersoll, Richard M. 2007. "Short on Power, Long on Responsibility." *Educational Leadership* 65 (1): 20–25. www.gse.upenn.edu/pdf/rmi/EL–RMI–2007.pdf.

Itin, C. M. 1999. "Reasserting the Philosophy of Experiential Education as a Vehicle for Change in the 21st Century." *The Journal of Experiential Education* 22 (2): 91–98.

Jackall, Robert, and Henry Levin. 1984. *Worker Cooperatives in America.* Berkeley: University of California Press.

Jackson, Bruce, and Susan R. Madsen. 2005. "Common Factors of High Performance Teams." Utah Valley State College.

Johnson, Curtis W. 1970. "An Analysis of the Faculty Perceptions of Organizational Influence Structure and Student Perceptions of Instructional Effectiveness." PhD diss. The University of Texas at Austin.

Johnson, Curtis W. 2010. "Civic Caucus Notes." *The Civic Caucus*, January 8.

Joseph, Claire. 2008. "High-Performance Norms: What Distinguishes the Best from the Rest?" https://community.gensurvey.com/content/HiPerNormsfall08.aspx.

Katzenbach, J. R., and D. K. Smith. 1993. *The Wisdom of Teams: Creating the High-Performance Organization.* Harvard Business School Press. Quoted in: Bolman, L. G., and T. E. Deal. 1997. *Reframing Organizations: Artistry, Choice, and Leadership.* 2nd ed. San Francisco: Jossey-Bass Publishers.

Kerchner, Charles. 2010. *Can Teachers Run Their Own Schools?* Creative Commons. http://creativecommons.org/licenses/by%E2%80%90nc%E2%80%90nd/3.0/.

Kernaghan, Kenneth, Brian Marson, and Sandford Borins. 2005. *The New Public Organization.* 3rd ed. Toronto, ON: Institute of Public Administration of Canada.

Kolderie, Ted. 1986. "Private Practice in Public School teaching. Book I: The Concept, Need and Design." Public School Incentives.

Kolderie, Ted. 1988 (October). Personal conversation wtih Albert Shanker.

Kolderie, Ted. 2005. *Creating the Capacity for Change: How and Why Governors and Legislatures Are Opening a New-Schools Sector in Public Education.* Bethesda, MD: Education Week Press.

Kotter, J. P., and J. L. Heskett. 1992. *Corporate Culture and Performance.* Quoted in: de Waal, Andre. 2005. "The Characteristics of a High Performance Organization." Maastricht School of Management.

Kouzes, James M., and Barry Z. Posner. 1988. *Leadership Practice Inventory Trainer's Manual.* San Diego: Pfeiffer and Co. Quoted in: Kusy, Mitchell, Louellen Essex, and Thomas Marr. 1995. "No Longer a Solo Practice: How Physician Leaders Lead." *The Physician Executive* 21: 11–15.

Kusy, Mitchell, Louellen Essex, and Thomas Marr. 1995. "No Longer a Solo Practice: How Physician Leaders Lead." *The Physician Executive* 21: 11–15.

Kyriacou, C. 1987. "Teacher Stress and Burnout: An International Review." *Educational Research* 29: 146–52. Quoted in: Neves de Jesus, Saul, and Willy Lens. 2005. "An Integrated Model for the Study of Teacher Motivation." *Applied Psychology: An International Review* 54 (1): 119–34.

Ladany, N., C. E. Hill, M. M. Corbutt, and E. A. Nutt. 1996. "Nature, Extent, and Importance of What Psychotherapy Trainees Do Not Disclose to Their Supervisors." *Journal of Counseling Psychology* 43: 10–24. Quoted in: Butler, Ruth. 2007. "Teachers' Achievement Goal Orientations and Associations with Teachers' Help Seeking: Examination of a Novel Approach to Teacher Motivation." *Journal of Educational Psychology* 99 (2): 241–52.

Lawler, Edward E., III. 1996. *From the Ground Up: Six Principles for Building the New Logic Corporation.* San Francisco: Jossey-Bass Publishers.

Leithwood, K., P. T. Begley, and J. B. Cousins. 1994. *Developing Expert Leadership for Future Schools.* London: The Falmer Press. Quoted in: Spillane, James P., Richard Halverson, and John B. Drummond. 2001. "Investigating School Leadership Practice: A Distributed Perspective." *Educational Researcher* 30: 23–28.

Leithwood, K., D. Jantzi, and R. Steinbach. 1999. *Changing Leadership for Changing Times.* Philadelphia: Open University Press, Buckingham. Quoted in: Barnett, Kerry, and John McCormick. 2003. "Vision, Relationships and Teacher Motivation: A Case Study." *Journal of Educational Administration* 41 (1): 55–73.

Lencioni, P. 2002. *The Five Dysfunctions of a Team.* San Francisco: Jossey-Bass Publishers. Quoted in: Wriston, Michael J. 2007. "Creating a High-Performance Culture." *Organization Development Journal,* Spring. http://findarticles.com/p/articles/mi_qa5427/is_200704/ai_n21291280/ .

Lens, Willy, and Saul Neves de Jesus. 1999. "A Psychosocial Interpretation of Teacher Stress and Burnout." In *Understanding and Preventing Teacher Burnout,* edited by R. Vandenberghe and A. M. Huberman. Cambridge: Cambridge University Press. Quoted in: Neves de Jesus, Saul, and Willy Lens. 2005. "An Integrated Model for the Study of Teacher Motivation." *Applied Psychology: An International Review* 54 (1): 119–34.

Levitt, B., and J. G. March. 1998. "Organizational Learning." *Annual Review of Sociology* 114: 319–40. Quoted in: McLaughlin, M. W., and J. E. Talbert. 2006. *Building School-Based Teacher Learning Communities.* New York: Teachers College Press.

Lezotte, Lawrence W. 1991. *Correlates of Effective Schools: The First and Second Generations*. Okemos, MI: Effective Schools Products, Ltd. www.effectiveschools.com .

Lieberman, Ann, and Lynne Miller, eds. 2008. *Teachers in Professional Communities: Improving Teaching and Learning*. New York: Teachers College Press.

Louis, K. S., and H. M. Marks. 1998. "Does Professional Community Affect the Classroom? Teachers' Work and Student Experiences in Restructuring Schools." *American Journal of Education* 106: 532–75. www.eric.ed.gov/ERICWebPortal/custom/portlets/recordDetails/detailmini.jsp?_nfpb=true&_&ERICExtSearch_SearchValue_0=ED412634&ERICExtSearch_SearchType_0=no&accno=ED412634.

March, J. G., and J. P. Olsen. 1989. *Rediscovering Institutions*. New York: Free Press. Quoted in: Weick, K. E., K. M. Sutcliffe, and D. Obstfeld. 1999. "Organizing for High Reliability: Processes of Collective Mindfulness." *Research in Organizational Behavior* 21: 81–123.

March, J., and H. Simon. 1958. *Organizations*. New York: Wiley. Quoted in: Ouchi, William, and A. Wilkins. 1985. "Organizational Culture." *Annual Review of Sociology* 11: 457–83.

Marmot, Sir Michael, et al. 2004. "Work, Stress, and Health: The Whitehall II Study." Cabinet Office. London: Council of Civil Service Unions.

Marr, T. J., and D. K. Zismer. 1998. "When Is a Physician Network a Group?" *Physician Executive* 24 (2): 25–29.

McLaughlin, Milbrey W., and Joan E. Talbert. 2001. *Professional Communities and the Work of High School Teaching*. Chicago: University of Chicago Press.

McLaughlin, Milbrey W., and J. E. Talbert. 2006. *Building School-Based Teacher Learning Communities*. New York: Teachers College Press.

McVicar, Brian. 2010. "Ionia Kindergartner Suspended for Making Gun with Hand." *mlive.com*, March 4.

Meyer, John W., and Brian Rowan. 1977a. "Notes on the Structure of Educational Organizations." In *Studies on Environment and Organization*, edited by M. Meyer. San Francisco: Jossey-Bass Publishers. Quoted in: Ouchi, William, and A. Wilkins. 1985. "Organizational Culture." *Annual Review of Sociology* 11: 457–83.

Meyer, John W., and Brian Rowan. 1977b. "Institutionalized Organizations: Formal Structure as Myth and Ceremony." *American Journal of Sociology* 83 (2): 440–63. Quoted in: Perrow, Charles. 1986. *Complex Organizations: A Critical Essay*. New York: Random.

Miller, D. 1993. "The Architecture of Simplicity." *Academy of Management Review* 18: 116–38. Quoted in: Weick, K. E., K. M. Sutcliffe, and D. Obstfeld. 1999. "Organizing for High Reliability: Processes of Collective Mindfulness." *Research in Organizational Behavior* 21: 81–123.

Molden, D. C., and C. S. Dweck. 2000. "Meaning and Motivation." In *Intrinsic and Extrinsic Motivation: The Search for Optimal Motivation and Performance*, edited by C. Sansome and J. M. Harackiewicz. San Diego: Academic Press. Quoted in: Butler, Ruth. 2007. "Teachers' Achievement Goal Orientations and Associations with Teachers' Help Seeking: Examination of a Novel Approach to Teacher Motivation." *Journal of Educational Psychology* 99 (2): 241–52.

Morgan, Gareth. 1998. *Images of Organization: The Executive Edition*. San Francisco: Berrett-Koehler Publishers / Thousand Oaks, CA: Sage Publications.

National Centre for Restorative Approaches in Youth Settings. "Restorative Approaches." Accessed July 17, 2012. www.transformingconflict.org/content/restorative-approahces-0.

National Commission on Excellence in Education. 1983. *A Nation at Risk: The Importance of Educational Reform*. www.ed.gov/pubs/NatAtRisk/index.html.

National Council on Teacher Quality. 2011. *State of the States: Trends and Early Lessons on Teacher Evaluation and Effectiveness Policies*.

NEA Commission on Effective Teachers and Teaching. 2011. *Transforming Teaching: Connecting Professional Responsibility with Student Learning*.

Neely, A. D., M. J. Gregory, and K. Platts. 1995. "Performance Measurement System Design: A Literature Review and Research Agenda." *International Journal of Operations & Production Management* 15 (4): 80–116. Quoted in: The Centre for Business Performance. Cranfield School of Management for the IDeA and Audit Commission Performance Management, Measurement, and Information (PMMI) Project. Literature review on *Performance Measurement and Management*. www.idea.gov.uk/idk/aio/306299.

Nelson, R., and S. Winter. 1982. *An Evolutionary Theory of Economic Change*. Cambridge, MA: Belknap. Quoted in: Weick, K. E., K. M. Sutcliffe, and D. Obstfeld. 1999. "Organizing for High Reliability: Processes of Collective Mindfulness." *Research in Organizational Behavior* 21: 81–123.

Neves de Jesus, Saul, and Willy Lens. 2005. "An Integrated Model for the Study of Teacher Motivation." *Applied Psychology: An International Review* 54 (1): 119–34.

Newell, Ronald J., and Irving H. Buchen. 2004. *Democratic Learning and Leading*. Lanham, MD: Scarecrow Education.

Newell, Ronald J., and Mark J. Van Ryzin. 2009. *Assessing What Really Matters in Schools: Creating Hope for the Future*. Lanham, MD: Rowman & Littlefield Education.

Newkirk, Thomas. 2009. "Stress, Control, and the Deprofessionalizing of Teaching." *Education Week*, October 21.

Nordgren, Lynn. 2010. "In Minneapolis the Teacher Union Is Driving Change." *Education Innovating* (blog), July 9.

Nordgren, Lynn. 2011. "Teachers, Charters Are Natural Allies." *Star Tribune*, December 11. Accessed on December 8, 2011. http://m.startribune.com/news/?id=135343148.

Olson, Ruth Anne. 1986. "Private Practice in Public Schools Teaching. Book II: The Experiences of Teachers and School Administrators." Public School Incentives.

Ouchi, William G. 2003. *Making Schools Work*. New York: Simon & Schuster.

Ouchi, William G. 2009. *The Secret of TSL*. New York: Simon & Schuster.

Ouchi, William G., and A. Wilkins. 1985. "Organizational Culture." *Annual Review of Sociology* 11: 457–83.

Perrow, Charles. 1986. *Complex Organizations: A Critical Essay*. New York: Random.

Peters, T. 1978. "Symbols, Patterns, Settings: An Optimistic Case for Getting Things Done." *Organizational Dynamics* 7 (2): 3–23. Quoted in: Ouchi, William, and A. Wilkins. 1985. "Organizational Culture." *Annual Review of Sociology* 11: 457–83.

Peters, T. 1980. "Management Systems: The Language of Organizational Character and Competence." *Organization Dynamics* Summer: 3–27. Quoted in: Ouchi, William, and A. Wilkins. 1985. "Organizational Culture." *Annual Review of Sociology* 11: 457–83.

Pfeffer, Jeffrey. 1998. *The Human Equation: Building Profits by Putting People First*. Harvard Business Press. Quoted in: Tomer, John. 2001. "Understanding High Performance Work Systems." *The Joint Contribution of Economics and Human Resource Management* 30 (1): 63–73.

Pink, Daniel H. 2009. *Drive: The Surprising Truth about What Motivates Us*. New York: Riverhead Books.

Piper, Karen. 2009. "Education 101: What Is a Charter School Authorizer?" Examiner.com, August 17. www.examiner.com/charter-schools-in-national/education-101-what-is-a-charter-school-authorizer.

Pithers, R. T., and G. J. Fogarty. 1995. "Occupational Stress among Vocational Teachers." *British Journal of Educational Psychology* 65: 3–14. Quoted in: Neves de Jesus, Saul, and Willy Lens. 2005. "An Integrated Model for the Study of Teacher Motivation." *Applied Psychology: An International Review* 54 (1): 119–34.

Prick, L. 1989. "Satisfaction and Stress among Teachers." *International Journal of Education Research* 13: 363–77. Quoted in: Neves de Jesus, Saul, and Willy Lens. 2005. "An Integrated Model for the Study of Teacher Motivation." *Applied Psychology: An International Review* 54 (1): 119–34.

Quinn, James Brian, Philip Anderson, and Sidney Finkelstein. 1996. "Managing the Professional Intellect: Making the Best of the Best." *Harvard Business Review* March–April: 71–80.

Reason, J. 1990. *Human Error*. New York: Cambridge University Press. Quoted in: Weick, K. E., K. M. Sutcliffe, and D. Obstfeld. 1999. "Organizing for High Reliability: Processes of Collective Mindfulness." *Research in Organizational Behavior* 21: 81–123.

Regan, M. D. 1999. *The Journey to Teams: A Practical Step-By-Step Implementation Plan.* New York: Holden Press. Quoted in: Jackson, Bruce, and Susan R. Madsen. 2005. "Common Factors of High Performance Teams." Utah Valley State College. www.theiahe.com/ documents/Common%20Factors%20of%20High%20Performance%20Teams.JCIBG.pdf.

Roberts, K. H., and D. M. Rousseau. 1989. "Research in Nearly Failure-Free, High-Reliability Systems: Having the Bubble." *IEEE Transactions on Engineering Management* 36: 132–39. Quoted in: Weick, K. E., K. M. Sutcliffe, and D. Obstfeld. 1999. "Organizing for High Reliability: Processes of Collective Mindfulness." *Research in Organizational Behavior* 21: 81–123.

Rochlin, G. I. 1989. "Informal Organizational Networking as a Crisis Avoidance Strategy: U.S. Naval Flight Operations as a Case Study." *Industrial Crisis Quarterly* 3: 159–76. Quoted in: Weick, K. E., K. M. Sutcliffe, and D. Obstfeld. 1999. "Organizing for High Reliability: Processes of Collective Mindfulness." *Research in Organizational Behavior* 21: 81–123.

Rochlin, G. I. 1993. "Defining 'High Reliability' Organizations in Practice: A Taxonomic Prologue." In *New Challenges to Understanding Organizations*, edited by K.H. Roberts. New York: Macmillan. Quoted in: Weick, K. E., K. M. Sutcliffe, and D. Obstfeld. 1999. "Organizing for High Reliability: Processes of Collective Mindfulness." *Research in Organizational Behavior* 21: 81–123.

Rosenholtz, S. 1989. *Teachers' Workplace: The Social Organization of Schools.* New York: Longman. Quoted in: Barnett, Kerry, and McCormick, John. 2003. "Vision, Relationships and Teacher Motivation: A Case Study." *Journal of Educational Administration* 41 (1): 55–73.

Roth, E. M. 1997. "Analysis of Decision Making in Nuclear Power Plant Emergencies: An Investigation of Aided Decision Making." In *Naturalistic Decision Making*, edited by C. Zsambok and G. Klein. Mahwah, NJ: Erlbaum. Quoted in: Weick, K. E., K. M. Sutcliffe, and D. Obstfeld. 1999. "Organizing for High Reliability: Processes of Collective Mindfulness." *Research in Organizational Behavior* 21: 81–123.

Rowley, Laura. 2003. *On Target: How the World's Hottest Retailer Hit a Bull's-Eye.* Hoboken, NJ: John Wiley & Sons.

Sagan, S. D. 1994. "Toward a *Political* Theory of Organizational Reliability." *Journal of Contingencies and Crisis Management* 2: 228–40. Quoted in: Weick, K. E., K. M. Sutcliffe, and D. Obstfeld. 1999. "Organizing for High Reliability: Processes of Collective Mindfulness." *Research in Organizational Behavior* 21: 81–123.

Sarason, S. B. 2004. *And What Do YOU Mean by Learning?* Portsmouth, NH: Heinemann. Quoted in: Newell, Ronald J., and Mark J. Van Ryzin. 2009. *Assessing What Really Matters in Schools.* Lanham, MD: Rowman & Littlefield Education.

Schein, E. 1983. *Organizational Culture: A Dynamic Model.* MIT Sloan School of Management Working Paper No. 1412–83. Quoted in: Ouchi, William, and A. Wilkins. 1985. "Organizational Culture." *Annual Review of Sociology* 11: 457–83.

Scott Morton, M. S. 2003. "The Interesting Organizations Project: Digitalization of the 21st Century Firm." In *Inventing the Organizations of the 21st Century*, edited by T. W. Malone, R. Laubacher, and M.S. Scott Morton. Cambridge, MA: MIT Press. Quoted in: de Waal, Andre. 2005. *The Characteristics of a High Performance Organization.* Maastricht School of Management.

Seifter, Harvey, and Peter Economy. 2001. *Leadership Ensemble.* New York: Times Books.

Sennett, A. R. 1896. *Carriages without Horses Shall Go.* London: Whittaker & Co.

Shell, G. R. 2006. *Bargaining for Advantage.* New York: Penguin Books. Quoted in: Wriston, Michael J. 2007. "Creating a High-Performance Culture." *Organization Development Journal*, Spring. http://findarticles.com/p/articles/mi_qa5427/is_200704/ai_n21291280/.

Sizer, Theodore R. 1984. *Horace's Compromise.* Boston: Houghton Mifflin. Quoted in: Ouchi, William G. 2009. *The Secret of TSL.* New York: Simon & Schuster.

Sizer, Theodore R. 1992. *Horace's School.* Boston. Houghton Mifflin. Quoted in: Ouchi, William G. 2009. *The Secret of TSL.* New York: Simon & Schuster.

Sizer, Theodore R. 1996. *Hope.* Boston: Houghton Mifflin. Quoted in: Ouchi, William G. 2009. *The Secret of TSL.* New York: Simon & Schuster.

Spillane, James P., Richard Halverson, and John B. Drummond. 2001. "Investigating School Leadership Practice: A Distributed Perspective." *Educational Researcher* 30: 23–28.

Sun, Christine. 2011. "Why We're Suing Minnesota's Anoka-Hennepin School District." www.splcenter.org/get-informed/news/why-were-suing-minnesota-s-anoka-hennepin-school-district.

Tamm, J. W., and R. J. Luyet. 2004. *Radical Collaboration.* New York: Collins. Quoted in: Wriston, Michael J. 2007. "Creating a High-Performance Culture." *Organization Development Journal,* Spring. http://findarticles.com/p/articles/mi_qa5427/is_200704/ai_n2129 1280/.

Tamuz, M. 1994. "Developing Organizational Safety Information Systems for Monitoring Potential Dangers." In *Proceedings of PSAM* II, vol. 2, edited by G. E. Apostolakis, and T. S. Win, 7–12. Los Angeles: University of California. Quoted in: Weick, K. E., K. M. Sutcliffe, and D. Obstfeld. 1999. "Organizing for High Reliability: Processes of Collective Mindfulness." *Research in Organizational Behavior* 21: 81–123.

Tannenbaum, Arnold S. 1968. *Control in Organizations.* New York: McGraw-Hill. Quoted in: Perrow, Charles. 1986. *Complex Organizations: A Critical Essay.* New York: Random.

Tannenbaum, Arnold S., et al. 1974. *Hierarchy in Organizations.* San Francisco: Jossey-Bass Publishers. Quoted in: Perrow, Charles. 1986. *Complex Organizations: A Critical Essay.* New York: Random.

Thomas B. Fordham Institute. 2007. "Where They Set the Bar." http://media.mcclatchydc.com/smedia/2007/10/18/07/614–20071017–NOCHILD.large.prod_affiliate.91.jpg. Accessed January 22, 2012.

Tomer, John. 2001. "Understanding High Performance Work Systems: The Joint Contribution of Economics and Human Resource Management." *Journal of Socio-Economics* 30 (1): 63–73.

Tomlinson, Carol. 2001. *How to Differentiate Instruction in Mixed-Ability Classrooms.* 2nd ed. Alexandria, VA: Association for Supervision and Curriculum Development.

Tucker, Marc. 2006. "Tough Choices or Tough Times: The Report of the New Commission on the Skills of the American Workforce." San Francisco, CA: Jossey-Bass.

Turknett, R. 2005. *Decent People, Decent Company.* Mountain View, CA: Davies-Black Publishing. Quoted in: Wriston, Michael J. 2007. "Creating a High-Performance Culture." *Organization Development Journal,* Spring.

Urbina, Ian. 2009. "It's a Fork, It's a Spoon, It's a . . . Weapon?" *New York Times,* October 11. http://www.nytimes.com/2009/10/12/education/12discipline.html.

Van Maanen, J., and S. Barley. 1984. "Occupational Communities: Culture and Control in Organizations." *Research in Organizational Behavior* 6: 287–365. Quoted in: Ouchi, William, and A. Wilkins. 1985. "Organizational Culture." *Annual Review of Sociology* 11: 457–83.

Van Maanen, J., and E. Schein. 1978. "Toward a Theory of Organizational Socialization." In *Research in Organization Behavior,* edited by B. Staw. Greenwich, CT: Jai Press. Quoted in: Ouchi, William, and A. Wilkins. 1985. "Organizational Culture." *Annual Review of Sociology* 11: 457–83.

Venn, J. J. 2000. *Assessing Students with Special Needs.* 2nd ed. Upper Saddle River, NJ: Merrill.

Weber, Max. 1968. *Economy and Society.* 4th ed. Vols. 1 and 3. Edited by G. Roth and C. Wittich. New York: Irvington Publications. Quoted in: Perrow, Charles. 1986. *Complex Organizations: A Critical Essay.* New York: Random.

Weber, Max. 1974. *The Theory of Social and Economic Organization.* Translated and edited by A. M. Henderson and T. Parsons. New York: Oxford University Press. Quoted in: Perrow, Charles. 1986. *Complex Organizations: A Critical Essay.* New York: Random.

Wehling, Bob, and Cari Schneider. 2007. *Building a 21st Century U.S. Education System.* Washington, DC: National Commission on Teaching and America's Future.

Weick, K. E., K. M. Sutcliffe, and D. Obstfeld. 1999. "Organizing for High Reliability: Processes of Collective Mindfulness." *Research in Organizational Behavior* 21: 81–123.

Wenger, E., R. McDermoot, and W. M. Snyder. 2003. *Cultivating Communities of Practice.* Cambridge: Cambridge University Press. http://books.google.com/books?id=m1xzuNq9RygC&dq=%22Cultivating+communities+of+practice%22&printsec=frontcover&source=bn&hl=en&ei=Bp7vSYjqAqKUMu29gfcP&sa=X&oi=book_result&ct=result&resnum=5#PPP1,M1 .

Westrum, R. 1988. Organizational and Inter-organizational Thought. Paper presented at the World Bank Conference on Safety Control and Risk Management. Quoted in: Weick, K. E., K. M. Sutcliffe, and D. Obstfeld. 1999. "Organizing for High Reliability: Processes of Collective Mindfulness." *Research in Organizational Behavior* 21: 81–123.

Wiener, Ross. 2003. "Making Sense of State AYP Lists." *The Education Trust,* September.

Wildavsky, A. 1991. *Searching for Safety.* New Brunswick, NJ: Transaction Books. Quoted in: Weick, K. E., K. M. Sutcliffe, and D. Obstfeld. 1999. "Organizing for High Reliability: Processes of Collective Mindfulness." *Research in Organizational Behavior* 21: 81–123.

Wilkins, A. 1983. "Organizational Stories as Symbols, Which Control the Organization." In *Organizational Symbolism: Monographs in Organizational and Industrial Relations,* edited by L. R. Pondy, P. J. Frost, G. Morgan, and T. Dandridge, 1:81–92. Greenwich, CT: Jai Press. Quoted in: Ouchi, William, and A. Wilkins. 1985. "Organizational Culture." *Annual Review of Sociology* 11: 457–83.

Wriston, Michael J. 2007. "Creating a High-Performance Culture." *Organization Development Journal,* Spring. http://findarticles.com/p/articles/mi_qa5427/is_200704/ai_n21291280/.

Xiao, Y., P. Milgram, and J. D. Doyle. 1997. "Capturing and Modeling Planning Expertise in Anesthesiology: Results of a Field Study." In *Naturalistic Decision Making,* edited by C. Zsambok and G. Klein, 197–207. Mahwah, NJ: Erlbaum. Quoted in: Weick, K. E., K. M. Sutcliffe, and D. Obstfeld. 1999. "Organizing for High Reliability: Processes of Collective Mindfulness." *Research in Organizational Behavior* 21: 81–123.

About the Authors

Kim Farris-Berg and **Edward Dirkswager** designed and led this investigation as senior fellows of the Center for Policy Studies (CPS). They were assisted by **Amy Junge**, associate at Education|Evolving.

Farris-Berg and Dirkswager have been following and documenting collective teacher autonomy for more than a decade.

Farris-Berg operates her own consulting practice where she focuses on education policy design. She is especially interested in analyzing where incentives can make a difference for public schools. Her forte is bringing the ideas and experiences of teachers and students into the process. Farris-Berg's work in this area has been acknowledged in the book *Disrupting Class*, in the *Stanford Social Innovation Review*, and in numerous other publications and venues. Farris-Berg earned a master's degree in public policy from the Humphrey Institute for Public Affairs at the University of Minnesota where she received the Lloyd B. Short Award for the Institute's best paper of the year and the joint Carlson School (M.B.A.)–Humphrey Institute award for best paper analyzing labor policy. She also holds a bachelor of arts degree, with honors, from the University of San Diego. Farris-Berg resides in Orange County, California, with her husband and three young children, and is just beginning her journey as a parent of children in public schools.

Dirkswager is a retired health care business executive and consultant with a long-term involvement in designing organizations to motivate those involved to produce high-quality, exemplary results, and superior service. He is the editor of *Teachers as Owners: A Key to Revitalizing Public Education* (2002), a practical guide for people interested in starting or encouraging the start-up of schools with teacher autonomy. Dirkswager holds an undergraduate degree in physics from St. John's University, Collegeville, Minnesota, and studied astrophysics as a graduate student at Yale University. He held executive positions in health care and government. Dirkswager has served on over twenty boards of directors, including Innovative Quality Schools, a chartered school authorizer. He was also chair of the board of the National Cooperative Bank in Washington, DC. Dirkswager is a lifelong learner, and as such he earned advanced degrees from Lumen Vitae International Center (Brussels, Belgium), Catholic University of America, and the University of Minnesota. He also served on the faculties of Loras College in Dubuque, Iowa, and University of St. Thomas in St. Paul, Minnesota. He and his wife reside in Minnesota.

Amy Junge is a former California public elementary and middle school teacher and assistant principal. As a teacher she was a member of the National Education Association (NEA), a teachers' union. She is taking a break from these roles to be a stay-at-home mother, and she continues to use her experience to consult on education policy matters on a part-time basis. Her role in this project was to bring the voice of a K–12 conventional school teacher and administrator into the investigation. Junge's accounts of her observations and thinking as she participated in this project are interspersed throughout this book. Junge earned a bachelor of arts degree from Northwestern University and a master's degree in religious studies from the University of California at Santa Barbara.

To learn more about *Trusting Teachers* check out our website

WWW.TRUSTINGTEACHERS.ORG.